LC

D1510867

New Horizons For The Teaching Profession

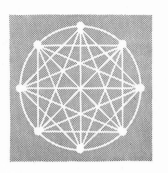

A report of the task force on
New Horizons in Teacher
Education and Professional
Standards ◆ 1961

Edited by
Margaret Lindsey, Ed.D.
Professor of Education
Teachers College, Columbia University

National Education Association of the United States

NATIONAL COMMISSION ON TEACHER EDUCATION AND PROFESSIONAL STANDARDS
NATIONAL EDUCATION ASSOCIATION OF THE UNITED STATES
WASHINGTON, D. C.

$3.00 cloth

(NEA Stock Number 52-128)

$2.00 paper

(NEA Stock Number 52-129)

Discount on quantity orders

Library of Congress Catalog Number 61-13285

Contents

New Horizons Project Task Force

Steering Panel

Margaret Lindsey, Director of the Project; Professor of Education, Teachers College, Columbia University, New York City.

Wendell C. Allen, Director of Teacher Education and Certification, Washington State Board of Education.

John R. Emens, President, Ball State Teachers College, Muncie, Indiana.

Charles E. Hamilton, Executive for Teacher Education, California Teachers Association.

Glaydon D. Robbins, Dean of Education, Moorhead (Minnesota) State College; Chairman of NCTEPS, 1959-60.

T. M. Stinnett, NEA Assistant Executive Secretary for Professional Development and Welfare; Executive Secretary, National Commission on Teacher Education and Professional Standards.

Ruth A. Stout, Assistant Executive Secretary for Professional Relations, Kansas State Teachers Association.

Florence B. Stratemeyer, Professor of Education, Teachers College, Columbia University, New York City.

Committee on Advancement of Professional Standards

Charles E. Hamilton, *Chairman.*

D. D. Darland, Consultant to the Committee; Associate Secretary, NCTEPS.

Frank Hildreth, Junior-High-School Vice-Principal, Des Moines, Iowa.

Frederick L. Hipp, Executive Secretary, New Jersey Education Association.

Dorothy McCuskey, Professor of Education, Western Michigan University.

Wendell Pierce, Superintendent of Schools, Cincinnati, Ohio.

Waurine Walker, Assistant Director, Division of Teacher Education, Texas Education Agency.

iv

Committee on Teacher Education: Pre- and Inservice

Florence B. Stratemeyer, *Chairman.*

Catherine Coleman, Director, Bureau of Teacher Education, Pennsylvania State Department of Public Instruction.

Russell Cooper, Dean, College of Liberal Arts, University of South Florida.

L. D. Haskew, Dean, College of Education, University of Texas.

Elizabeth Anne Meek, Classroom Teacher, Wheeling, West Virginia.

Sister Mary Emil, I.H.M., Executive Secretary, Sister-Formation Conferences, National Catholic Educational Association.

Dwight Teel, Assistant Superintendent of Schools, Milwaukee, Wisconsin.

Committee on Accreditation of Teacher Education

John R. Emens, *Chairman.*

W. Earl Armstrong, Consultant to the Committee; Director, National Council for Accreditation of Teacher Education.

Morris L. Cogan, Director, Secondary-School Apprentice Teaching, Graduate School of Education, Harvard University.

Margaret P. Godfrey, Principal, Sarah J. Rawson School, Hartford, Connecticut.

J. T. Kelley, Director, Division of Teacher Education, Certification, and Accreditation, Florida State Department of Education.

E. Dale Kennedy, Executive Secretary, Michigan Education Association.

Committee on Certification and Professional Performance of School Personnel

Wendell C. Allen, *Chairman.*

Robert N. Bush, Professor of Education, Stanford University, California.

William H. Flaharty, Deputy Commissioner of Education, Connecticut State Department of Education.

Jay E. Greene, Examiner, Board of Examiners, New York City Board of Education.

Margaret Knispel, Classroom Teacher, Beaverton, Oregon.

Howard Nostrand, Chairman, Department of Romance Languages, University of Washington.

Forrest Rozzell, Executive Secretary, Arkansas Education Association.

Committee on Identification, Selective Admission and Retention in Teacher Education

Ruth A. Stout, *Chairman.*

Earl Anderson, Chairman, Department of Education, College of Education, The Ohio State University.

William Edson, Director, Student Personnel Office, College of Education, University of Minnesota.

S. A. Kendrick, Vice-President, Examinations and Research, College Entrance Examination Board, New York City.

Donald Roush, Dean, College of Education, New Mexico State University.

Katherine Stapp, Classroom Teacher, Danville, Illinois.

Preface

IN 1946 the National Education Association established a National Commission on Teacher Education and Professional Standards. This Commission was charged with responsibility for carrying on a continuing program for the profession in matters of selection and recruitment, preparation, certification, inservice growth, and the advancement of professional standards, including standards for institutions that prepare teachers. By 1958 many of the original goals set by the Commission had been accomplished. Momentum toward the achievement of others was adequate to promise their accomplishment in the foreseeable future.

During the period when progress was being made by the Commission and other groups toward higher standards in the teaching profession, events at home and abroad were beginning to have a more-than-usual impact upon education in the United States. A new era in the relationships of nations began to emerge, complicated and confused by conflicting ideologies and the striving of millions of the world's peoples for freedom and economic well-being. Competition in the development of nuclear energy and the exploration of outer space began to occupy a position of central attention and to demand increasing amounts of the nation's resources in both money and manpower. World population was expanding at an unprecedented rate.

In the United States one-time agrarian people were moving to the cities and their rapidly growing suburbs. New sets of problems related to community structure, the place of the family, communication, transportation, and interfamily competition emerged. The rate at which new knowledge was being developed and old knowledge given new meanings was rapid. A new climate of respect and prestige for intelligence was developing.

One of the cumulative effects of conditions in other parts of the world and at home was a renewed and serious concern about education of children and youth. Many who had formerly expressed little interest in the nation's schools and colleges began to take an active part in efforts to determine policies. Others who had always been active in discussions about education found reason in the prevailing conditions for increasing their activity. Old controversies over purposes of schools, selection of content, school organization, standards to be met, and the selection and preparation of teachers took on new significance and added dimensions. Implications of technology for the solution of problems in school organization, utilization of personnel, and instructional methods and materials served to accentuate the urgency of these problems.

Though not always using the same words or taking similar approaches, both the public and the profession were expressing deep concern about the standards held by the teaching profession. Demands that the quality of education in schools and colleges be improved indicated a strong need for the profession to speed up action in certifying to the public the competence of its members. If the profession did not meet this need, it was already apparent that nonprofessional influences would rush in with proposals to solve problems which were clearly professional problems and which should be solved by the profession.

It was in this setting that the National Commission on Teacher Education and Professional Standards began to re-examine its purposes, goals, and procedures. Analysis of what had been accomplished in the preceding decade and of what needed to be done, if the profession was to assume more fully its responsibility for the quality of education, resulted in a proposal which ultimately became the Project on New Horizons in Teacher Education and Professional Standards.

Development of the Project

The scope of the project was defined by the original responsibilities assigned to the NCTEPS in 1946. However, for purposes of study the original responsibilities were organized into these five areas: (1) advancement of professional standards, (2) teacher education, both pre- and inservice, (3) accreditation, (4) certification, and (5) identification, selective admission and retention of professional personnel.

With appointment of a project director, the first step in development of the project was taken. An outstanding educator in each of the five areas was invited to join with the executive secretary and the chairman of the NCTEPS and the project director as a steering panel. At its first meeting in August 1959, this panel stated the purpose of the project as follows:

To develop definitive statements in the areas of responsibility assigned to NCTEPS that would serve as guides for action programs

at the local, state, and national levels by TEPS and other profes-
sional organizations and individuals toward the complete pro-
fessionalization of teaching.

"Definitive statements" was interpreted to mean analysis of values
and assumptions underlying policies and proposals; examination of
the evolution of concepts, current status, and trends; tentative projec-
tion of polices; and proposals for action.

Also during its first meeting, the steering panel explored possible
content in each of the five areas and planned steps to be taken in
getting the project under way.   One step was that of organizing a
national committee in each area with membership representative of
all segments of the profession and geographically distributed throughout the United States.   By early October 1959, all committees were
organized and an orientation conference for all participants was held.
Here, T. M. Stinnett, speaking for the NCTEPS, charged the participants with the critical importance of the project and expressed
the hope that it would reach horizon-level accomplishment.   In separate work sessions each committee examined its assigned area and
projected procedures for carrying out responsibilities.

All participants in the project were committed to a principle of
widespread involvement insofar as it was possible within time and
manpower limitations.   To this end a questionnaire soliciting reactions and suggestions in each of the five areas was sent to a sample
of institutions preparing teachers, to professional organizations having
interest in one or more of the areas, and to selected individual members of the profession.   Responses were thoughtfully prepared, often
through special meetings of college faculties, state commissions on
teacher education and professional standards, and other such groups.
Data from this questionnaire were analyzed and results were submitted to all five committees for their use.

About the same time, a printed brochure describing the project
and requesting reactions was distributed.   This brochure drew forth
numerous inquiries, many statements of support, and provocative
questions and suggestions.

At each of the seven regional TEPS conferences held in 1960, a
paper discussing assumptions behind the project and raising questions
about professional responsibility was presented.   This was followed
by discussion focused on tentative recommendations submitted by
each committee.   A summary of these discussions was forwarded to
all committee members.   Essentially the same procedure was used
in getting reactions and suggestions from an assembled group at the

1960 conference of the American Association of Colleges for Teacher Education.

Between November 1959 and March 1960 each committee held a work session. Generally, tentative drafts of statements on aspects of the areas for which the committees were responsible were prepared and exchanged in advance of these work sessions. At these sessions the committees sought to reach agreements on issues, to determine the nature of their reports, and to set and assign responsibilities for completion of the reports.

A pamphlet presenting preliminary recommendations was published in June 1960. This served as the basis for a report to the National Education Association at its annual convention and to the annual meeting of State TEPS Chairmen the same month. Wide distribution of this pamphlet resulted in careful study of the preliminary recommendations. The effect of reports from the field, indicating clear support of some proposals, serious questions about others, and rejection of still others, was to cause major modification in the final report of the project group to the NCTEPS.

By August tentative drafts of full-length reports were ready and all committee members came together for a work conference. At this time criticisms of reports were considered, issues were analyzed and agreements were reached on their treatment, and plans were made for completing the present report to the NCTEPS.

The steering panel met with the NCTEPS at three sessions held during the period the project was being developed. The first time, a proposal for carrying on the project was presented for reactions and suggestions (August 1959). Six months later a complete report of what had been done up to that time and some preliminary recommendations were the content of discussion (February 1960). The third meeting was devoted to the panel's report of major recommendations and to joint discussion of them (August 1960).

Following the August (1960) meeting, committees made final revisions of their reports, taking into account the many reactions and suggestions from groups and individuals in the profession, as well as specific suggestions of the NCTEPS.

This Report

This is a report of the New Horizons Project, made by a task force assigned a specific responsibility by the NCTEPS and asked to report its findings and recommendations to the NCTEPS. It is intended to present recommendations, to provide a rationale for them, and to propose action that might be taken by individuals and groups toward more complete professionalization of teaching. The NCTEPS has not yet taken action on the recommendations presented. Before them lies the task of deliberation on the recommendations and the development of policy statements to guide activities in the years immediately ahead as the profession accelerates its progress in the advancement of professional standards.

Members of the task force hereby express their appreciation for the opportunity to be associated intimately with a significant undertaking. Appreciation is expressed to the NEA for the grant which made the project possible, for the co-operation and support of officers and professional staff throughout the development of the project; to the Commission and its executive secretary and professional staff for facilitating in many ways the work of the project group; to those in the field who responded to requests for suggestions and criticisms—representatives of other professions, as well as educators.

Margaret Lindsey

Margaret Lindsey, Editor
Director of the Project

CHAPTER 1

Introduction

THE CHARGE GIVEN to the individuals responsible for this report was to define new goals and to propose action to advance the standards of the teaching profession. Many individuals contributed to the execution of this charge through discussions at various conferences and through written reactions to preliminary reports. Responsibility for what appears in this document, however, must be borne by the task force to whom the assignment was given by the National Commission on Teacher Education and Professional Standards. A few comments about this task force and its responsibility are in order.

Members were selected to ensure a representative total group and, as far as possible, representative subcommittees. First, there were representatives from all segments of the teaching profession—classroom teachers and administrators at the elementary-school, secondary-school, and college levels; teachers of both professional and academic subjects in teacher education programs; and staff members of state professional associations and of state departments of education. Second, all geographic regions of the United States were represented. Third, each problem area encompassed in the project was represented by individuals whose leadership in that area had been recognized. A complete list of the working members is to be found on pages iii through v.

As background for reading this report, it is important to understand how the task force resolved certain problems faced—interpretation of the designation of the project, agreement on recommendations, and coverage of the area for study.

Interpretation of New Horizons

The term *new horizons* was employed initially by T. M. Stinnett, executive secretary of the NCTEPS, in his original letter to the NEA Board of Directors requesting a special grant to carry on the project. The term was emphasized at the first conference of working members when Dr. Stinnett presented them with their charge.

A persistent point of discussion in the early stages of the project was the question, "What is a new horizon?" It became clear that what to some was "new" to others was "old." It was subsequently assumed that this would be equally true for readers of the report. The problem of presenting entirely *new* horizons was further complicated by the necessity of placing various recommendations in a meaningful context. For example, in order to clarify a proposal on internships some picture of the total program of preservice teacher education had to be presented. A recommendation that the profession accelerate its concern and support for the National Council for Accreditation of Teacher Education could not be made understandable apart from some consideration of the total process of accreditation. Consequently, inclusion of such general background material makes it even more likely that readers will find "old" horizons among the new. The risk has been undertaken deliberately, however, in the interest of clearer communication. Each reader may find in the pages of this report some concepts, interpretations, and suggestions for action that are relatively new to him.

Agreement on Recommendations

From the outset the intention of those selecting committee personnel was to appoint individuals whose points of view differed on major issues confronting education and the teaching profession. Thus, by design, controversy was introduced into the project. While efforts were made to identify precise points of disagreement and to resolve controversy wherever possible, it was not expected that all committee members would agree with all proposals receiving majority approval, either within a single committee or within the task force as a whole.

This expectancy proved to be accurate. Two comments must be made about this fact. First, participants testified that where conflict was dealt with openly in developing proposals the end product was better than it would have been had all placidly agreed from the beginning. Second, although all the final recommendations presented in this report are supported by most committee members, there are individuals who would take exception to specific recommendations.

Coverage of Assigned Area

The report is organized around the five areas originally designated by the NCTEPS in its assignment to the task force. While all five areas are essential components of a whole, which might be labeled "professional self-discipline," they do not equal the whole. In other words, there are important aspects of professional self-discipline not included in this particular project. For example, failure to deal with professional accreditation of elementary and secondary schools, with the nature of professional organizational structure, or with criteria for membership in the profession to any considerable extent and with directness is failure by deliberate decision, not by oversight. The basis for the decision resides in the charge to the task force.

Furthermore, those areas that are included are interrelated in complex, though highly desirable, ways. When selection of professional personnel is treated with any degree of completeness, attention must be given not only to early identification of able youth, but also to selection that is an integral part of programs of preparation at all levels and to selection on the basis of performance throughout the career of the educator. Similarly, the purposes and means of professional accreditation cannot be considered fully without including the relationship of this process to preservice programs of preparation and to licensure and employment of teachers and other educators. Regardless of how the total content of the five areas is cut, overlapping, though reduced to a minimum, persists because each part is so integrally related to each other part and to the whole. The duplication in idea development that remains is viewed as necessary to completeness of discussion in each area.

Plan of the Report

Chapter 2 is a brief statement of definition of the profession as viewed by the task force. The perspective of the profession presented here is basic to understanding and interpreting the ideas appearing in the remainder of the report. A sketch of some pertinent factors in education's setting today, with implications for the teaching profession, is provided in Chapter 3. Chapters 4, 5, 6, 7, and 8 are basically the reports of the five committees associated with the project. Preparation of professional personnel is considered in Chapter 4. The focus of Chapter 5 is accreditation of preparatory programs. Licensure, as a key process in professional discipline, is discussed in Chapter 6. Chapter 7 deals with the continuous selection of professional personnel from early identification of able youth throughout the career of the educator. Chapter 8 considers policies and procedures incumbent upon the teaching profession if it is to assume its full responsibility in the development and enforcement of standards. Finally, an image of the teaching profession in the decades ahead is presented in Chapter 9 as a summary of recommendations from the New Horizons Project.

CHAPTER 2

The Teaching Profession, 1961

1,400,000	teachers in public elementary and secondary schools
220,000	teachers in private elementary and secondary schools
130,000	school administrators, supervisors, consultants, researchers and other specialists in elementary and secondary schools
350,000	professional personnel in higher education institutions
25,000	professional staff members in professional organizations, in government offices of education, and in private agencies with educational programs

2,125,000   *This is the size of the teaching profession, 1961.*

Who Are Included?

The statistics presented above imply what to many is a new concept of the body constituting the teaching profession. The implication is deliberate, for this is the perspective of the potential teaching profession as viewed by those responsible for this report. Included are all teachers, supervisors, administrators, researchers, consultants, and other specialists engaged in professional services in schools and colleges, in professional associations, in government offices of education, in voluntary accrediting agencies, and educators working in organized programs in business and industry.

What Qualifies a Professional?

To draw broad limits around the group of people who may be encompassed in a profession is one way of defining it. For more accurate definition, however, qualifications of individuals making up the professional body must be examined. An individual who qualifies as a professional, regardless of the particular profession of which he is a part:

Is a liberally educated person.

Possesses a body of specialized skills and knowledge related to and essential for the performance of his function.

Is able to make rational judgments and to take appropriate action within the scope of his activities, and is responsible for the consequences of his judgments and action.

Places primary emphasis upon his service to society rather than upon his personal gain.

Actively participates with his colleagues in developing and enforcing standards fundamental to continuous improvement of his profession and abides by those standards in his own practice.

Practices his profession on a full-time basis.

Is engaged in a continuing search for new knowledge and skill.[1]

The teaching profession should be no exception in requiring its members to qualify by these standards.

What Unites a Diversified Profession?

More than two million specialists in education are bound together by a chain of common purpose: to provide the best possible education for the citizens of this nation. Commitment to this socially significant purpose predisposes individuals toward a pursuit of excellence in the performance of their specialized functions. Group commitment to this purpose creates an atmosphere of freedom and respect, an atmosphere in which each individual is challenged, as well as protected, in using his full potential for scholarly and imaginative approaches to his tasks. If the broad strokes painted in this picture of the profession are not entirely accurate as of now, the least that can be said is that the conditions implied are to be desired.

Within this body there exists differentiation in function and consequent variation in specialization, but such differentiation does not entail differences in status, prestige, or quality of contribution to the central purpose. The work of the first-grade teacher who opens wide new vistas for groups of children year after year is not more or

---

[1] This list of qualifications of a professional was derived from analysis of statements of such qualifications in several professions, including education.

less important than that of the research scientist who confines his teaching to tutoring two advanced doctoral students each year; it is different in kind. The contribution to the improvement of the educational program made by the school superintendent who succeeds in securing a sufficient allocation of funds for a new junior high school is not greater or smaller than that made by the faculty planning the program for that new school; it is different in kind. So it might also be said of the work of college teachers, of staff members of state departments of education, and of executive secretaries of state teachers associations.

The scope and complexity of educational programs in this country, where responsibility for this social institution is decentralized, are such as to make diversity in function a continuing necessity. Furthermore, effective performance of various functions calls for a high degree of specialized preparation. To illustrate, because an individual is a superb teacher of young children does not mean necessarily that he will be equally effective as a college teacher, for college teaching calls for some specialized skills different from those demanded of the teacher of young children. It does not follow automatically that because one is effective as a superintendent of schools he will also be effective as a college president. It cannot be assumed that the good high-school teacher is also competent to serve as a curriculum co-ordinator for the school system, for the functions of this office require additional and a different kind of specialization. Each different function in education, although calling for some abilities in common with all others, demands a degree of specialization directly related to that function.

To improve educational opportunity in this country it is imperative that all who by profession participate in educating children, youth, and adults come closer together in association so that mutual understanding and respect can be fostered and commitment to common purpose can be made an explicit guide for group and individual action. While groups need to unite in common purpose, diversity among groups must be maintained and freedom for group and individual operation must continue to be valued and guarded. Actually it is doubtful that an atmosphere of freedom for any one group can prevail without the association of all groups in promoting such freedom. To put it another way, any one group continuing to work in isolation will eventually find its arena of freedom reduced in size and its opportunity to contribute to the total task of education diminished. For example, college faculties concerned with the preparation of classroom teachers will increase their scope of freedom and their impact on education when they work constructively with other groups in the profession, such as elementary- and secondary-school teachers and administrators. Learned societies will find that they can be more influential in decision-making with regard to school programs and preparation of teachers when they work with, not in isolation from or against, other groups making up the teaching profession. Professional educators will discover that they can enhance their contribution to collegiate programs when they work with and respect the contribution of liberal arts professors.

A profession is more than a mass of competent individuals, for a profession as a whole has responsibility for the quality of its unique, definite, and essential social service and for the development and enforcement of standards in the continuous selection, preparation, and performance of its members. Such responsibility can be assumed adequately only when a profession has some structure and organization, including machinery for policy formulation and enforcement in discipline of its individual and group members.

The Subject of This Report

The responsibility of these more than two million educators, diverse in function and specialization, for the quality of educational opportunity made available to fifty-six million children, youth, and adults in the United States is the subject of this report. More specifically, the pages that follow present recommendations, with underlying rationale, on what the teaching profession should do in assuming more fully its responsibility for improving the quality of education through its own self-discipline.

Before turning attention to the recommendations in each of the five areas encompassed by the project, a brief look at special responsibilities of the teaching profession in this decade is presented in Chapter 3.

Responsibilities of the Teaching Profession in the Sixties

The Setting

MOST CITIZENS in the United States realize that good education is critically important to the survival and improvement of democracy in the world and at home. But education has become an enormous, complex enterprise, and it costs more than many people want to pay. Even among those who believe that an educated citizenry is crucial, there is concern about keeping costs at a minimum while at the same time improving the quality of education. Such concern prompts the giving of much advice, often by nonspecialized persons. Some educators wish to take a careful look at what is involved in increasing the quality of educational opportunity. They are aware of urgencies growing out of rapidly developing knowledge, not only about what is important to learn but also about how people seem to learn what they learn. These people believe that fundamental improvement of education involves more than widespread utilization of technical devices, reorganization of schools and personnel, or development of a national curriculum.

At a time when concern about the education and its cost is general, when evidence of effectiveness of current programs is inadequate, when different approaches to problems of education are suggested in all segments of the population, and when everything surrounding the educational enterprise changes almost overnight, the task of making decisions about education is complicated. At such a time, the question of who makes what decisions and how takes on more than passing significance.

Our Educational System Is Situated in a Democracy

If, in truth, there are values inherent in democracy that make it different from other forms of society, such values must surely dictate

9

differences in the purposes and procedures of major social institutions in a democracy as compared with those in other ideologies. That the teaching profession being discussed in this report is situated in a democracy in the United States and not in any other form of society elsewhere in the world is the most significant fact in its setting. Moreover, that it is situated in American democracy at a particular time in history is important, for by now experience with our form of democracy is sufficient to have made possible identification of priorities and to have brought about new and increasingly insightful interpretations of basic tenets.

Our democratic setting includes a commitment to equality of educational opportunity for all, a commitment that gives rise to some of our most perplexing problems in education today. It encompasses a concept of respect for the integrity of each human being, a concept that truly sets our society apart from many other forms of social, economic, and political organization. It embraces a commitment to the protection of individual freedoms as well as protection of individual-group relationships. It includes a principle of grass-roots involvement in decision-making, a belief in keeping decisions close to the point of operation. While placing unquestionable confidence in the intelligence of the citizenry, it fosters a principle of respect for specialization. In this democratic setting decisions about education must be made, and both the decisions and the processes of arriving at them must be consistent with its basic value commitments.

In a Democracy Good Education
Is Critically Important

A long exposition is not required to illuminate or support the critical importance of education today. The proportion of people needed in various kinds of work to sustain and improve our economy has undergone drastic modification in recent years. Fewer unskilled laborers are needed; many more semiskilled, skilled, and professional people are demanded. Even if this were the only condition to be considered, it would be clear that more education for more people is important. But this is not the only factor to be taken into account.

Our democracy depends upon intelligent participation. Because this is so, each citizen, insofar as his capacity permits, needs to understand and be able to accept his responsibility as a participating member. Ability to accept such responsibility is composed of considerable knowledge, basic skills of various kinds, and positive attitudes. To ensure that people take seriously and are prepared to assume their responsibilities of citizenship is a major purpose of education.

> The degree of effective liberty available to its people should be the ultimate test for any nation. Democracy is the only means so far devised by which a nation can meet this test. To preserve and protect the democratic process in the United States is therefore a primary goal in this as in every decade.
>
> The democratic process functions only when the individual accepts his full responsibility as a citizen by forming considered opinions on public policy and by active participation in the choice of public representatives.[1]

Achievement of this purpose is more critical in a democracy than in any other social order.

Many things going on in the world around us serve to underscore the urgency of education. If this nation is to assume its appropriate role in the exploration of outer space and nuclear energy for peaceful purposes, and if we are to survive in the face of world competition to divert such explorations to other than peaceful purposes, our educational programs will have to produce men capable of doing the job. Perhaps time will prove that the most serious competition in the world is not these kinds of explorations but rather competition for the intellectual and value commitments of people. Today it is certain that both scientific explorations and intellectual commitment are important, and it is equally certain that both make education a focal point for concerted effort.

Confronting change that is unprecedented in speed and scope, the United States finds itself without ready solutions to many new problems, both domestic and foreign. It is doubtful that any previous period in history has had greater demands for creativity and innovation. To develop individuals who have what it takes to deal effectively with these problems requires education of high quality. Beyond these evidences of the critical importance of education is the fact that an affluent democratic society cherishes for all its members a good life, a life that is enriched by each individual's fulfillment of his potential. There can be no question that education is crucial at this time.

---

[1] The President's Commission on National Goals, *Goals for Americans,* © 1960 by The American Assembly, Columbia University, New York, N.Y. (Englewood Cliffs, N.J.: Prentice-Hall, Inc., publisher), p. 4.

Our System of Education
Is a Complex Enterprise

Commitment to equality of educational opportunity for all citizens accounts, in considerable degree, for the development of free public schools in America and for the complexity of our present educational system. To what extent the founders of the common school anticipated some of the contemporary problems in society's efforts to provide equality of educational opportunity is a matter for educational historians. Even if their perceptions were enlightened beyond the times in which they worked, it is doubtful that the founders could have envisioned an educational program, beginning with the preschool years and extending through post-high-school years, and encompassing all the children of all the people. It is unlikely, also, that they could have conceived of a future where purposes of the free educational system would become progressively more complex and multiple. But these things have happened. Today fifty-six million individuals, of all ages, present themselves for organized education, not only in elementary and secondary schools, but in preschools, colleges and universities, technical institutes, and adult programs.

There is more to the bigness and complexity of the educational program than size alone, however. When all the children present themselves to the school to be educated, the resulting population is one covering the entire range of human variability. Differences among individuals are not confined to native capacity to learn. They extend through all aspects of development, from physical vigor to value orientation. This population includes those called adjusted as well as those judged to be maladjusted by social standards; those who have suffered deprivation as well as those who have been blessed with abundance of spiritual and material well-being; those who think, feel, speak, and act in patterns of one culture and those whose thinking, feeling, speaking, and acting are indigenous to another culture.

Providing only for the middle range of each of such differences would present problems enough. Because we are committed to equality of educational opportunity, we must provide the best we can for all. Clearly, providing equality of opportunity for all does not suggest an educational program geared to the least common denominator. It suggests, rather, a program that is challenging to each individual, one that is appropriate to his particular abilities and needs. What is challenging to the ten-year-old who is talented in science is not likely to be the same as that which challenges the ten-year-old who is severely limited in his control of fundamental processes of communication. Similarly, what may be best for the high-school student headed for a career in medicine may not be best for the young humanist. Quite obviously, a commitment to equality of opportunity demands differentiation in the opportunities provided.

Further, there are a variety of exceptionalities in this mass population, each of which calls for special arrangements, often of very particular kinds. Consider the problems of providing for those who are handicapped in one way or another—physically, mentally, or emotionally. Think of the range of specific handicaps in any one of these types. Exceptionalities also include those who are gifted; not only those who are generally intellectually gifted, but also those who are gifted in special areas or abilities, such as those talented in creative arts of all kinds. Again, equality of opportunity, properly interpreted, demands programs to challenge all those who fall within the range of exceptionality.

To organize, administer, and conduct a mass educational program that actually provides for equality of opportunity has been one of the great American experiments. In the judgment of many, it has been an experiment which makes America unique among the nations of the world.

The Cost of Good Education Is High

The battle for free public education providing equality of opportunity for all the children of all the people has never been won in this nation. Clear evidence of this fact is found in the nature of the public's financial support of education. Because the school population has grown more rapidly than the general population, mounting costs of education appear to be disproportionately large. The magnitude of the educational enterprise, including schools at all levels and in all communities, has precipitated increased need for improvements in organizational structure and management. Size alone accounts for some of the increased demands for personnel, for buildings and equipment, for materials. But size does not account for all the increased demands.

Differentiation of program called for, if the needs and abilities of all are to be taken into account, creates an additional claim on the dollar set aside for education. Caring for extreme differences, those who are atypical or exceptional, is a relatively expensive part of the program. Providing educational opportunity during the preschool and post-high-school years similarly places stress on the school budget of the local community and of the nation.

Accompanying the growth of the educational program in size and complexity has been an increase in the kind and amount of specialization required of those to whom the public assigns responsibility for carrying on the program. The supply of competent teachers has frequently been inadequate to demand. Concern about the important roles played by teachers in their daily work with youngsters has led, on the one hand, to provision of specialized help for them in the form of consultation and supervision. On the other hand, there have resulted all sorts of demands that teachers be more highly selected and better prepared for their tasks. But to encourage able young people to prepare for teaching and to retain them in the profession make necessary increased financial rewards. The same can be said for those who administer the educational program.

Furthermore, in the present setting there are clear needs for specialized personnel in addition to those who teach, supervise, or administer. Contemporary knowledge about human beings and learning suggests that some individuals, a surprisingly large percentage of them of school age, need very special kinds of help—psychological counseling and various remedial health services, for example. That the intellectual development of these pupils is deterred unless their specialized needs are met suggests that such specialized services may be essential if the school is to fulfill its central responsibility for the intellectual development of pupils. It takes highly specialized educators to organize, administer, and perform these services. Competent personnel cannot be secured for such purposes unless financial rewards are consistent with those available in other occupations demanding such services.

Even with this brief recounting of some of the characteristics and demands of America's program of mass education, it is immediately clear that such a program is expensive. Just how expensive it appears to be at the present time is colored by competing demands for the dollar. While the gross national product has been climbing steadily, and it might therefore be assumed that more money could be made available for the support of education, new demands on the national budget and on individual budgets are made by parallel conditions. Chief among these is the drain on financial resources brought about by efforts in the preservation and improvement not only of our own nation's way of life, but of democracy throughout the world. Consequently, the cost of free public education for all comes in for more critical examination than would be true if the economy did not have to support unprecedented programs of national survival. However, one is inclined to conjecture that even if the times did not demand placing priority on national security in allocating funds, the problems of adequate support for the institution of education in our society would continue to be pressing.

Under these conditions it is natural that the attention of laymen and educators alike should turn to a search for means whereby the quality of education would not suffer while its cost was being held at a minimum. Within this context people tend to deal with the cost of education from different perspectives. To some, cost is the overriding concern. It would appear that these people, few though they are, would have us sacrifice basic democratic values, disregard our heritage, woefully limit our goals, and stintingly provide a minimum education at as little cost as possible. Among these people are those who seem to discount the need to educate all the children of all the people. Either they do not believe in this democratic commitment or they simply want someone else to pay for it. Others, many of whom accept a principle of equality of opportunity, allow their concern with rising costs of education to dominate their thinking.

Most people in the United States are deeply and sincerely concerned about our educational program. They believe fundamentally that this society can and should provide good education for all. They want for all citizens educational opportunity of the highest quality. That this is true can be stated with confidence. With equal confidence, however, it can be stated that by and large the citizens of this nation do not yet realize all that is involved in providing the quality and scope of educational opportunity viewed as ideal. Financial support of education has never been equal to the ideal of equality of opportunity. In this sense the struggle to provide optimum educational opportunity for all has not yet been won in this nation.

Advice on Education
Is Plentiful

Because education of the young is so important, because making the ideal of equality of opportunity a reality takes more than we have yet been willing to give in both human and material resources, and because the cost of education places stress on the economy, many people offer all kinds of advice on education. For the most part these people are concerned, in a central way though not entirely, with maintaining and improving the quality of education with a minimum outlay of funds. Advice comes freely from those who are informed and have special competence to deal with problems in education; it comes just as freely from those who are uninformed and nonspecialized.

Much of the advice, presented in concrete proposals, relates to utilization of technological developments in teaching, to reclassification of pupils in schools, and to new schemes for the deployment of staff personnel. Primary among the technological developments are two: educational television and teaching machines. One who has had experience in teaching or who understands the complexities of learning would not seriously propose that educational television could replace the teaching staff to any appreciable degree. On the other hand, the real student of education and of teaching could not fail to see the contribution to education that can and should be made by appropriate use of television. What is lacking at present is research on exactly how television may best be employed in the educational program and substantial, accurate reports both as to cost and effectiveness of current experiments with its use.

Teaching machines, from simple, mechanical, toy-like devices to complex electronic laboratories, are proposed as means for cutting down the amount of time a teacher devotes to routine activities and for making a larger amount of independent learning possible for pupils. Observations of these aids to teaching and learning reveal, as is true with television, that they have positive potential for contributing to the educational program at some levels and in some areas. Real study of the particular contributions that might be made by widespread use of such devices has scarcely even begun.

Advice is forthcoming also on the regrouping of pupils. Proposals in this category tend to suggest one of two means for regrouping: Pupils should be classified on the basis of ability, thus supposedly increasing the efficiency of the teacher and ensuring attention to the needs of pupils. Or, pupils should be grouped in large sections for certain kinds of experiences, in smaller groups for other kinds of experiences, and dealt with individually for still other purposes. Most of the current suggestions on regrouping are not novel when viewed by themselves. What gives them novelty at this time is their combination with other proposals (on television, for example) and the emphasis some of their proponents place on them as ways of reducing the cost of education.

Various schemes for differentiating functions or roles of teachers are also being advocated. Common among such schemes is that often referred to as "team teaching." Schemes of this sort generally would increase the size of the pupil group in a class and provide a team of teachers, each with a different level of preparation and competence. Their roles in guiding the learning of youngsters would be differentiated primarily on the basis of what is judged (by advocates of the plan) to be professional activities, requiring fully prepared professionals, as compared with routine or technical services, requiring a technician instead of a professional.

The kinds of proposals just discussed do not often occur isolated from one another. More frequently they are suggested as "a package" and the interrelationships among them become part of a proposal.

While the public and educators alike are being advised to accept and implement proposals on utilization of television, teaching machines, homogeneous grouping, and "team teaching," advice of another dimension is being heard from some educators. This is advice of caution, calling for deliberation, study, research, experimentation, and analysis as bases for modifications. Advisers in this group also recognize the need for improvement in the educational program. They do not reject, nor do they discount the importance of various proposals such as those mentioned earlier. From their point of view, as they examine what is of significance to be learned in schools and colleges, they are convinced that much more is involved in fundamental improvement of education than the adoption of new devices or the reorganization of class groups.

It may be helpful, in understanding the advice of caution as compared with the advice of immediate and widespread utilization of technological developments, to look at the kinds of questions that seem to be of concern to various advisers. A few of those who propose immediate and wholesale modifications seem to be asking only one question: How can we reduce the cost of education? Others in this group are concerned with meeting the continuing shortage of qualified personnel. Still others appear to be asking fundamental questions, such as these: How can we make sure that the intellectually gifted youth of the nation have challenge to develop their full potential? How can we have more students profit from really great teachers?

The caution suggested by those advisers asking for more deliberate and careful consideration of all proposals is expressed well in Jerome Bruner's report of a conference on educational methods sponsored by the National Academy of Sciences:

> Yet there is always a question as to the purpose of any particular device—be it a film of paramecia or a slide projection of a graph or a television show on the Hoover Dam. *The devices themselves cannot dictate their purposes.* Unbridled enthusiasm for audio-visual aids or

for teaching machines as panaceas overlooks the paramount importance
of what one is trying to accomplish. . . . The objectives of the curriculum and the balanced means for attaining it should be the guide.[2]

Educators advising caution insist upon the focus suggested by the
conference group quoted. So they ask questions like these: What
should schools and colleges help students to learn? Are some things
more important than others? What are our bases for wise decisions
on what is to be learned through organized education? What do we
know about how people learn that will help in making productive
decisions on roles to be played by teachers, by material aids, by
various instructional methods?

This group of educators advises caution, but not because the questions raised by the first group are unimportant. Instead, believing
that "the objectives of the curriculum and the balanced means for
attaining it should be the guide," they insist upon re-examination of
their questions as a basis for moving to proposals on how technological developments may best be used to advance the purposes of education, on how schools should be organized to create the most
advantageous environment for learning, or on the kinds of responsibilities teachers must assume in helping students learn.

Someone may ask why, after all the years of analyzing results of
experimentation, research, and experience, it still is necessary to
spend time on clarification of what the schools and colleges should
help people to learn. Hasn't this question been settled? Like so
many questions basic to social, economic, and political institutions,
this question has been settled to the satisfaction of some people in
the past. But past answers are not good enough for today and tomorrow. Today's answers must take account of what we know today.
The truth of this statement is made crystal clear in a brief examination of today's expanding knowledge.

The Explosion of Knowledge Has Serious
Implications for Educational Programs

The "explosion of knowledge" in today's world is a common topic
for discussion. What is usually meant is that new information, new
facts, new principles are being introduced at a rapid pace, often
extending or displacing entirely established generalizations and sometimes initiating whole new bodies of knowledge or new organizational
structures for old bodies of knowledge. That such an explosion is

---

[2] Jerome S. Bruner, *The Process of Education* (Cambridge, Mass.: Harvard University Press, 1960), p. 87-88.

taking place is apparent even to the man on the street. It is markedly more apparent to those engaged in education. They must re-examine their concepts of knowledge and its place in the school; they must discover what this explosion of knowledge means for the educational program.

In view of the current accretion of new knowledge and the probability that the future will see even more rapid development of knowledge, one thing is clear. The school cannot hope to teach all the knowledge pupils will need in the years ahead; teachers in preparation cannot hope to acquire all the knowledge they will need to teach. What knowledge, then, should prospective teachers be expected to acquire? Similarly, what knowledge should students be helped to learn? Even if it were possible (and it is not) for students to acquire the presently available knowledge, this would be inadequate for the future. Or, to state it from another perspective, if the educational program sets as its primary goal helping students to acquire today's organized bodies of knowledge, the goal falls far short of what students will need in the future. If acquisition of today's knowledge is inadequate, what should the educational program strive to help students accomplish with regard to knowledge?

One answer to this question is found in the proposition that what students need to learn in any field of knowledge is how to go on learning in that field. But what does this proposition mean? First, an individual is unlikely to go on learning in a field unless he feels strongly motivated. Second, unless a person is equipped with methods of inquiry required in a field, he cannot go on learning in an independent and creative manner. Third, until an individual has a base of what is known, he is severely handicapped in advancing his knowledge.

What motivates individuals to continue to examine, explore, experiment, analyze, innovate, discover, create? Put simply, such motivation is a product of what the individual is by reason of his past experience and his aspirations, and of the intellectual and psychological climate in which he is situated. To be highly motivated to continue to learn, the individual must already have learned through experience that there are unknowns, that searching for new ideas, relationships, or modes of behavior is exciting and rewarding. He must be in an environment where his teachers demonstrate intellectual curiosity, where they share their own searchings, excitements, and rewards. He must be in an environment where the expectancies place priority on independent, creative exploration into fields of knowledge.

What about the required equipment for successful inquiry? There are general and specific aspects of this equipment. On the general side, there are those skills, abilities, and predispositions basic to all intellectual inquiry, such as skills of communication, ability to see logical relationships, whether they be quantitative or qualitative, tendency to withhold conclusions until all data are in, ability to locate and the disposition to utilize a range of sources of evidence. General equipment, constituted of skills and abilities like these, is necessary for all people in their roles as citizens in a democracy and as human beings seeking self-fulfillment. For those individuals who are going to make deeper exploration into any given field of knowledge, additional equipment is required. This equipment is often unique to a field and includes understanding of the kinds of questions that have particular relevance, control of the methods of inquiry that hold special promise for the field, and familiarity with pertinent sources and their use.

It has been suggested that a base of what is already known in a field is essential to further exploration in that field. What is this base? Earlier it was stated that neither teachers nor students can be expected to learn all that is now known in a field of knowledge. What is it, then, that should be known as the base for continued learning? It is proposed by some scholars that every field of knowledge has its own structure composed of relationships which may be stated as principles or generalizations regarding the data of the field; that the number of those principles is small; that they serve both as the beginning understanding of a field and as the center of the advanced scholar's exploration of new knowledge in a field.[3] If this be true, perhaps the needed base for inquiry is the comprehension of principles, with depth of comprehension determined by the level of the inquirer.

There is more to be said about today's expanding knowledge than that it is accumulating in quantity. One important idea is illustrated by this incident: A homemade bomb went off in a telephone booth on a busy corner in the city. When those responsible were rounded up and questioned, it turned out that a sixteen-year-old boy, attending high-school classes for the gifted in science, had constructed and placed the bomb. The point of the illustration is simply the old question of "Knowledge for what?" It is the same question that troubles many persons in all parts of the world right now in the form of

---

[3] *Ibid.* For those interested in this concept of structure, analysis of it will be found in Chapter 2. The statement made here is the author's interpretation and, therefore, should not be ascribed to Bruner.

"Nuclear energy for what?" Thus it may be said that a necessary part of knowledge, if it is to contribute to advancement of civilization (or to enhancement of the individual), is a value orientation, a morality with respect to its use.

What has been said here about knowledge in general applies just as truly to fields that are foundational to teaching (psychology, philosophy, sociology, anthropology, and so on) and to the accumulating body of knowledge that is called by some the discipline of education. Because this is true, it follows that those who teach or perform related services in education must also deal with the specialized knowledge of their profession as scholars continuing to learn.

Thus far we have been discussing some of the particular conditions surrounding education today that appear to have special implications for the teaching profession, its role and responsibilities in the sixties. Let us turn now to a closer look at some of those responsibilities.

The Responsibilities

Conditions surrounding education and educators at this time present problems difficult to solve. Answers to most questions about education are not easily arrived at, nor does it appear that they can be clear-cut, black or white. For example, can or should this nation continue in its efforts to provide equality of educational opportunity for all? If so, by what organization of the school, by what classification of pupils, by what assignments to teachers, by what selection of purposes? Or, to take another illustration, is it impossible to supply the number of qualified teachers needed in the nation's schools and therefore necessary to develop plans that can be carried out with fewer professionals? Or, one more example, how can technological developments be used to best advantage in the educational program?

Who is responsible for making decisions on such questions? In considering the placement of responsibility it is important to take account of the social setting—democracy as developed in the United States. In that setting, the people are granted the right and the responsibility to make decisions affecting their welfare. Decisions about education fall in this category. So also do many basic decisions about medicine, law, and economics. As society has advanced, as institutions (such as education) have become more complex, and as knowledge has been accumulated, it has become necessary for the people to delegate their rights (responsibilities) of decision-making in specialized areas to those who are expert in those areas. When the people delegate a right, they still possess the right. They have simply asked their representatives to assume responsibilities for them, often because they feel unprepared.

A perplexing problem for the personnel of many specialized services and agencies in our society is that of determining when the people are prepared and competent to make decisions and when they are not. Or, to put it another way, which areas of decision may appropriately be dealt with by the public and which areas actually call for a degree of specialization beyond that characteristic of people in general? It may even be said that this problem is more perplexing for educators than for any other group because of the marked tendency for all educated people to view themselves as experts in education.

Because society has set up a formalized agency to carry on the education of the young and because the public must provide financial means for conducting that agency, the public has a stake in and a responsibility for its effectiveness. The question is, At what points should the public assume responsibility for decisions on education and at what points should the public turn to the profession or grant the profession of specialists responsibility for decisions? It is important that the public and the profession have clear concepts of their respective roles and that each support the other to the end of providing the best possible educational opportunity for all.

The division of major responsibilities in decision-making about education, as presented in the chart on page 23, is suggested as a point of departure for consideration of this very important problem.

Primary obligations of the public include establishing broad policies regarding education, determining purposes it desires to have this social institution accomplish, and providing working conditions that facilitate achievement of goals. The profession should provide appropriate leadership in public decision-making in each of these areas. For example, though the public may have certain kinds of evidence on the cost of the education it wants for its children and youth, the profession may have additional data and should assume leadership in securing consideration of these data when they are crucial to decisions on allocation of funds for schools.

Again, the public may make unrealistic demands on schools through lack of specialized knowledge or failure to make careful analyses of priorities in functions to be served by formal education. In matters of direction and goals, it is the responsibility of the profession to take leadership in working with the public through providing additional information, introducing new questions, and presenting analyses of alternative proposals. The profession is obligated, fur-

The Profession's Responsibility		The Public's Responsibility
joining with the public in	{ establishing public policy regarding education determining purposes of education providing working conditions conducive to productivity }	joining with the profession in
assuming autonomy for	{ determining and utilizing best means for achieving agreed-upon purposes ensuring competent professional personnel }	granting the profession the right to make and carry out decisions in
joining with the public in	{ evaluating achievement of purposes appraising public policy regarding education }	joining with the profession in

This analysis is based on the definition of a professional as stated in Chapter 2.

ther, to create public understanding of working conditions necessary for carrying on the business of education effectively.

A clear distinction must be drawn, however, between the public's responsibility for decisions on education as public policy and the public's relation to execution of that policy. When it comes to determining the means for accomplishing purposes agreed upon by the public and the profession, the public should, with complete confidence, give autonomy to the profession. Where decisions call for expert or specialized knowledge, a principle of respect for specialization or expertness is not without precedent. The public may decide as policy to provide preventive medicine for all children and youth, but the public does not presume to determine exactly how this policy shall be implemented. Decisions on best means for executing the policy are left to specialists in medicine who have the expertness necessary for intelligent choice. The public may decide that schools should help all pupils to achieve maximally in the communication skills, but the public must then allocate to the profession the responsibility for carrying out this policy. Similarly, the public may require that those who carry on the educational program be qualified, but decisions on the meaning of "qualified" and procedures assuring that only qualified personnel serve in the educational program belong to the profession.

This is the true meaning of professional autonomy: that the profession is granted by the public the right to make and carry out decisions that call for professional expertness. Assignment of responsibility is accompanied by accountability. When the public grants to the profession autonomy in determining means to be employed in achieving purposes, the public may, and indeed should, be concerned with whether or not its policies and purposes are being implemented effectively. Here, too, the profession should assume initiative and leadership in working with the public in continuous examination of the educational program in terms of co-operatively determined policies and purposes.

In granting to a profession responsibility for making decisions important to the general welfare, the public places a high degree of confidence in the profession. This confidence is based primarily on an assumption that there is professional expertness derived from a body of knowledge which is unique to the profession and without which expertness would be absent.

One of the most challenging tasks confronting the teaching profession at this time is making more explicit the content of its expertness, particularly the body of knowledge basic to it. To suggest this as an important task is not to imply that there is any question about the central premise of expertness unique to the teaching profession. Rather, it is to indicate that the present level of sophistication with respect to all professions, and particularly the teaching profession, makes necessary re-examination of professional expertness and its foundations.

In every profession there are basic questions peculiar to the ends and means of the social service to be rendered by it. As such questions have arisen in teaching, the profession appropriately has sought help from available organized bodies of knowledge such as philosophy, psychology, and sociology. In the future, these disciplines will continue to contribute valuable data for use by educators, and the teaching profession will wisely employ such data in dealing with its unique questions and problems.

However, the process of relying on other disciplines for data needed to deal effectively with questions and problems in teaching is by itself inadequate for now and the future. As experience with this process has accumulated over the years, several significant things have happened. First, organized bodies of knowledge on which the teaching profession has typically drawn were not (and are not now) systematized with reference to questions peculiarly pertinent to teaching. Scholars in education, seeking help from such bodies of knowledge, have had to assume responsibility for translation of data into its relevance or significance with reference to their particular questions. Translations have often been inaccurate, inappropriately applied, and misleading. On the other hand, scholars in the various disciplines, sympathetic to the need for translating data of their fields into useful forms for education, have often based their efforts to translate data on inaccurate, inappropriate, and misleading concepts of schools and teaching. With the rapidly increasing knowledge about problems in education and the explosion of knowledge in the several disciplines, the problem of bridging the gap between data in various disciplines and their implications for schools and teaching has become even more difficult. The question of who is responsible for such bridging has become more pressing.

Second, accumulated experience in utilizing knowledge from other disciplines to solve problems in education has made evident that very few, if any, questions in teaching can be answered by application of data from a single discipline. The scholar in education has learned that he must draw not on one body of knowledge but on several if he is to arrive at effective answers to his questions about the ends and means of his professional tasks.

A third conclusion from experience is implied in the second. It seems quite clear that if data from other disciplines are to be used appropriately in dealing with questions about teaching and learning, the point of departure in examining other disciplines must be the educator's questions. It is the question to which an answer is sought, or the issue on which resolution is desired, or the problem on which help is needed that must serve as the central criterion in selection and use of data from other fields of knowledge. Such questions, issues, or problems do not always arise from practical operations in education. They may, and frequently do, come to light in theoretical analyses by scholars in education. Too, they often are prompted by new findings in one or more of the several disciplines. Regardless of the source of such questions, however, their answers should be sought by taking off from the questions and utilizing whatever knowledge holds promise for contributing to their answers.

Fourth, and finally, experience in drawing from other disciplines in efforts to solve problems and answer questions about the ends and means of educating the young has produced a new body of knowledge that is peculiar to the tasks of professional educators. This body of knowledge includes questions which are uniquely revelant to teaching and schooling. It not only encompasses new categories for existing knowledge, but it also includes some distinctly new knowledge.

The challenge confronting the teaching profession referred to here, then, is that of defining this new body of knowledge which is peculiar to the tasks of professional educators. Considerable progress is currently being made in efforts to define teaching and to describe and categorize the discipline of education. The teaching profession needs to direct major energies in hastening this progress. Definition of the expertness peculiar to the professional educator is fundamental to the advancement of professional standards on all fronts. Furthermore, if the public is to place responsibility for the quality of education in the profession and have confidence in the profession's ability to assume this responsibility, the public must be assured of the profession's expertness. Such assurance will not be complete until the expertness is clearly defined.

Mr. and Mrs. Jones are citizens in a small community. As part of "the public," they place confidence in the teaching profession by granting to it, through their elected representatives, certain responsibilities. But, they are more than part of the public. They are parents of children who must attend the local school. In sending their children to school, they must perforce rely upon the competence of the professional educators working in that setting to provide the best possible education for their children. If Mr. and Mrs. Jones are to maintain confidence in the profession, they must know that their own children are being guided by qualified personnel who perform with excellence each day. In granting autonomy to the teaching profession, the public assumes that the profession can and will be accountable for the competence of all its members. As part of the public, Mr. and Mrs. Jones share this assumption. As parents of children attending a local school, they believe that those professionals conducting the education of their children are competent because they assume the profession is responsible for the competence of each and every member.

Implications of these assumptions for the teaching profession are quite clear. There is, indeed, a highly specialized kind of expertness possessed by the professional scholar in education. The profession is responsible for ensuring that its members possess this expertness and that their individual practice is consistent with it. This responsibility can best be guaranteed by the profession through the development and enforcement of standards of selection, preparation, and performance of all its members.

CHAPTER 4

Preparation of Professional Personnel

THE MORE THAN TWO MILLION persons identified in Chapter 2 as members of the teaching profession are individuals. They teach mainly in school and college classrooms, but they also teach in predawn sessions on television, in industry, in hospitals and at the bedside in individual homes. They teach children and youth, graduate students and other adults who seek continuing education. Some do not appear to be teaching, and others facilitate and contribute indirectly to teaching; they serve as materials specialists, co-ordinators of instruction, supervisors, administrators, researchers, consultants. Each, in his individual role, is competent because of the development of his unique potential in relation to the qualifications required of all professional educators. The challenge on the new horizon in the development of programs for continuous preparation of professional personnel is to identify clearly and to develop the critical imperatives for all educators, capitalizing upon the great asset found in the uniqueness and variations in human beings.

Goal Imperatives for Professional Educators

The new horizon reveals the teacher and other educators as professionals. The essential qualifications of a professional person have been outlined in Chapter 2. These standards apply to members of the teaching profession and have special meaning for the professional educator. Four of them merit further consideration in delineating goals to serve as guidelines for programs of preservice preparation and inservice growth.

Being a Liberally Educated Person Has Special Significance for the Professional Educator

Individuals achieve as educators because of the persons they are quite as much as because of the technical knowledge and skills they possess. What the professional educator is and does as a person is a dynamic factor in every educational function that he carries out. His effect upon others is contingent upon his behavior as a person. This applies not only to the direct teaching function but to the esteem in which the teaching profession is held and to the educator's role as a citizen contributing to the education and improvement of society. Being an educated person, then, for the professional educator means:

> Focus on a personality and what the professional educator is and does as a person—his attitudes, ethical standards and value commitments, life-shaping interests, mental health, and self-understanding.

> A liberal education that actually liberates and affects a person.

Individuals are always persons apart from their professional allegiances and responsibilities, but in a unique and special way the professional educator is a person within a profession.

The Professional Educator Has Advanced and Technical Knowledge Basic to Discharging His Special Functions

The professional educator, as any other professional, possesses advanced and technical knowledge essential to discharging effectively the exacting and difficult obligations of his functions. The professional educator must:

> Know his teaching field (or field related to his special function) as fact and as discipline.

> Be a specialist in the teaching-learning process, in understanding learners.

> Know education, what it can do and what it should do for people.

Specifically, the professional teacher of history knows history and its related fields, knows it to an advanced and technical degree, knows it as fact and as discipline. He knows learners, and learning, and materials which facilitate learning, all to advanced and technical degrees. He knows education, what it can do and what it should and must do for twentieth century America. He possesses technical skill in historical interpretation, in explanation, in causing others to do both valuational and comparative thinking. Such are characteristics of one earmark which identifies the professional educator: advanced and technical knowledge. "Advanced" is measured not from where the student begins but from where the profession is stationed, and is determined not from what is laid out but from what is learned.

On the new horizon, advanced knowledge in the three areas will be a part of the preparation of *every* professional educator. College teachers will be as concerned with genuine understanding of learning, learners, and the role of education as they have in the past been diligent about advanced and technical understanding of their teaching field. Work in the field of specialization will not be lessened, but provision will be made in the preparation of college teachers for consideration of all three areas. The same applies to the preparation of special service personnel. For example, the preparation of the superintendent of schools on the new horizon will include study in depth in such areas as human growth and development and the workings of the human mind, in sociology and fields relating to education as a community institution. Work in these areas is basic to his leadership role in the areas of curriculum development and business administration.

The Professional Educator Is Able to Make Far-Reaching Decisions Within a Framework of Personal Independence

The professional educator is cast in the role of making far-reaching decisions of grave import within a framework of personal independence. It is the professional educator who must decide what shall fill the fleeting hours when school is in session and, to a degree, what shall be a part of out-of-school activity:

What is important for learners to learn, for particular learners to learn, and to what degree.

What tools and methods can be employed to help learners achieve desired goals.

How to guide individuals so as to create a desire to go on learning, to develop ability to deal with the new and the unknown.

Automation for schooling may proceed apace, as may the automation of medical diagnosis and treatment. But the professional on the newest horizon currently envisioned still will be making far-reaching decisions. Some of his choices will be simplified by automation, some may even be directed by centralized authority and other controls, but in essence the professionally prepared educator will remain an independent, trusted individual whose checks and balances are essentially internal. His success in making what prove to be sound decisions will be the measure of his status as a professional.

As a consequence, the professional educator is educated to make decisions, exercise choices, render judgments. Good intentions are necessary but insufficient. Skill in decision-making, or even in decision-initiating, is to be cultivated assiduously, but that in itself is not enough. Preparation of the professional educator demands provision for deep immersion in the sutff of which decisions are compounded, wide familiarity with the choices which are possible, ceaseless practice in testing the pronouncements of authority and tradition in the light of moral and intellectual standards, and a deep personal commitment to a system of values.

Such are characteristics of the second earmark of the professional educator. With few external sanctions, he is entrusted with a very precious possession belonging to other people to handle as he sees fit. Because he is a professional, people impute to him the competence and integrity necessary to serve as a trustee for the very stuff of which their lives are made. Stature as a professional, then, means stature consonant with such trusteeship.

The Professional Educator Is a Person Committed to Moral and Intellectual Excellence, to Teaching Scholarship

To be fitted for trusteeship, a person must be captured by an ideal, a self-image committed to moral and intellectual excellence. The needed image is that of a teaching scholar who:

Has a genuine interest in learning and in continuing to learn.

Has the urge to share knowledge in ways to help others, in turn, to develop competence and genuine interest in learning.

Professional educators hold trusteeship for the precious ingredient of scholarship in our society. Hence the educator on the new horizon must be not only a scholar, but a scholar with a special flair.

That special flair is suggested by the two attributes just named. One is actual possession and continued acquisition of the knowledge the educator needs to discharge effectively his professional responsibilities. A genuine interest in knowledge, in the process of becoming learned, is not to be confused with mere mastery and accumulation of facts. Rather, it is an interest in learning based upon seeing relationships among facts and their relevance for use. It is an interest in learning buttressed by knowing how to learn and by intellectual curiosity. Such interest is caught, as well as taught. Today's teachers in elementary and secondary schools reflect rather faithfully the zest, the inquiringness of mind, the adventurousness in pursuing higher learning which were displayed by their college professors. They carry into their classrooms to appreciable degree the atmosphere of their college campuses. Their successors will continue to do the same. The professional educator on the new horizon will be characterized by a new degree of contagious interest in learning.

The second attribute is the urge to share knowledge in ways to help others develop competence and genuine interest in learning. This characteristic distinguishes the educator's scholarship and that of other professionals. Members of most professions, unless they carry a teaching role, do something *to* and *for* others that these individuals cannot do for themselves. By contrast, the educator works *with* others so as to help them to develop powers similar to his own, to develop scholarly interest and competence and the ability to go on learning. In a recent statement, Philip Phenix, while suggesting that this fundamental difference "sets teaching beyond professionalism," further clarifies the difference in this way:

> The pupil in this respect occupies a radically different position from that of a surgeon's patient or a lawyer's client. The professional person does what another is not expected to do; the teacher does what the other is expected to do. The professional person is related to others externally; the teacher is related to his students inwardly. The professional person acts essentially independently; the teacher works reciprocally. These are the differences that set teaching beyond professionalism.[1]

While Phenix is speaking directly of those who carry a teaching role, the characteristics of teaching scholarship must be equally known and understood by other professional educators. For example, those who counsel and work with teachers (supervisors, principals, superintendents) must have a clear understanding of the essential elements of teaching scholarship and must themselves be teaching scholars. In like manner, those who develop instructional materials must know what the teacher seeks to achieve and how he conceives his role. In fact, the resources for learning developing outside the school and the increasing scope of instructional materials within the school are potent factors in changing the teacher's role. His function is no longer that of being a major source of data. On the new horizon the teacher's role is that of bringing insight to situations and helping

---

[1] Philip H. Phenix, in a paper presented at the Connecticut State TEPS Conference, January 1960.

others to reflect intelligently, to weigh and to judge, to see through data and arrive at sound interpretations. This means helping learners to reflect upon and intellectualize their experiences. It means helping individuals learn how to learn; it means sharing knowledge in such a way that hunger is increased, not satiated. This role is much more difficult and much more challenging than that of presenting descriptive materials.

What do the four qualifications of the professional educator just discussed, and the further characteristics of a professional noted in Chapter 2, mean for the preparation of professional personnel? This question is the focus of the remainder of the chapter.

Planned Education Required

Competence to teach and to carry out other functions of the professional educator cannot be conceived as a by-product of becoming a well-educated person. To realize the goals under discussion requires a distinctive organization of learning experiences.

Planned Education Is Designed Education

The proposition that the preparation of professional educators is designed education suggests that much more is required than the presently all too common hit-or-miss collections of courses, credits, degrees. Persons who steer their way through college with degree requirements in a catalog as their guide are seldom fitted as professionals thereby. All too often the focus is on the degree rather than on the competence required of the teaching scholar and the needs of the particular student to achieve that competence. Explicitly, designed collegiate preparation for the professional educator should have three major characteristics. First, it should have constant validation and challenge from what teachers and other educators do, should do, and can do as individuals and as members of the teaching profession. Planned to accomplish certain purposes, the origin of the design is found in the demands of the profession served. Courses and other learning opportunities are developed and related one to the other in ways thought best to achieve the desired goals.

Second, planned education should provide for selection and guidance of learning opportunities with reference to the particular capabilities and needs of the individual student. Education for the teaching profession shortchanges students when it fails to extend them to their fullest capacities for learning. With regard for the over-all plan of the educational program, the individual student, with guidance, should design the program best suited to his needs and concerns. Each student, undergraduate or graduate, comes to his study with a particular background and individual competences. The teacher education program should permit and encourage persons to proceed at differing rates, with differing ranges of penetration into areas of intellectual endeavor, and in combinations appropriate to the individual.

Third, within the framework of the imperatives of teacher education, there should be opportunity for variety in planned programs. The uniqueness of each college—its particular student body, its faculty, its special educational problems—conditions the design that will best achieve the agreed-upon goals. Further, each program of planned education must be responsive to advances in knowledge and to the developing findings of research. No college, however, should be permitted to continue to prepare teachers which cannot provide a planned program that leads to the development of highly qualified teachers. Such a program must be philosophically based, scientifically designed, and constantly evaluated with reference to accepted professional standards.

Planned education, then, is a distinctive organization of objectives and learning opportunities for persons who are to be prepared as neophytes in the teaching profession and later, through advanced study and profitable experience, to become increasingly competent practitioners in that profession. Planned education is required equally for the preservice education of the teacher, for his continuing inservice education (both college work and activities sponsored by the school system), and for his education if he changes his function in the teaching profession.

The Dimensions of Designed Education Are Derived from the Fundamental Concerns of the Teaching Profession

The preceding discussion suggests that the demands of the teaching profession are constant referents in designing teacher education programs. The discussion of goals suggests that planned education for professional educators should:

Focus on what teachers and other educators should *do* as individuals and as members of the profession.

Have concern for what the educator *is* as a person, for development of the individual personality.

Permit and encourage individuals to proceed at differing rates, with differing ranges of penetration in areas of study, and in combinations appropriate to the individual.

Further exploration of the distinctive characteristics of the teaching profession suggests two other dimensions which should affect the design of teacher education programs.

First is the dimension of going beyond knowledge to action. It is not enough that professional preparation provide for understanding what the teacher and other educators should do. Performance is highlighted, sought for, criticized, evaluated, and nearly guaranteed before a stamp of approval is put upon a graduate. In the preparation of professional personnel, the educative cycle is considered incomplete until it has entered the phase of demonstrable competence to perform.

Second is the dimension that provides a balance between the practical and the possible. Professional preparation must never lose sight of the practical, though it should feed upon visions of the possible. In particular, teacher education can become so concerned with the vision of what the best teachers can do that it loses sight of what beginning teachers can do. In like manner, the preparation of educators to function in roles other than teaching must be viewed in relation to the competences required to begin effectively to carry out their trusteeships. In each instance, the critical factor is determining what is required to *enter* successfully and dynamically upon a particular career in the teaching profession and what is required to continue to grow and function effectively. This does not mean lowering sights; it means aiming at the right target to begin with.

Together, these two dimensions suggest a preservice program designed so that:

Provision is made for each member of the teaching profession to demonstrate through direct experience—student teaching and internships—his competence to perform in his chosen professional role.

The focus throughout the program is on what is essential for a *successful beginning* in the profession, including a grasp of his role sufficient to enable the neophyte to see and then seize the opportunities presented to him by practice in the profession.

For the educator in service who, as part of his program of continuing growth, engages in informal professional activities or in an organized program of advanced study, the design should also provide for demonstration of competence and should be focused on what is essential for the individual's steady progress in personal and professional growth.

All five dimensions (the two listed above and the three named at the beginning of the section) can be, in fact must be, achieved by every institution which assumes the responsibility for preparing persons who are professional educators. Some institutions will incorporate these dimensions in undergraduate programs for the education of teachers for elementary and secondary schools and for undergraduate-graduate preparation of college teachers to work in undergraduate liberal arts colleges. The same dimensions will be part of the design of graduate programs for the preparation of college teachers to work in schools of education and other teacher preparing institutions, and in graduate programs for educators preparing for special functions such as those represented by the fields of supervision, administration, and curriculum co-ordination. The same dimensions, with essentials for *continuing* individual growth replacing essentials for a successful *beginning* in the profession, will give focus to inservice programs for professional educators.

Planning the Program Requires the Co-operative Efforts of All Who Share in the Preparation of Professional Educators

The goals sought and the indicated dimensions of preparation suggest that the student's entire program must be considered professional preparation. When viewed from the perspective of new horizons, professional preparation cannot be limited to the work offered by a department of education. These offerings contribute to the preparation of the professional educator, but they do not accomplish it and are not uniquely responsible for it. No college has yet produced even satisfactory beginning teachers by merely adding offerings of a department of education to a nonprofessional curriculum.

The program must be conceived as a unified whole. All departments of a college or university, to the extent that they participate in teacher education, must share in the development of the program. The unique contribution of the arts and sciences to the teaching profession (to the professional educator as a person and in his "teaching" role) makes it necessary that those who teach general education or basic work in liberal education share in designing the teacher education program. Helping the prospective teacher, supervisor, or administrator to explore a field of specialization so that he can help others to know and understand that field requires the efforts of the specialist in that field. But those who are competent in general education, as well as those who have special background in professional education, must share in decisions regarding proposals for work in an area of specialization. Decisions must be made regarding knowledge most useful to the teacher, and proposals and policies in each area must be viewed in relationship one to another as they make up the total program.

In like manner, work in professional education has interlocking relationships with work in general education and specialization that require co-operative program-planning. Educational theory takes on meaning as it brings learners and major fields of knowledge into relationships that lead to needed behavioral change. All teaching methodology rests primarily upon concepts of learners, of learning, of educational goals. Educational theory and methodology being developed in relation to the various teaching fields and that offered through work in professional education need to be mutually understood and related. Then, too, education and its role in a culture are a part of the concern of the historian and the sociologist in looking at social institutions, as they are of the economist and the anthropologist.

The significant part to be played by the various aspects of the college program, and their interlocking relationships, make it crystal clear that the education of members for the teaching profession is the responsibility of the whole institution. Each institution in its own way should provide for co-operative approaches to planned program development. An institution-wide council on teacher education, representing the various academic fields and professional education, is a useful means for establishing program policies. In a university organization co-operative effort may be facilitated by including as faculty members of the school of education—either through a joint appointment or in an advisory (voting) relationship in program-planning—representatives from departments and schools offering work for future professional educators. Another useful way of strengthening co-operative efforts is team-taught courses offered jointly by the school or department of education and the appropriate department in the arts and sciences, for example, educational sociology, philosophy of education, and educational psychology. Whatever plan is used for co-operatively developing the program for professional educators, some group must function in a leadership role; the school or department of education should have that responsibility.

Everybody's business is nobody's business! The faculty members of the department of education are the logical persons to give the needed leadership and exercise a co-ordinating function because the preparation of professional educators is their major responsibility. They should be the best-informed and most soundly prepared in the field of teacher education as a whole enterprise. As a group answerable for *part* of that education, they should take the leadership in bringing to fruition the co-operative efforts of all who participate in the development of members for the teaching profession.   In making this proposal it is equally clear that the department of education cannot and should not take exclusive responsibility for the education of teachers.

The nature of the needed co-operative efforts can be more clearly seen by looking at the content and experiences to be included in the program of professional preparation.

A Sharp New Emphasis on the Acquisition and Control of Knowledge

The explosion of knowledge discussed in Chapter 3 bears directly upon work in each aspect of the program of professional preparation: general education, specialization in the teaching field, and professional education.   The growth of knowledge in each of these areas makes it impossible to acquaint the student with all that is known in a field, let alone anticipate what new knowledge will become available and necessary for the professional educator's effective functioning in the future.   This fact and its correlative—the need to go on learning, to have the competence to learn things as yet unknown, and to help others build that competence—point to a new horizon in the acquisition and control of knowledge.

Significance for Decision-Making and Use By the Educator as a Person and a Professional Is the Key to Content Selection and Design

Significance for high-quality use is proposed as the central criterion for content selection and organization on the new horizon.   The rapid and continued growth of knowledge makes necessary selection from all that is available.   The basis of selection is found in the concern for going beyond knowledge to action, a distinctive feature in the preparation of a professional educator.   Knowledge becomes something to be used; its acquisition goes beyond knowing to the ability to analyze, to synthesize, to evaluate, to apply.   The challenge on the new horizon lies in effecting the needed balance between awareness and understanding of the fields of knowledge as disciplines and the ability to use knowledge functionally.

Significance in terms of the goals sought—enthusiasm for learning, intellectual curiosity, ability to meet the challenges of new situations, willingness and ability to think and to act in keeping with tested values—suggests the selection of content basic to understanding:

> The methods of inquiry required in a field, questions that have particular relevance; tools and procedures by which facts, concepts, and propositions are analyzed, related, and evaluated; pertinent sources and their use.

> The fundamental structure of the discipline or field as found in the major principles or generalizations regarding the data of the field.

> An essential morality regarding the use of the data of the field; a value orientation.

The criterion of significance, in terms of the decisions to be made and action to be taken by the professional educator as a person and as a professional worker, applies equally to each area of the program of professional preparation.   What the criterion might mean for general education, specialization, and professional education is considered in the sections that follow.

In GENERAL EDUCATION *Man's Common Concerns Determine the Selection and Interrelationship of Knowledge from Various Fields*

The imperative for general education on the new horizon is to add to the traditional acquaintance with the major fields of knowledge a new dimension, that of *significance*.   Those responsible for designing general education must select within the various fields of knowledge— the humanities, the life and physical sciences, the social and behavioral sciences—those concepts, principles, and supporting information which will serve the distinctive goals of this area of professional preparation and have relevance for the activities and decisions of the individual, the citizen, and the educator in his professional role.

General education is liberal education that is functional in the twentieth century.   General education is an effort to use the "major divisions of man's intellectual and spiritual resources"[2] to illuminate

---

[2] Earl J. McGrath, *The Graduate School and the Decline of Liberal Education* (New York: Bureau of Publications, Teachers College, Columbia University, 1959), p. 3.

personal problems and those of the society in which men live. It is focused on the needs and responsibilities which men have in common; it applies to those aspects of development which help the individual to become a more alert, cultivated, and responsible individual and citizen. Five comprehensive goals are indicated.

The first and overarching goal of general education is to develop understanding and use of major ideas and principles of the various divisions of knowledge as they bear on the range of common human concerns. In achieving this goal, other objectives are also central:

Developing intellectual curiosity.

Becoming acquainted with resources for continuing inquiry and study in a field, and how to use them.

Gaining an appreciation and respect for all areas of knowledge.

Acquiring experience with synthesizing and integrative properties of knowledge.

Second, general education should cultivate those skills and habits of thought which constitute intellectual competence, for example, the ability to think logically and clearly, to gather relevant data, to draw conclusions from facts established. The student should gain understanding of and competence in using the different forms of reasoning employed in the various fields. One criterion of the educated man is that he recognizes that there are essentially different modes by which men *know,* each of which has its advantages and its limitations. General education should help to achieve that important balance which will keep individuals from acting blindly on a few facts or procrastinating because complete evidence is not available. Becoming a disciplined and independent thinker also calls for the development of certain other attributes which suggest the following objectives:

Having a disposition to examine, inquire, analyze.

Being willing to admit one's convictions and having ability to defend them.

Acting on principle and daring to be different in supporting convictions.

The third goal, to develop skills of communication and effective interaction with others, encompasses two kinds of objectives. Every individual needs sufficient command of communicative skills (lingual, numerical, and graphic) to be able to express his ideas clearly and to understand and intelligently utilize the rapidly developing mass media.   Then there are the skills that relate to a wholesome quality of interaction with others.   These are the skills basic to effective interpersonal relationships.

The fourth goal of general education is to help the individual to examine intellectually his value system.   Ever-increasing material standards in a world of tension and uncertainty create special needs for sensitivity to value issues and a personal responsibility for value judgments.   The student may have essential knowledge, the skills of intellectual workmanship, and intellectual curiosity.   Yet these rational processes may be of little worth unless tempered by moral responsibility and guided by values which derive from and fit into a reasoned view of existence.

The scope of general education makes possible a fifth objective: to help the individual gain perspective regarding the relation of an area of specialization to other fields.   As the student becomes acquainted with the range of fields of knowledge and comes to understand their content and methodology, he gains perspective on the unique contributions of the various areas in dealing with the common concerns and activities of man.   Thus he gains understanding of the relation of his area of specialization to other fields.

Taken together, the five goals of general education provide orientation to the major fields of knowledge, call attention to critical issues and problems, point to the interrelatedness of knowledge, focus on major ideas and principles and on methodology important in the decisions which individuals must make.

General education has unusual urgency for the professional educator.   Members of the teaching profession as persons need the same general education important for all thoughtful people.   For the educator as a professional, however, general education has unusual urgency.   The teacher stands before his pupils in a special way, as a symbol and example of the educated person in the best sense of that term.   If he is a rounded and informed person, with lively curiosity in many fields, he will stimulate students to join him in these interests. Further, his broad educational background will make him sensitive to nascent pupil interests.   Then, too, the teacher's central and critical role in the twentieth century, that of helping learners to intellectualize their experiences, gain new insights, and develop the motivation to continue to learn and the ability to cope with the unknown, requires a new dimension in his own general education.   General education has an equally important and similar significance for educators who, in their roles as administrators, supervisors, and curriculum co-ordinators, are a symbol of the educated person whose background provides sensitivity to teachers' concerns and competence to help teachers reflect positively on their work in guiding the general education of children and youth.

General education has extra usefulness for the teacher and other educators, including curriculum co-ordinators and specialists in instructional materials, because the teaching of a particular field is enriched when it can be related to developments in other areas, thus enabling the learner to perceive larger meanings and generalizations than can be found in a single subject. Such correlation and integration of materials is possible only when the professional educator is himself a broadly educated person.

Unless the educator has a real understanding of the basic ideas and pervasive problems of the community and larger society he is ill-fitted to comprehend the place of education and to carry his proper role in the education of that society. Tomorrow's teacher will increasingly share in community councils and take an active role in community development. If he is to counsel wisely regarding educational efforts he must have understanding of the way people think, their behavioral patterns, how they are motivated and how change is brought about. While the student's work in educational theory and practice will focus on these problems, many basic concepts will emerge from his general education.

Substantive content from various fields is brought together as it bears on situations of wide human relevance. To achieve the goals of general education, content is selected so as to bring the student face to face with major issues and forces affecting men's lives. Concepts and principles from various fields are looked at in relation to their contribution to the student's understanding of and ability to deal with those issues and forces and the problems and situations which they create. Focus is on the meaning of content in terms of adjustment and behavior, and the relevance of knowledge to the student's world is made explicit. As this is done the student becomes acquainted with the major fields of knowledge and is provided some experience in the means by which he may continue to use each field. The "ways of knowing" of a discipline are discovered and understood both by working directly in a discipline and by using the discipline as a resource in dealing with man's common concerns.

Work both in interdisciplinary studies and in separate disciplines can help the student realize the goals of general education. Content in a single discipline approach should be organized with cognizance of the broad implications of that field of knowledge. For example, the study of government would include consideration of such items as hidden persuaders in choice of political leaders, current ideals and regulatory agencies, economic resources and governmental power, effects of sociological population demands. Active participation in the political process and in carrying out the obligations of community membership should be an integral part of such a study.

Selected materials in an interdisciplinary approach might be organized in various ways: around problems, social institutions, fundamental processes. For example, cognizance of the basic process of continuity in all life (what it means in history, in education, in the arts) can have great value and significance in meeting the changes and uncertainties of contemporary life. "Bias" (what it is, its roots and causes, how to meet and deal with it) is a force significant in the life of every individual. The approach might be through study of such processes or through consideration of problems in which these processes are important factors, for example, present tensions which separate races and nations.

New horizons for general education do not support vagueness or superficiality; exactly the reverse. Dealing with a range of knowledge from various fields means sound intellectual exploration of carefully selected content. Emphasis is on the major concepts and principles of the several fields which the learner makes his own by thinking through factual information to its meaning in use. Students should be encouraged to pursue in greater depth particular aspects of an area of study. The term "general" is used because the material studied is relevant to human beings in general rather than to a particular person, group, or circumstance.

General education is a lifetime objective. The general education envisioned on the new horizon is neither terminal nor merely introductory. Work of a provocative nature, designed to achieve the unique goals of becoming an informed and interesting person and a capable and active citizen, should be available at all levels, with a depth of inquiry appropriate to the maturity and experience of the learner. In a rapidly changing society general education must be carried on at all levels of maturity and with all levels of intellectual sophistication.

Work in general education cannot be relegated exclusively to the first two years of college, nor should it be the sole responsibility of the undergraduate college. It should be a part of each college year, of inservice education of the professional educator, and of adult education programs, with provision for courses and noncourse activities appropriate to the changing maturity level of the learners. The college should not suggest, by a program that offers general education only in the first two years or a graduate program which fails to include opportunity for general education, that general education is a hurdle to be met and that once met it is no longer an important part of education. True, as the student determines his field of specialization less time may be given to formal arrangements for general education, but at no time should his program preclude continuing study toward a more complete achievement of the goals of general education.

The Content of SPECIALIZATION *Is Selected for Significance in Making Decisions Relating to the Teaching Field*

An essential part of the preparation of any person aspiring to the teaching profession is specialization in a teaching field or function. As noted early in the chapter the educator should indeed be a scholar, but a scholar whose first and most absorbing passion is inducing learning by others. This suggests that the nature, extent, and intensity of specialization cannot be considered in abstraction from the way in which the field of study affects the various decisions the teacher must make. Characterized by both depth and breadth, specialization must extend beyond mere compliance with a traditional "major" or "field of concentration" program. For the professional educator *significance* in the specialization component of the program of professional preparation must be viewed in two ways: there are the dimensions of the field of specialization itself, and there are the dimensions of the field as an area affecting work in school or college.

Specialization requires thorough understanding of the field as a discipline. One important dimension of specialization is that of the discipline of a given field of knowledge. Each of the basic fields of human knowledge has a certain way of coming into contact with or laying hold of reality. The study of literature, for instance, gives the student a mode of grasping human reality by a kind of joint exercise of affectivity, imagination, and reflection. This is to be contrasted with the social scientist's effort to grasp some of the same realities through the more exclusively rational techniques of observation, enumeration, and classification proper to his science. The philosopher strives to know the identical social facts through a cooly questing kind of intelligence which relies for its raw material only on the garnered data of common experience.

To know a field as a discipline the teacher-to-be and other educators must know not only what it is, but what it is not, for knowing the limitations of a discipline is part of its mastery. This means that its method and approach to reality must be studied more carefully. Its tools, its sources, its modes of operating, its distinctive kinds of evidence, its objectives and conclusions must be studied in detail and with continuous self-consciousness.[3] This calls for a much more careful approach to a field than can be tolerated for those who will not become specialists in learning and the inducement of learning in others.

To achieve these goals means to approach the selection of content and its organization in a new way. In commenting on recent recommendations of the National Academy of Science and the National Science Foundation, a member of the Amherst faculty indicates something of the nature of the needed new emphases:

> The first, soundest, and virtually unanimously repeated recommendation is that natural science curricula must give up the debilitating fetish of subject matter coverage. It is no longer educationally sound to try to cover the entire spectrum. We must make judicious selection of subject matter. The selection must be neither haphazard nor eclectic. It must be addressed to the clearly articulated goal of allowing a logical, coherent, and clearly motivated development of the conceptual structure of the discipline. It must reveal the evidence on which conceptual schemes are based, the connections between such schemes, and the questions which are not answered, the results which are not achieved. It must generate an adequate vocabulary and leave the student with the capacity to traverse himself, when the need is encountered, those compartments of subject matter which can no longer be included in the formal course.[4]

Such understanding of a field of concentration is essential also because there is a love of learning and an appreciation of scholarship which can come only from exploring a whole field with some thoroughness and from investigating deeply some aspect of it. The

---

[3] This competence includes and appears to go beyond what Professor B. Othanel Smith would call grasp of the "logical structure" of a subject. In "A Joint Task: The Preparation of a Teacher," *Journal of Teacher Education* 10:192; June 1959, he states: "The intellectual discipline of the teacher lies in his command of the logic of his teaching subject. By this I mean his command of the logical procedures by which facts, concepts, propositions, and arguments are analyzed and evaluated; his command of the logical and symbolic dimensions of explanation and prediction. And I mean his control over the operations and procedures of analysis and evaluation by which judgments—both practical and moral—are examined and justified."

[4] A. B. Arons, "What Should Be the Shape of Things To Come in the Natural Sciences Curriculum?" *Current Issues in Higher Education, 1959* (Washington, D. C.: Association for Higher Education, a department of the National Education Association, 1959), p. 124.

"discipline" or manner of thinking and knowing characteristic of a certain subject can hardly be acquired in a way making possible its independent and original use, short of some prolonged acquaintance with the field. For the teacher, as well as for any other educated person, it is important that there be this sharpening up of some one set of capacities. For the teacher in an age of continuing education it is especially important that he have the ability to do independent and original thinking in some one field, that he have the tools and guidelines for continued exploration in some one area.

One set of dimensions, then, in the selection of significant content in a field of specialization is found in the penetration that provides understanding of how the various elements of the field are ordered and related, that builds awareness of the field as a discipline having a method and approach to reality. The second set of dimensions relate to the field as an instructional area.

Specialization requires understanding of the field as an instructional area. The second set of dimensions governing content selection suggests that the knowledge included for study should embrace the generally recognized basic concepts, principles, and supporting information that are fundamental to guiding the learning of children, high-school or college youth, or adults and to helping them reflect upon and intellectualize their experiences. The expansion of knowledge and the increased complexity of many fields point to emphasis on controlling ideas rather than details. Acquisition of knowledge must be of a nature to make it possible (a) to explain the "why" rather than to teach content empirically, and (b) to recognize the full import of learners' questions and deal with them so as to satisfy and further develop intellectual curiosity. Unless educators are prepared to grasp the larger issues of a field, to select and use knowledge in thinking through and dealing with situations and problems, and to continue their own development in the field of specialization they will in a relatively short time find their knowledge out-dated and their work with learners hampering rather than helpful. Knowledge which relates to and extends beyond that which the educator will teach is selected because of its relevance for the decisions which he must make relating to curriculum and teaching.

Viewing the field of specialization as an instructional area not only suggests content selection within a field but also offers guidance in the choice of the field of specialization and in the patterns of courses and other experiences. This dimension, of course, is not constant in a world of exploding knowledge and changing educational programs. Teaching fields not only differ among themselves, they differ in themselves in different periods.   Although it might have been said quite positively some years ago that geology, astronomy, and Russian were not important areas of specialization for the educator, this is not at all clear in the space age.   With changing needs and new developments in knowledge, school and college curricula must be revised and brought up to date.   Some fields of concentration at the college level, which have no correlates in the lower schools, may be unsuitable as areas of specialization for prospective teachers in those schools. Further, the developing concept of general education in elementary and secondary schools, as well as at the college level, suggests that for many educators specialization needs to encompass broad aspects of a field of study and even of several fields.   Selecting the area of specialization, therefore, requires knowing the way in which the field of specialization is now and should be reflected in the curriculum.

Acquaintance with the field as it is now and is likely to be reflected in the curriculum also gives direction to the pattern of courses and other experiences to be included in the specialization component of the student's program.   A point made by the Commission on Mathematics of the College Entrance Examination Board supports this position:

> It is true that prospective teachers need to re-examine Euclid from a modern point of view and to appreciate such things as the rigid requirements for construction problems laid down in Euclid.   However, it is a sacrifice of time sorely needed for more modern mathematics to follow a traditional college geometry sequence.   Non-Euclidean geometries, topology, and the elements of differential geometry would be far more appropriate for teacher education than the usual "advanced" Euclidean geometry.[5]

Equally true, unless attention is given to the field of specialization as an area of instruction, traditional "majors" may leave great gaps in the educator's needed competence.   For example, "No one would think of producing a surgeon who had never heard about the colon since his freshman biology course, but there seems to be no compunction about turning out English teachers who haven't had any study of written exposition other than freshman composition."[6]   Take another illustration from the experience of the the same author:

---

[5] College Entrance Examination Board, Commission on Mathematics, *The Education of Secondary School Mathematics Teachers* (New York: the Commission, September 1957), p. 11.

[6] L. D. Haskew, "Planning Institutional Programs," keynote address to the Regional Conference of the National Commission on Teacher Education and Professional Standards, in Oklahoma City, January 18, 1960.

Recently one of our officials examined the transcripts of a large number of applicants who had college degrees with majors in history. He turned over *seventeen* of them before he found one which acknowledged that any history ever occurred below the equator and *twenty-four* before he found one which admitted the existence of China.[7]

The specialization component of the program for teachers and other educators might well provide for areas of concentration or work within areas that range beyond the traditional choices. For example, the literature written for adolescents has special significance for the teacher of high-school youth; the study of speech is important to both the elementary- and the secondary-school teacher. Conversational language rather than intensive formal grammar study is indicated in the field of foreign languages for the teacher working in the elementary school; for many teachers an exploration of the principles of linguistics to develop understanding of many ways of thinking will be more important than extended study of a foreign language. Needs such as these can be met only if the student's program in the teaching field is carefully designed.

Specialization in professional preparation has both common and differentiating elements. What has been said thus far applies to specialization of all educators. Supporting the recommendation made in Chapter 8 that the educator's professional responsibility includes refusal to undertake work for which he is not prepared, the question must be asked, What differences should there be in the specialization of educators working in different parts of the educational system? Should specialization for the teacher working in the elementary school be different from that for the teacher in the secondary school? How should the specialization for the college teacher of philosophy, sociology, or psychology differ, if at all, from that of the teacher whose work is in a field such as educational philosophy or educational sociology?

The *elementary-school teacher* is called upon to help children develop insights in a variety of fields, to reflect on almost the total range of their experiences. To achieve the breadth of understanding suggested by the various areas included in the program of the elementary school, and at the same time to attain the depth of exploration required for teaching scholarship, poses a difficult problem. To realize the values and satisfactions that come from intensive study of a field, and at the same time to gain the needed breadth, on the new horizon the specialization of the elementary-school teacher should be a composite of study of *one* field in depth, as discipline and

---

[7] *Ibid.*

as specialized content, and more intensive study of the various aspects of general education. Further, study of general education as part of the prospective elementary-school teacher's specialization would be in the nature of increased understanding of the various fields as prerequisite to becoming more sensitive to children's concerns, more competent in dealing positively with their almost endless questioning "why," more understanding of the issues and problems which can have meaning for them.

Work in depth, or specialization, for the elementary-school teacher or teacher-to-be might be in one of the foundations of education, for example, child growth and development. For the student specializing in this area, work would include study in such basic underlying behavioral sciences as biology and psychology, study in applied fields such as educational psychology and child development, together with direct experience in laboratory situations. For other students preparing to teach in elementary schools, specialization might relate directly to an area of the elementary-school curriculum, for example, children's literature, music, art, life science, dramatics, or history. For still others, specialization might be focused on building competence in dealing with certain needs common to elementary-school populations, such as speech or remedial reading.

Specialization for the elementary-school teacher should not mean surrender of the self-contained classroom as the organizational focus of the elementary school. A valid reason for more intensive study in a single field, in addition to the intellectual enthusiasm and self-confidence and psychological security which derive from having explored the dimensions of at least one discipline, lies in the ability of each faculty member to be a resource person for pupils and for other teachers.

The prospective *secondary-school teacher,* who is consciously preparing to teach in a core program or in a smaller high school in which he likely will be asked to work in a variety of fields, should specialize in a broad teaching field. This may take the form of a broad area such as the social sciences, or it may be in the nature of penetration in a single field with supporting study in ancillary disciplines. However, if the teaching field is to be truly unified and strengthened by the reciprocal illumination of allied arts and sciences, the program must be more than a casual juxtaposition or collection of courses. The characteristics of depth must be consciously striven for in terms of deliberate analysis of the interrelationships of the subjects.

Those students who can be relatively sure of placement in a larger situation in which the secondary-school curriculum is organized by separate subjects, or one in which integrated and core courses are taught by a team of teachers representing different fields, may specialize in a single discipline. But even in these situations supporting study in broad fields is to be desired.

Specialization for the *college teacher* may be in a single field or in the integration of knowledge from related fields. This specialization will be broader or narrower according to the student's interests and the position for which he is preparing. Those college teachers who teach philosophy or sociology or psychology to the liberal arts student clearly must be specialists in these disciplines. On the other hand, those college teachers who work in fields which are a part of the foundations of education (psychological, social, philosophical, historical foundations of education) should be scholars in the basic discipline and in the related field of education. For example, the teacher of philosophy of education must have scholarship in the main divisions of philosophy and in the history of general philosophy *and* scholarship in the philosophy of education. They have a dual scholarship in the field of teaching specialization.

All that has been said of the field of specialization as discipline and as content applies on the college level. In addition, inasmuch as the doctorate should be the objective for the college teacher, specialization should also include attention to the acquisition of tool skills needed in pursuit of graduate study. In fact, study in the field of specialization should make its appropriate contribution to preparation for graduate study for all educators whose planned educational program includes advanced study.

Specialization for those who plan to work on the more advanced graduate level may well provide more varied patterns of preparation. The more mature students with whom the college teacher will work need contact with a variety of teachers, including some research specialists who may be less polished in the techniques of classroom administration but who can illustrate in their persons the joy in pursuit of knowledge and who are skilled in developing and guiding the imagination and creativity of their students. In each instance specialization for the doctoral candidate must be developed with regard for the particular responsibilities he will be called upon to discharge.

Specialization has an intrinsic relationship to general education, not an accidental one. Specialization builds upon early work in general education. Its content is selected with reference to that which has preceded in the student's program; it is designed to help the student use appropriately his previous experiences in new and expanding situations.   Most students will first meet the area which is later to become their specialty as one of the major fields drawn upon in general education.   That aspect of the field, first explored as a part of general education, is widened and sharpened through work in specialization.   Further, such goals of general education as building skills of logical analysis and of reasoned and orderly consideration of ideas, of effective communication, of intellectual curiosity and a positive attitude toward learning are extended through activities in the area of specialization.

The foregoing suggests an interlocking relationship between general education and specialization, a point which will be considered more fully in a later section.   Suffice at this point to note that the interrelatedness of the two areas raises many points of inquiry on the part of those designing the program of professional preparation. For students whose specialization is in one or more of the fields included in general education, should the work in general education be waived in favor of first-level courses in specialization?   In order to build on work in general education, should specialization be deferred to the senior college or graduate program?   On the new horizon, the answers to these questions would be No.   The importance of general education for all persons has been noted, as has its significance throughout the educational program.   Specialization, while contributing to some of the goals of general education, has its unique objectives.   The challenge on the new horizon is twofold.   It lies first in providing opportunity for the student to enter work in specialization when he is ready and has made at least a tentative decision regarding his area of special interest.   For some individuals this will be in the freshman year, for others in the senior college, and for still others at the graduate level.   The second challenge, and the more difficult to meet, is to select content and develop the work in specialization so as to build on the understandings and skills already gained in general education, whatever the extent of the previous work in general education.   It is a challenge that requires an effective program of student guidance and provision for co-operative development of the educational program.

The Content of PROFESSIONAL EDUCATION
Is Selected for Significance in the
Performance Responsibilities of the Educator

Professional education, the third aspect of the total program of professional preparation, deals with a study of learners, learning, the school or other educational institution, and the meaning and purposes of education.

The field of education has many of the earmarks of the newer disciplines such as political science, economics, and sociology. The body of substantive knowledge that bears on the teaching-learning process and the role of education in society comes from many fields: psychology, biology, sociology, anthropology, philosophy, and others. A derived discipline in the sense that it draws upon other fields, education is developing as a discipline in its own right as noted by Whitehead in a statement made some ten years ago:

> We are only just realising [sic] that the art and science of education require a genius and a study of their own; and that this genius and this science are more than a bare knowledge of some branch of science or of literature.[8]

Education as a discipline must deal with its own phenomena and develop its own rules of evidence and ways of knowing and of grasping reality. Work in professional education then, like general education and the area of specialization, should:

Be maintained at a high intellectual level of rigorous and disciplined study.

Be taught in a "liberating spirit" in the sense that the educator possesses intellectual curiosity and genuine interest in continuous learning; taught to inspire the desire to learn and develop the "tools" necessary to increase insights and to envision and grasp both new goals and better ways of achieving desired ends.

Place emphasis on the control of ideas rather than details; on the use of facts in arriving at principles and generalizations rather than specific techniques and procedures.

Contribute to general education through the development and reinforcement of skills of logical reasoning and problem-solving, and through providing all students an opportunity to develop understanding about the role of the school and the work of the teacher in twentieth century America.

Substantive content in the field of education must provide for new dimensions in decision-making by the professional educator. Decisions which educators have been making practically since the begin-

---

[8] Alfred North Whitehead, *The Aims of Education,* Mentor Books, M 41 (New York: New American Library of World Literature, 1949), p. 16. (© 1929 by The Macmillan Co.; used by permission.)

ning of time (what to teach, how to teach, how to evaluate learner growth) take on new dimensions in a world of mass media, exploding knowledge, rapid communication, atomic potential. They require different knowledge and different ways of using knowledge. In some instances new areas of decision are created. The discussion which follows looks at new dimensions in time-honored areas of decision-making and explores more recently developing concerns of the teaching profession.

Decisions in education must be based on *a vision of the possibilities of education in twentieth century society.* The answer even to the age-old question of what to teach is not a matter of the simple selection of instructional content. Underlying the decision are such matters as the goals of democracy, the implication of America's place in the community of nations for the role of the school, the basic social trends that affect education, a vision of the school (college) as a social institution, and the meaning and purpose of education.

Further, the educator as an individual and as a member of the teaching profession, alone or in co-operation with others, must face developing pressures on organized education to expand its role as social conditions create new needs or other institutions are unable to carry out their functions. The role the school can and should perform in the remainder of the century must be clarified. Teachers and other educators need to be equipped to respond discriminatingly to pressures, aware of the unique function of the school to help learners intellectualize their experiences, yet mindful of the need for each learner to be cared for physically, emotionally, and socially, as well as intellectually.

Educators today, more perhaps than at any other time in history, must also understand the issues of public policy that bear upon education. What should be the response to demands of the public for more science and mathematics, to proposals that teachers in these areas have more advanced preparation than teachers of the arts or social studies and be given added remuneration? What should teachers and administrators do if, in relation to the Supreme Court decision regarding desegregation, schools are instructed by the state governor to close? What should a teacher do in relation to a bond issue for new schools? The list of such questions could be extended; each requires decisions involving reflective thinking about the school as a social institution.

Another area of decision-making is developing from the growing body of advice referred to in Chapter 3. This includes criticism of and proposals for education from the informed and the uninformed, from within the profession and from laymen. The educator needs to be able to analyze critically each proposal, to see the hidden persuaders, to judge in terms of the goals sought through education in a democratic and rapidly changing society, and to test in the light of what is known about learning.

A second aspect of professional education basic to decisions which the educator must make is *how to use basic educational principles relating to the nature of the learner and the learning process in a wide range of situations.* Work in the area of the mental, emotional, social, and physical behavior of children and youth, and the psychology of learning and of adjustment and personality development has long been a part of professional education, but often a most ineffective part. To deal adequately with the widely diverse individuals, who will make up the predicted enrollment when nearly all youth are in school for at least twelve years and 40 per cent or more of high-school graduates continue in college, will make rigorous demands on educators' knowledge of human behavior. They must be as perceptive as possible of human variations, of the needs of each learner and the forces affecting his concerns and purposes. To help with this very difficult task on the new horizon, it is necessary to be sure that work in this area includes such matters as judging which of a student's concerns are typical and part of the growing-up process and which are more deeply rooted problems; sensing when the needs of the learner call for support and encouragement and when freedom to struggle alone makes for greater growth; understanding something of attitude structure and change; recognizing factors that affect the learner's perception of situations and of people and that condition his purposes; comprehending the struggle which individuals may have between the values and mores of their subculture and those of the larger culture of which they are also a part, understanding how values are developed and changed; knowing how to study the "personality" of a group, its culture, cohesion, and potential productivity, and the essentials of group psychology.

Study of learners should include consideration of adult behavior. Professional education should help the teacher, supervisor, administrator, and those working in professional organizations to recognize that basic educational principles apply to work with parents, professional colleagues, and other adults as truly as to work with children and youth. The same basic principles which govern the learning of the young child—the significance of purpose, individual differences, transfer of learning through similarity and generalization, response in terms of perception—are central in understanding and in modifying the thinking and behavior of teachers and other educators as they work together in committee, at faculty meetings, or in professional organizations. The same principles apply as the teacher works with parents to help them interpret their child's progress or to help them see that closing the public schools is not a sound answer to the desegregation issue.

Effective use of basic educational principles is required in the teacher's role of maintaining genuine contact with the learner's mind and imagination and helping him to deepen his insights. To perform this role calls for new emphasis on cognitive learning. The psychology of cognition needs to be explored along with selected materials from the fields of philosophy and logic. There is need to understand the nature of concepts and generalizations and how one teaches for concept development. This emphasis is not to be interpreted to mean that attention should no longer be given to the problems of personal adjustment and mental health. Both emphases are needed; both, in balance, are important aspects in guiding learning.

Using educational principles in helping learners develop "visual literacy" is still another area of importance on the new horizon made necessary by the rapidly developing use of media of a visual nature—television, video tape, films, and filmstrips. How to observe becomes quite as important as how to read; both are imperatives in the 1960's. Study of the processes of visual communication and their effect on decision-making, on attitude and value-building, and on ways in which personal identification takes place need to be included in professional education.

More than any other new dimension in this area, theoretical knowledge relating to learners and learning must "come alive," and the gap between theory and its use in the everyday activities of the educator must be closed. Three things are required:

1. A study of the nature of the learning process leading to the development of a set of principles or generalizations for use in guiding teaching and learning.
2. The use of these principles in study of various areas of decision-making of the educator.
3. The implementation and testing of principles in situations involving firsthand experience on the part of the student.

A third aspect in professional education on the new horizon is *understanding the underlying rationale of different educational programs and how to bring about changes in curricula.* One of the major areas of decision for the educator as teacher, administrator, curriculum co-ordinator, or materials specialist relates to determining the nature of the educational program, the selection of curricular content, and its organization to facilitate desired learning. Whether projecting a curriculum or studying educational programs and curricular patterns used by others, the educator must consider the rationale underlying each. What are the perceived purposes of education and the role of the school? What are the goals likely to be realized? What is the conception held regarding the nature of the learner and the principles of learning accepted and implemented? To answer questions such as these means a critical analysis of curricular plans, a seeking to understand the thinking back of positions taken, much more than just knowing that different programs exist and being able to describe them.

Tomorrow's educator needs to know how to work with others in bringing about curricular change, as a member of a curriculum committee, as an interpreter of change to parents, and as a guide of children and youth. Attention should be given to such problems as (a) how to bring about change when sharp differences in basic philosophy exist among staff members, when there is little leadership given by those holding leadership or status positions, and (b) how to function effectively in carrying out one's responsibility to learners when curricular requirements and practices are more or less rigidly prescribed.

The educator also needs to see the aspect or part of the curriculum with which he is concerned in relation to the total educational program. This means both the learner's total program of work at any given time and that which preceded and that which is to follow. It also means knowing relationships between course work and noncourse aspects of the curriculum, between the program and out-of-school activities, and between the work of the teacher and that of other specialists. Understanding the scope of the educational program and the work of those who share in its implementation is needed for the educator to conceive adequately his own special function and to be an active and responsible member in carrying out that function. The various facets of the total educational enterprise must be reflected upon in terms of basic concepts and principles held.

A fourth aspect of professional education relates to *teaching methodology and the selection and use of instructional materials.* On the new horizon teaching methodology means asking the right questions more often than giving the right answers; it means implementing a set of educational principles rather than focusing on specific techniques. Teaching methodology refers to the processes selected to build bridges connecting learners with the desired learning. Effective selection of these processes means much more than choosing one of several techniques or procedural patterns. Teaching methodology refers to ways of working with learners to help them find answers to their concerns through clear thinking and critical insight. It means asking the questions which will guide learners in finding answers and which will open new avenues. It means identifying inconsistency, questioning assumptions, adding meaning by giving an illustration or by asking for the application of ideas to practical situations, locating points of difficulty, making comparisons to sharpen differences or similarities, raising questions of values and focusing attention on consequences of acts or areas of needed inquiry, and assisting in the formulation of propositions, hypotheses, and generalizations. The goals of scholarship desired, the controls and intellectual powers needed in a changing world in which each individual must deal with the unknown and continue to learn require that study of methodology focus on developing skill in the use of means such as those just mentioned. Further, there is the need to explore how to use these means of facilitating learning when this focus is respectively on developing concepts and generalizations, on achieving attitude and value development, on gaining skills, and on growth in aesthetic sensitivity and appreciation.

In the foregoing is to be found an answer on the new horizon to the age-old query regarding the nature and place of general and special methods courses in the preparation of teachers. The methodological means named should be the central concern of any work in general methods. They take on significance for use, however, as they are directly related to the nature of the learner, the basic principles governing learning, and the goals to be achieved. This being the case, separate courses in general methods might well be replaced by larger block courses. One such might be a block in which goals, learning principles, and methodological means are related in study of the selection and organization of curricular experiences. Another organizational form for relating work in these several areas might be a block in which the focus is on kinds of experiences and ways of guiding them to achieve the different aspects of growth noted above: gaining skills, developing concepts and generalizations, building or modifying attitudes and values, and growing in aesthetic sensitivity and appreciation. Different institutional groups will want to experiment with other arrangements, keeping in mind that the focus at all times should be on the implementation of basic educational principles rather than on how-to-do-it techniques, and that the methodological means have worth only as they are effectively related to learners and goals. When this focus occurs the teacher will gain the tools and insights needed for planning prior to teaching and for developing and carrying out plans with learners. Only as the educator can relate the several critical factors in a teaching-learning situation will he gain the needed security and competence to make the decisions required in the new and different situations that he will face, situations created by the uniqueness of each group of learners, by the changing social scene, by the developing bodies of knowledge, and by instructional materials that change over the years.

If work in general teaching methodology is provided for in this way, is there a place for special methods courses relating to an area of specialization? Previous proposals that work in the area of specialization be selected with reference to the decisions the educator must make suggest that work in special methods, or the implementation of general methodological means in a particular field, might properly be a part of the work in specialization. First, the college teacher working with students in a field of specialization is teaching "how to teach" by his own methodology. The historian, the scientist, or the mathematician who participates in teacher education communicates to his students both content and method. In fact, his teaching may be more potent in conveying concepts and convictions about teaching methodology than anything he may say. However, provision should also be made for direct and self-conscious consideration of special problems of teaching methodology that the student is experiencing and the situations that he envisions in his role as teacher. Work in a field of specialization, taught by college teachers who understand both the specialized methodology of the field and appropriate learning theory, would seem to afford the best opportunity to investigate the living relationships between "substance" and "process" in education.

Closely related to teaching methodology are the decisions which must be made regarding the selection and effective use of instructional materials. In an age of television, teaching machines, and a wide range of instructional materials available in home and community settings, the challenge is selecting the instructional medium or material which most effectively and efficiently serves to achieve the desired learning and using the right medium, at the right time, in the right way. First and foremost the educator must come to see instructional materials as resources to facilitate learning, of value only as they assist in achieving desired goals. The central question is not whether television is effective but in what learning situations and for achieving what goals does it serve better than other media? In like manner, the critical questions to be asked regarding teaching machines are: What can they do? What can't they do? What are the unknowns? What can be achieved through the teaching machine that cannot be done through use of the scrambled book? What can be achieved through use of the scrambled book that is not already available in the text that supplies answers?

Through work in professional education the educator must be helped to assess critically materials and media in terms of goals to be achieved and what is known about the nature of the learning process. What kinds of materials can be programmed for use in teaching machines? How does the need for reinforcement relate to such factors as maturation and recognition of learner purposes? In television instruction (which, even with the best intercommunication now available, is essentially a one-way, sequenced, and paced presentation of information) is adequate provision made for teacher-pupil and pupil-pupil interaction, for learners to present their views for immediate discussion and evaluation? How important is discussion for the kind of insightful learning needed today? These and other questions must be raised by the educator as he makes decisions regarding instructional materials of all kinds.

From such analyses, providing a critical and constructive study of various media of communication, the educator gains perspective in a world of developing technology that affects learning both within and without the school. He will not reject new developments as threats to his role, nor will he accept them without good reason. He may find it is his function to use them more creatively than envisioned by those developing them. He will devise sound ways of preparing learners to use these materials for maximum profit to themselves. He will keep abreast of experimental evidence regarding new developments and perhaps engage in some experimentation himself. As a more experienced educator he may help to sensitize producing agencies to the kinds of materials most needed by the profession. But the teacher alone has the skills of sparking and leading discussion, of guiding human interaction, of helping individuals to intellectualize their experience, of responding face to face, and of sharing with learners the excitement of exploring new worlds.

A fifth aspect of professional education is *becoming an intelligent consumer of educational research and engaging in practical experimentation*. The discipline of education, like other changing and developing fields of knowledge, does not have final and fixed answers to the many problems confronting members of the teaching profession. The professional educator is constantly raising questions and exploring new and better ways of working. His teaching scholarship requires study of available research as a regular part of the investigation of an educational problem. It requires modifying practices when judgments are not adequately supported by data and setting up new hypotheses for experimental testing.

Necessary both to intelligent evaluation and use of the research of others and to his own seeking of new insights and carrying on practical field experimentation is a growing understanding of the modes of thought in education. On the new horizon, ability to use educational research as a tool is essential for all educators. Engaging in action research is a part of both undergraduate and graduate preparation, as well as of inservice education. Such ability must be developed to a level and with an intensity appropriate to the individual's stage of maturity and the kinds of decisions his professional endeavors require.

A sixth aspect of professional education is *becoming a responsible member of the teaching profession.* Chapter 8 of this report is devoted to a consideration of policies and procedures incumbent upon the teaching profession if it is to assume its full responsibilities and maintain the stature of a major profession. This stature is achieved only as individuals and groups of professionals discharge their particular obligations. Helping the prospective educator to understand what is involved in membership in the profession and to develop commitment to contributing to the progressive improvement of that profession must be taught as well as caught. Provision must be made for reflection on such matters as these: the essentials of a profession, the individual member's role in helping to set standards and in their maintenance, the purpose and operation of professional organizations, the function of accreditation and the work of recognized accrediting groups. Each student should have active membership in a professional organization and should share with members of the faculty in selected activities of other organizations.

Finally, *continuing preparation for intelligent participation in community life as a spokesman for education as well as a private citizen* should be part of professional education. The educator has always been a spokesman for his profession and for education with the public. The potential scope of his efforts and need for exercise of them have sharply increased with the growing public interest in education noted in Chapter 3. Only as the professional educator speaks out can the public become informed and have sound bases for judging the growing number of statements about education found in the press and popular magazines and made on radio and television. In conversation with laymen, in public forums and open meetings of the board of education and other civic groups, through participation on panels on radio or television, through the school page of the newspaper or through writing in professional and popular journals the educator creates in the public mind an image of the profession and an understanding of what education does and why. What he does in this area may be quite as important as what is done in the classroom, for what he does may make possible or impossible what he can do for children and youth. There is need to develop competence to carry this role effectively.

Work in professional education can also contribute to the educator's effective participation in community life. One such function, emerging as a result of developments in television, is that of helping to set up educational television programs for the community. This and other community activities in which the educator may bring his professional competence to bear need not be limited to the more experienced members of the profession or to the persons of leadership status. The critical factors in such participation are the creativity and insight of the individual himself. Some beginning teachers may have that competence as a result of their work with instructional materials. Students, at any point in their initial or continuing preparation, who show special interest in working with community members on educational or related civic enterprises should have the opportunity to develop needed competence.

The foregoing seven areas are suggested as those requiring new emphases in the professional education aspect of pre- and inservice professional preparation. A discussion of substantive content would be incomplete, however, without explicit reference to the fields making up the foundations of education. As viewed in this discussion, the social and philosophical fundations, history of education and comparative education, and the psychological foundations are seen as important resource areas on the undergraduate level and as fields of direct study as organized bodies of knowledge in graduate programs. The social and philosophical foundations, together wtih the psychological, contribute data for the decisions the educator must make. This interlocking relationship has been alluded to from time to time in the preceding pages. Throughout the student's study of professional education he should be helped to use all these fields, together with historical and comparative education, as important resource areas in dealing with educational problems. A student with special interest might study one of the fields more intensively as an organized body of knowledge. In general, however, it is suggested that intensive study of these areas as organized bodies of knowledge, combining "ways of knowing" of education and the particular academic field, be deferred to graduate study or inservice education. For many undergraduate students it would be helpful toward the close of the preservice program to have an opportunity to integrate previous experience in these areas. Such a period of reflective study should help the student to see current educational issues more clearly, to test his awareness of specious educational arguments, to react to new ideas or proposals in the light of past history and current needs, to begin developing a philosophy of life and of education, his own values and point of view.

All areas of professional education meet, in a special way, in full-time student teaching. This and other professional laboratory experiences give new meaning to theoretical concepts as they are implemented in carrying out the activities of the educator. These firsthand experiences, however, also draw upon concepts and principles developed through work in general education and the field of specialization. For this reason, the place and nature of student teaching and other direct experiences on the new horizon are considered in a separate section rather than as a part of professional education. This section follows immediately after discussion of two other points relating to professional education: the degree to which the work should be differentiated for those who have different goal-functions, and the time required for professional education if the indicated competence is to be developed.

Differentiation of work in professional education should be a matter of emphasis. The common elements in the activities of teachers who work with younger and older children, with high-school and college youth suggest the desirability of a considerable degree of common experience in the field of education. This is further emphasized by the need for every teacher to see the educational program as providing experiences which have continuity for the learner. The basis of differentiation lies primarily in the *intensity of study* within certain areas. For example, the prospective secondary-school teacher in his study of learners would give special attention to the adolescent, while the elementary-school teacher would focus on younger children and the college teacher would look intensively at the adolescent of college age. Each, however, needs to know the growth patterns of the age level immediately preceding and following. The same might be true of study of the curriculum and would apply to student teaching. In a number of areas the needed differentiation can be met through differentiated assignments and independent study related to course work.

Another aspect of differentiation which must be considered by those who are looking at new horizons is what work in professional education should be included in *preservice education* and what should be included as a part of *advanced study and continuing education*. To begin to teach requires some understanding and competence in each of the areas outlined in the immediately preceding pages: the role of education, the nature of the learner and the learning process, educational programs and their rationale, teaching methodology, instructional materials, educational research and experimentation, professional membership. For the prospective teacher the focus is on concepts and principles basic to his discharging of responsibilities as a beginning teacher. In his continuing work in professional education as a graduate student or through inservice activities, there will be exploration of new perspectives on these responsibilities, attention to those more likely to be undertaken by the experienced teacher, and opportunity to look at the foundational fields and theories of education as developing bodies of knowledge. To illustrate, the beginning teacher needs to know something of the teacher's role in the community. As a young teacher, because of circumstances or his interests, he may find himself called upon to be a spokesman for education in group discussions. In advanced graduate study, because of past experiences and other activities in which he would like to engage, the teacher's program may include intensive study of politics and the teacher's role in it. Experiences with learners may have raised questions that lead to advanced work in human growth and development and the psychology of learning. He may now be ready to test his educational beliefs through systematic study of major philosophies of education.

As was noted in the case of general education, content is selected for study by the undergraduate with his interests and needs in mind; later study deals with the same and related areas in the new dimensions provided by experience and maturation. Widening horizons resulting from maturation and experience suggest an emphasis in inservice and graduate work in education that is qualitatively different in both substance and method.

Still another aspect of differentiation relates to providing special experiences in professional education that may be required to prepare educators for newly developing roles such as *team teaching, television teaching, working with the gifted learner, serving as a reading specialist*. Whether special work is required and what it should be rests upon what is sound education, upon what is an educative rather than a miseducative experience. Applying this criterion, what is indicated in the areas of team teaching? First, it should be recalled that the rapid expansion of knowledge, the widening range in abilities found at all levels of the educational system, the focus on study in depth with opportunity for each individual to achieve his maximum potential, and the interlocking relationships among disciplines in dealing with important issues and problems all indicate the need on the new horizon to use team teaching at the secondary-school and college levels. However, this is a concept of team teaching on a horizontal basis where each member of the team is professionally prepared; each is a teacher in his own right, although each may represent a different area of specialization. It is a concept of peers rather than of individuals having different levels of preparation. The only exception to be made is that one member of the team might be a prospective high-school or college teacher who, as a student teacher, would be learning how to engage in team teaching. As such, he would be under the special guidance of one member of the team whose added function it would be to guide the neophyte in planning for his cooperative teaching responsibility and in reflecting upon and critically evaluating the work. Being a "practicing" team member suggests that the primary specialization is in professional education, in providing direct experience with team teaching in student teaching or other laboratory experience. A further need is that of implementing study in self-understanding and effective interpersonal relationships in meeting the situations which are necessarily a part of being a member of a teaching team.

Approached negatively, professional education might well include critical study of proposals for team teaching in which various functions are performed by "teachers" having different levels of preparation and, in some instances, little or no professional background. This proposal has grown up around the teacher-aide concept and suggestions that the school might be more efficiently managed by having large lecture sections for certain work. John Fischer states the problem:

> It is being suggested that schools might be more efficiently managed if for certain purposes large classes of several hundred students were assembled for lectures by outstanding teachers, to be followed by small discussion groups led by other instructors of presumably lesser stature. . . . what we dare not forget is that the mass lecture will necessarily produce a common effect upon the students. Indeed that is its principal purpose. Since the lecturer will be chosen for his superior skill, we

may assume that the process of making the students alike will be well handled.

But what of the rest of the cycle? Stimulating the individual responses of students will be the business of the discussion group. Here, by definition, the instructor will not be the equal of the lecturer. Shall we be setting up a scheme with a built-in bias in favor of mass indoctrination? Do we want to use our best manpower to produce uniformity and only our lesser resources in the cause of individuality? [9]

Is this the kind of team teaching desirable on the new horizon? Can critically reviewing students' written work or guiding independent study be viewed as less significant educative experiences and therefore justifiably guided by a teacher with "a lower grade of leadership capacity"? These and related questions must be asked and answered in terms of beliefs regarding the nature of an educative experience. Granted the problems attendant upon increased enrollments at all levels, educators must identify, in terms of what is known about a sound educational program, alternatives to be checked and tested experimentally. Perhaps there is a place for the large lecture situation with small discussion groups guided by equally competent teachers. Perhaps a teacher can, within a sound educational program, work with a larger group if he is afforded high-level secretarial and clerical assistance and adequate instructional tools. These, of course, are considerations important for all educators, not just those who expect to engage in team teaching.

The mass lecture just referred to raises some of the same questions as those connected with the special preparation of teachers for television. Here, too, there is need for experimentation to discover how the medium can be used to provide for the teacher's unique role in guiding learning, the interaction of teacher and learner when the student's response is being formed. The television teacher must not only be a master teacher himself but his preparation must provide understanding in depth of what technically can be done with the medium, sensitivity to the ways in which different teachers work, development of high-level interpersonal relationships and ability to work co-operatively with others, self-understanding in relation to gaining needed satisfaction by working with teachers and away from direct contact with children and youth. Preparation for work in this medium should be delayed until after successful teaching experience in face-to-face relations with learners and some acquaintance with teachers and their work in various teaching situations.

---

[9] John H. Fischer, from an address to graduates at the Convocation of Teachers College, Columbia University, June 1, 1960, p. 7.

Areas of preparation such as self-understanding and effective interpersonal relationships are not unique for television teaching. The difference, as in other teaching roles already referred to, is one of intensity and depth of study. The same is true of the teacher planning to be a reading specialist or to work primarily with gifted learners. The former, of course, must know the reading field in depth, must know how to work effectively as a consultant with a wide range of teachers, and must see his area of specialization in relation to the other activities of the learner. Likewise for the teacher of gifted pupils who must know in greater depth than others the particular characteristics of these pupils and what they mean for selection, organization, and guidance of learning experiences. Because the reading specialist must see his work in relation to the other activities of the pupils with whom he works, and because the teacher of the gifted will gain increased understanding of the important differences, it is suggested that preparation for such specialization should be delayed until after some teaching experience.

Time is required if study of professional education is to affect behavior. The question is frequently asked, Can adequate study of professional education be postponed to the fourth or fifth year of preservice preparation? As viewed on the new horizon the answer would be No, even if the total amount of time allocated were the same as that provided over a four- or five-year period. The reason for this response is twofold. First, there is need for ideas about teaching to mature and to be tested before the student undertakes responsibility for the trusteeship of the teacher. This point must not be confused with the issue of the amount of time given to work in professional education. The proposal relates to the importance of time between the introduction to professional problems and having to cope with them as a member of the profession. There is need to think about them, to see what they mean in various situations. Opportunity to reflect over a period of time must be weighed against immediacy of use, the argument often advanced by those who favor delaying study of professional education to the year of graduation. The second reason for suggesting that the student be introduced to work in professional education as soon as he has chosen to enter teaching relates to the significance of beginning work when his professional purpose is clear. When the student has selected teaching as his profession, the motivation that comes from exploring what is involved in teaching enhances rather than detracts from the values gained from work in general education. This is true because of the special significance of general education for the teacher.

To allow for differences among students, provision must be made for variable and flexible plans for the beginning of and for the length of time in study of professional education. For many teacher candidates professional education should be a part of each year of the preservice program. Equal provision, however, should be made for students to elect to teach at variable points in their college programs. In each instance two essentials must be taken into account. First, provision must be made for adequate exploration of the basic areas of professional education prior to assumption of full teaching responsibility. For the student who is delayed in making a vocational choice this may mean an added period of study. However, the length of time in and of itself is not important. The focus should be on the competence required to begin to teach and to continue to grow as a professional. Therefore, the second essential in guiding the student in areas basic to the work of the teacher is to tailor programs to meet the background and maturity of the individual student.

Direct Experience Gives Meaning to Ideas and Closes the Gap Between Knowing and Doing

Significance, as used in the preceding discussion, refers to the selection and organization of the content of professional preparation in terms of its importance for the educator as a person and as a professional. Significance has another meaning that relates to the educative cycle being incomplete until it has entered the phase of demonstrable competence to perform. For the professional educator "control" of knowledge means going beyond "knowing" to using knowledge in making the far-reaching decisions required by his role. For him, knowing has value in the power it provides for a mature quality of action. It is the emphasis given by Kubie in his consideration of education for maturity when he refers to the mature person as the individual who is able to derive meaningful concepts from abstract and isolated facts and to use them constructively for human welfare:

> Every educator knows scholars who lack the least quality of human maturity and wisdom, yet who are technical masters of their own fields, whether this field is the humanities, art, music, philosophy, religion, law, science, the history of ideas, or the languages by which men communicate ideas. The measure of our wisdom about living is determined neither by the breadth of the area of our knowledge nor by the sharpness of the focus of our specialization.
>
> . . . .
>
> Moreover, we know that the essence of maturity can come only through the insight which arises out of the interaction between living and

blundering, and then of studying and dissecting of our blunders. Neither living without self-study nor study without living is enough.[10]

Direct experience has the dual purpose of giving meaning to ideas and concepts for which the individual has little or no conceptual background and of providing an opportunity to test his ability to implement understanding in action.

Student teaching and other professional laboratory experiences have long sought to carry this dual function as a part of professional education. On the new horizon, direct experience should be an integral part of each aspect of the program of professional education: general education, specialization, professional education.

Course work, as well as independent study not directly related to course work, should include direct experience. When the focus is on ability of the individual to act on thinking, there is need to experience forces and situations. Direct experience in dealing with a wide range of persons and circumstances is needed in addition to using knowledge functionally in classroom activities. The student in his classwork in art, for example, will try communicating through art rather than only reacting to great masterpieces; through direct experience he will gain added understanding and skill as he works with community hobby clubs or shares in redecorating the college dormitory or planning a lounge or social center. His understanding of political science, as a part of course activities, will require not only a study of both sides of a controversial issue but taking a stand, marshalling facts to back his stand, and being willing to be counted. Through direct experience he becomes an active participant in political matters: working on a school bond issue, sharing in the nationwide movement of the Citizenship Clearing House,[11] working with a pressure group, or some other aspect of political life in the community. His study and use of critical thinking in a course in sociology will be applied to testing current pronouncements and those growing out of tradition; his direct experiences might include work in a settlement house to give added meaning to class discussion of the nature of juvenile delinquency, how it can be prevented, and how it is currently being treated. In his study of writing he will give a large part of incourse time to writing, possibly with direct experience in sharing in the writing of a college brochure, working in the editorial offices of a publishing house or on a newspaper. From class work and

---

[10] Lawrence S. Kubie, "Are We Educating for Maturity?" *NEA Journal* 48: 60-61; January 1959.

[11] A movement to involve students of government directly in political activity.

through direct experience he will discover the real meaning of rhetoric and grammar.

In the area of professional education, study about community resources moves to the use of such resources with boys and girls. Knowing about the work of the teacher becomes experiencing the life of a teacher and determining on valid grounds (testing in action) whether one is by temperament and competence suited to the teaching role. Learning about the use of anecdotal pupil records changes to the reality of helping a teacher keep such records and knowing the realism of including this activity in the teacher's busy schedule of activities. Findings in the field of child growth and development come alive in counseling children in a camping situation. And the list might be extended.

Involving the student in planning his own program of activities and in planning co-operatively with peers in a class or other group affords another important direct experience. Only as the student shares in co-operative planning does he learn to plan co-operatively. To understand the meaning situations have for an individual and to help him to learn to plan, the college teacher must provide for the student to be cast in the role of a co-teacher. This role is practically mandatory on the new horizon because of the information which the student will have which is only partly known to the teacher. It has the further essential of providing opportunity for the student to use his knowledge gained in one area as it bears on another. This has special merit in preparation for the teaching profession where the several parts of the program are so closely interrelated and where a unique quality of the teaching profession is helping learners develop powers similar to those of the teacher.

Throughout his program the student will, through his use of knowledge, learn how to learn. Further, in trying to formulate ideas for himself he will know that uncertainty which is basic to creativity and essential to taking a stand and acting on it. He will also know the excitement and satisfaction that come from being able to use knowledge in news ways and, to a degree, to contribute new knowledge (at least new for him).

The total collegiate environment and the larger community in which the college is located provide important direct experiences. The college that has its focus on individuals using knowledge for intelligent action makes conscious use of the collegiate community. Students are provided a responsible part as members of the community. Membership and leadership in clubs and organizations, real (not perfunctory) participation in student government, membership on student-staff committees responsible for forums, collegiate publications, curricular development, recreational and social activities— these and other aspects of the total life of the college can provide significant opportunities to extend the meaning of knowledge and test its meaning in use. They are opportunities for communicating rather than only learning about communication, for bringing about change rather than merely learning the steps and factors essential in change, for applying basic democratic concepts in group situations rather than studying about group dynamics, for managing money rather than just talking about principles of buying and spending.

So intangible an item as the intellectual climate of the college provides a direct experience. To achieve the imperatives of preparation for the teaching profession requires a climate that leads to student behavior in which high quality performance is the norm, rich intellectual and aesthetic stimulation is found out of class as well as in class, independent study and inquiry are parts of the college mores.[12] Most important, perhaps, is learning to be a dedicated person, a citizen-teacher with enthusiasm for working with and for people. Is the student participating in noncourse activities and giving freely of his time and energy, or does he limit his efforts to those which bear directly on his personal progress? Even though he gives all the correct answers when talking about the educator's role and the importance of zest, loyalty, and dedication as characteristics, what does his behavior in the college community suggest?

The personal set of values on which the student acts, and other goals, are extended when the community includes the town or city in which the college is located. He realizes what it means to be a member of a community through community service projects sponsored by the college, such as participating in a school bond drive and activities related to an election of governmental officers. Through such projects he learns how to achieve a desirable balance between community life and one's personal-professional responsibilities. Such experiences, however, take on meaning only when carefully guided, when students' responses are noted by teachers and reactions made to them. They provide an opportunity to put knowledge to work.

A full-time period of student teaching is required in addition to the direct experiences which are a part of collegiate life and of incourse work. The foregoing discussion suggests:

---

[12] The work in progress of C. Robert Pace, of Syracuse University, is illuminating on this point. Preliminary findings point to the fact that the atmosphere of some colleges is intellectually invigorating, while that of others is comfortable and placating.

That direct experiences should be a part of each year of collegiate work and each aspect of the program.

That such experiences should grow out of and be an integral part of incourse work, as well as a part of independent study.

That such experiences must be individualized, carefully planned and guided, with opportunity for analysis and reflection upon what has been experienced.

These experiences, however, should not be viewed as a substitute for the student teaching experience. Rather, they develop readiness for the more complete responsibility of student teaching. On the new horizon:

Provision should be made for at least one and possibly two periods of full-time student teaching. The value of two student teaching experiences—one relatively early and one toward the close of the program—should be tested; the purpose of the first would be to give direction to further work and make it more meaningful, while the second would have as a focus the student's ability effectively to use his knowledge and skills in guiding learning.

The length of the student teaching period and where it is placed in the professional sequence should be an individual matter governed by the maturity and previous direct experience of the individual student. For most students the work should *not* be delayed until the last semester of the program.

The nature of experiences to be included in student teaching should provide direct contact with the range of the educator's activities.

Observation as an experience separate from participation should come late rather than early in the student's program. The complexity of teaching makes observation of limited value until the student has firsthand contact with a teaching-learning situation.

Student teaching should be under expert supervision, jointly carried by a representative of the college and the field situation.

The need for full-time student teaching applies equally to the prospective teacher working at any level of the educational program, including the college. Equivalent direct experiences should be provided for those whose professional roles are to change from that of classroom teacher to such roles as principal, curriculum co-ordinator, materials specialist, supervisor, superintendent.

Perhaps one other point needs clarification. Full-time student teaching is not to be interpreted to preclude a parallel seminar in which problems met in student teaching are considered. Some of the content of professional education would be studied in the seminar rather than through other courses.

An internship should be provided; it is, however, not a substitute for student teaching. In addition to competence demonstrated in student teaching and follow-up study to remove weaknesses uncovered, there is need of proficiency demonstration through an internship. Under the joint supervision of the college and the field, considerations such as the following should govern the internship:

The internship is held to be a privilege, not a right. The intern must:

show qualifications for teaching in the given area or at the given level.

meet all requirements (except experience) which might be set for any candidate for a regular teaching position in the given situation.

During the internship the student assumes full responsibility (under guidance) for from one-half to three-fourths of a teaching load, thus providing opportunity to *study the total range of the teacher's work.*

The intern should receive monetary compensation proportionate to his teaching load and in harmony with the salary schedule for beginning teachers.

The purpose is to assure a high level of competence through providing opportunity for complete responsibility of the educator's role under guidance, with parallel advanced study. The internship also provides further demonstration of proficiency.

Until more substantial evidence is available, there is need to experiment with varied patterns of internship. One such pattern would be a five-year unified undergraduate program in which the fifth year would be an internship leading to the bachelor's degree and a first-year salary differential to recognize the extension of work in depth at the undergraduate level. A second pattern might be a five-year unified program with half time in the fifth year given to an internship and the other half to advanced study applicable toward a graduate degree. A still different pattern and one toward which the profession may gradually move is a six-year unified program, with the sixth year providing internship opportunity and leading to the master's degree. These and other patterns need to be explored and experimentally tested, as do various ways of organizing the total design of the program for the preparation of professional personnel.

A Unified Program: Erasing Artificial Lines Dividing Various Parts

General education basic to continuing growth as a person, specialization providing scholarly knowledge of the subjects or areas to be taught, professional education leading to understanding and skill in professional performance—each part must continue to be integral in both pre- and inservice programs of all professional educators. But their interrelatedness must be recognized and the program of professional preparation must be designed to erase the unnatural and unnecessary dividing lines.

Each Aspect of the Program Has Goals Which Are Held in Common With the Other Areas

The new emphasis on the acquisition and control of knowledge suggested in the preceding sections points to outcomes that cut across areas. General education, specialization, and professional education can and should make an important contribution:

To developing intellectual curiosity—a positive attitude toward learning and a disposition to examine, inquire, and analyze.

To building skills of logical analysis and of reasoned and orderly consideration of ideas.

To acquiring experience with the synthesizing and integrative properties of knowledge.

To gaining an appreciation and respect for all areas of knowledge; becoming acquainted with resources for continuing inquiry and how to use them.

To acting on principle, in terms of an examined and intellectually grounded value system.

To building skills basic to effective interpersonal relationships.

Such goals should deliberately be made objectives of each of the major aspects of the program.

Some Unique Outcomes of One Aspect of the Program Are Contributed to By Other Areas

While all parts of the program have certain goals in common, some of the unique outcomes of one part are contributed to by another area. As already indicated, general education is focused on the needs and responsibilities which men have in common. One area of wide human relevance is the role of education in American society. The student as individual and citizen, as taxpayer and potential parent needs to understand the central role of education in a democracy and the role of the school in relation to other community institutions. He needs to comprehend the essentials of a good educational program, to see these in relation to educational costs, to envision something of the way in which school and home can and should work together. Further, knowing something of the nature of the learning process and of human growth and development will give increased insight concerning the student's own behavior and that of others in the college and larger community. Thus professional education contributes to the unique goals of general education.

General education, in turn, contributes to the area of specialization in helping the student to see the relationships between his teaching field and other fields of knowledge. His area of specialization is enriched because, through his own breadth of knowledge gained in general education, the student can perceive larger meanings and generalizations than can be found in a single subject. Other aspects of the interlocking relationship between general education and specialization and between general education and professional education have already been referred to in suggesting that general education has special urgency for the educator.

The goals of professional education, too, are served by other aspects of the program. Every college teacher engaged in the preparation of teachers, whether the field is general education or an area of specialization, by his own teaching is contributing to the professional education of the student. Further, educational theory takes on meaning as learners and major fields of knowledge are brought into relationship. Then, too, the proposal that work in special methods be provided as an integral part of an area of specialization points to another relationship in which the two areas seek to achieve common goals. The special teaching methodology of a field needs to be developed in relation to the basic educational principles under consideration in professional education; teaching methodology rests primarily upon concepts of learners, of learning, of educational goals.

This interlocking of the several parts of the program of professional preparation is important both in determining the work of each area and in designing the total program.

Balance Without Compartmentalization Is Required in a Unified Program

On the new horizon the program of professional preparation cannot be compartmentalized into neatly labeled blocks of courses in general education, specialization, or professional education. Nor can general education and other aspects of professional preparation be defined by certain numbers of credit hours. The present fruitless quest to provide balance by allocating a certain per cent of the total program to each area will be replaced by a program:

That is co-operatively designed by the total group responsible for the preparation of educators.

That is balanced to provide for realizing designated goals in achieving competence to deal with the range of decisions of the educator as a person and as a professional.

That recognizes a variety of ways of achieving the desired goals, of which courses are only one.

While this seemingly more nebulous way of providing a balanced program may at first thought be less satisfying than a specific allocation of time or credit, it will not long remain so when the spurious quality of any such designation is recalled. Perhaps 40 to 50 per cent of the preservice program should be devoted to achieving the objectives which are general education. This, however, is a far cry from allocating such proportions of credit time to courses designated "general education courses." To continue with this area as an illustration, in one college basic work in general education may consist of extensive, carefully planned courses; in another the goals may be achieved by fewer general education courses supplemented by non-course activities.

There should be, without doubt, some collegiate courses and non-course experiences designated to give *primacy* to the objectives of general education. However, as noted earlier, they can be so constructed and taught that other purposes are served simultaneously. The same would be true of the areas of specialization and of professional education. On the new horizon, when only high-quality colleges having dedicated and informed staffs are permitted to engage in teacher education, wide leeway should be exercised in making arrangments for the interlocking three major parts of the program of professional preparation.

Time Is Required to Achieve the Desired Goals in Balance

Length of a program is not an arbitrary figure but is contingent upon what is to be achieved and the kinds of experiences required to realize the desired goals. Assuming a unified, effectively interrelated program and careful selection of students to be admitted to the program:

For most elementary- and secondary-school teachers the preservice program should be five years in length.

For most college teachers and those preparing for work in administration or supervision, or special assignments such as materials specialist or curriculum co-ordinator, the preservice program would be three years beyond the baccalaureate degree.

The increased depth of scholarship required to gain the control of knowledge indicated as necessary to begin work as a teaching scholar and to continue to gain in professional stature suggests a five-year unified program as initial preparation for most students. The equivalent of five years would seem to be needed for the preparation of both elementary- and secondary-school teachers, even if content is carefully selected with reference to significance. As colleges move toward this horizon, every effort should be made to improve present four-year programs through focused selection of content and well-designed curricular arrangements. Further, continuous experimentation should take place testing the length of time needed with reference to increasing the efficiency of learning, selecting students of especially high caliber, and modifying the curricular design. Within any five-year program students should be allowed to proceed through the program at differing rates and provision should be made to accommodate the student of advanced ability.

The five-year initial preparation for membership in the teaching profession is, of course, but the beginning of a program of continuous preparation. What continuing education means on the new horizon is considered in a later section dealing with inservice education. Likewise, the expectation that the doctorate will be normal preparation for college teaching and other specialized functions will be included in the last part of the chapter.

A New Concern for Individuals: Their Uniqueness and Maximum Development

The uniqueness of the individual educator, as a person and as a professional worker, must be preserved deliberately. It is out of individuality that change and progress come. For each educator to become the most effective individual and the most productive professional he is capable of becoming is a deeply personal matter.

The Student Must Have Greater Responsibility for His Own Education

The significance of the involvement of the learner in his own learning, in the goals of decision-making, in the development of power to go on learning and to deal with the unknown point to the importance on the new horizon of placing greater responsibility on the learner for his education. Several changes in professional preparation are indicated if this is to be done as one step toward fulfilling the mandate to capitalize on human variations.

The concept of involvement requires that the college teacher's role be responsive rather than controlling. This is made necessary both by the goals of helping individuals develop insight and power to use knowledge rather than gaining knowledge alone and by what is known about the learning process. Kenneth E. Boulding describes the interactive process:

> The accumulation of knowledge is not merely the difference between messages taken in and messages given out. It is not like a reservoir; it is rather an organization which grows through an active internal organizing principle much as the gene is a principle of entity organizing the growth of bodily structures. The "gene," even in the physio-chemical sense may be thought of as an inward teacher imposing its own form and "will" on the less formed matter around it. In the growth of images, also, we may suppose similar models. Knowledge grows also because of inward teachers as well as outward messages. As every good teacher knows, the business of teaching is not that of penetrating the student's defenses with the violence or loudness of the teacher's messages. It is, rather, that of cooperating with the student's own inward teacher whereby the student's image may grow in conformity with that of his outward teacher.[13]

The effective teacher helps the student take his next step. Viewed in this way teaching is more than telling; in fact, telling is but a very small part of teaching. Teaching ceases to be something done to

---

[13] *The Image,* © 1956 by the University of Michigan Press, Ann Arbor. p. 18.

another; it is something that the learner does for himself, using the help and guidance of his teachers and the material resources of the environment. And an important aspect of teaching is providing an environment which fosters high motivation to learn. As noted in Chapter 3, such a learning environment is one:

In which priorities are placed on creativity and imagination.

In which the individual discovers through his experiences that there are unknowns and that searching for new ideas, new behavior, new insights and relationships is rewarding.

In which those who guide learning demonstrate intellectual curiosity and share their own searching, not using students to realize the intellectual pursuits of the teacher, but using those pursuits to help the student achieve his goals.

In terms of what has been generally accepted for some time regarding the learning process, responsive rather than "controlling" teaching is not a new horizon. Its implementation on the college level, however, would indeed achieve a new horizon.

Student counseling and guidance have a central role and new dimensions when the learner takes greater responsibility for his education. College teachers who work with students in their courses in ways to respond to them share in the counseling process. Through co-operative planning they help individuals and groups to set goals that are both realistic and challenging. Through evaluative procedures provision is made for self-assessment and further guidance in making class and personal program plans. On the new horizon, examinations need to be something done *with* the student in determining progress and planning next steps, rather than something done *to* him. They should be designed to provide another opportunity to apply knowledge to new situations, not simply to report knowledge to others. New efforts should be made by college classroom teachers and evaluation specialists to use their combined skills in developing tests and other evaluative materials which provide the student opportunity to use his knowledge in responding to situations similar to those he now faces and will face later as a citizen and as a professional. Attention should be given to the use of a wide range of evaluative instruments, not only those of a written nature.

In addition to the counseling and guidance role of the college teacher in relation to his teaching responsibilities, it is suggested that each student have a faculty adviser who works closely with him over the period of time he is in college, and that student and adviser seek the counsel and help of other staff members at appropriate times. In this relationship it is important:

That the student be helped to set personal and professional goals based on self-understanding.

That provision be made for systematically planned personality assessment and guidance given in modifying self-understanding and self-other relationships.

That a program of course and noncourse activities, on and off campus, be co-operatively developed with the student and tailored to meet his needs and interests.

Opportunity for unhurried, independent study must be a built-in part of every student's program. The spirit of inquiry and investigation depends upon margins of time for reflection. When the student is involved in co-operatively planning his activities, when he helps to identify and clearly sees his goals, he becomes a more responsible agent in carrying out his responsibilities and time for reflection can replace the currently customary rapid succession of assignments and fixed due dates for all students. In addition to time for unhurried reading and reflection, a part of each student's program should allow for independent study that makes it possible for the individual "to use his own best powers in his own unique way." At times it may be a period for "catching up," at other times for exploring a special interest or more intensive investigation of an aspect of class work. It is time which makes it possible to pursue a problem or an interest wherever it may lead, rather than stopping short in order to work on a term paper or some other assigned task. Many educators never have this type of experience until the development of the doctoral thesis. This point in graduate study is a too-long-delayed experience for the professional educator in the 1960's.

As students at both the preservice and inservice levels take a larger part in their education and become more involved in planning and carrying out their activities, there will be increased attention given to the uniqueness of each learner.

Human Variations and Uniqueness Require
Flexibility in Arrangements

Those who prepare teachers, and the teachers they prepare, talk easily about the worth of the individual and the importance of individual fulfillment. The goals are important; their realization is less easily assured and attained. The expanding college population, showing a widening range in human variations within a single college and between colleges, offers a challenge to find new ways to recognize uniqueness and provide for the maximum development of each individual.[14]

Different students will gain needed competence through different kinds and arrangements of experiences. Reference was made early in the chapter to the need for programs of professional preparation to be carefully planned to accomplish certain goals. The design is developed to have essential unity and coherence; it is not an accumulation of miscellaneous courses and credits which may meet the requirements for a degree. The critical task within the over-all structure of the collegiate curriculum is to plan a program for the individual student which has coherence and unity in terms of his special aptitudes, capacities, needs, and experience background. Certain considerations emerge as important in achieving this task.

First, different students will gain the needed competence through *different kinds of experiences.* No longer can it be assumed that a course meeting regularly through an academic year for three or more hours a week is the only channel for teaching and learning. Nor can it be assumed that all duly credited scholarly pursuits must take place at the college. This shrinking world will, in the years ahead, make study around the world an integral part of some students' programs. While working on campus some of the desired ends of the educational program will best be met for some students by opportunity to move ahead through independent study and counseling conferences with an adviser or instructor; others will need the more complete guidance found in a carefully developed course. Some will gain the needed understandings through discussion of basic intellectual concepts; others, lacking an experience background, will need firsthand contacts against which to reflect ideas. Recognizing this type of differentiation and flexibility, provision can be made for the more mature student who decides to enter the teaching profession at a somewhat later period in life. Provision should be made for some individuals to carry out this delayed decision, meeting the requirements of the professionally competent educator through work which recognizes their variants.

Provision for individual differences also means *differences in the time when an activity will be undertaken,* as well as in the *length of*

---

[14] Studies in progress by T. R. McConnell at the University of California show clearly the range of human differences in present college populations.

time spent in the activity. For example, the point of beginning work in an area of specialization and in professional education depends upon when the idea of becoming a professional educator is first clarified as a goal. Similarly, the placement of student teaching should vary in terms of the readiness of the student rather than in terms of the fact that he is a senior or is entering the last semester of the junior year. The student's competence and maturity, rather than his classification as a freshman or junior, should determine the time when any activity is undertaken.

Human variations also mean differences in the length of time spent in a given activity. Some students will need to explore an area of work thoroughly; other students, for whom the work is a check on background gained in other experiences, may require much less time. Some students at a given time may be using a discipline as a resource, while others are at the point of intensive study of the field as discipline and an organized body of knowledge. Through differentiated assignments, special-interest projects, guided independent reading, and participation in selected parts of a course, the effort and length of time given to various aspects of a course will differ for individual students. Differences in rate of growth also suggest a flexible length of time. This last factor needs especially to be studied in relation to differentiation in the length of the student teaching period and other laboratory experiences. A question might well be raised regarding the currently common practice of a fixed period of time for student teaching, usually in terms of a set number of calendar weeks.

Differentiation in time length also applies to *flexibility in length of the total program* for different students. While recommending a five-year, unified preservice program, as will be recalled, students with differing abilities should be allowed to proceed through the program at differing rates.

Tailoring a program to the individual student is facilitated when the program itself has certain characteristics. More than provision for flexibility is required to capitalize on the uniqueness of the individual and to provide for his maximum development. Three characteristics are suggested as central to new horizons. The first relates to the value of having *clinics, studios, and laboratories in the major fields of knowledge* available for independent student and staff use and for use by class or smaller groups. With each staffed by a teacher having a teaching specialization in the particular area, the student would find in these centers a rich resource of well-organized, up-to-date materials. Both the materials and the counsel of a teacher "steeped" in the content and methodology of the field would be available.

Another provision which merits exploration is that of *varied types of participation in course work*. A student might engage in a course as a full participant carrying all course responsibilities, as an auditor seeking help with a problem or the realization of a particular goal, or as a class member for selected units of the course. Different students would participate in different courses in different ways, as determined by each student and his adviser. In fact, a student might enroll in a course more than once, engaging in different activities in keeping with his changing purposes and developing insights as he matures.

Having fewer courses and developing larger blocks of work also merits experimental study. One such larger block might be *integrating seminars*. These would take different forms. One might be a seminar in which the major purpose would be to provide students having a common teaching field an opportunity to integrate their work in various fields and deal with the questions which this type of experience creates. Such a seminar might be staffed by a teaching team made up of a representative of general education, of the students' teaching specialization, and of professional education.

Another type of seminar might focus on the same purpose at a different depth and also serve a group counseling function. Such a seminar would be made up of one or more staff members and their advisees. It becomes a group means of helping an adviser to be informed about the responses of his advisees to the varied course and independent activities in which they are engaged, and to provide for them a sounding board through which they can be helped to see new implications, new directions, and next steps, and to sharpen the problems to which further attention should be given. Such a problem-raising and integrating seminar might continue throughout a student's college program.

These and other proposals which will emerge as college staffs seek ways to implement the principle of individual differences have merit for undergraduate as well as for graduate programs. When made an integral part of programs for professional preparation, human variations and uniqueness are seen as an opportunity rather than as a burden.

Evaluation of Student Progress Will Be Qualitative Rather Than Quantitative

When the program of professional preparation is focused on the development of a person whose control of knowledge goes beyond knowing to action, competence must be judged by qualitative rather than quantitative measures. When the focus is on the individual, his uniqueness, and maximum potential no specified number of courses in a field, of semester hours of work, of total accumulation of credits can guarantee or indicate professional competence.

The present lock step of uniform credits will give way to direct reporting of competence. This means a whole new emphasis on an analysis of the essentials of competence, an analysis that identifies the various elements which contribute to competence and at the same time recognizes the relationships among them. This new emphasis is made necessary by the fact that different combinations of elements make for equally effective functioning as professional educators. The task is one of both analysis and synthesis in relation to individuals.

A further new horizon lies in the kind of data gathered to identify and report competence. *Descriptive records must replace* the usual assignment of *grades.* Some beginnings along this line have been made in describing a student's work in student teaching and other laboratory experiences. Much still remains to be done: what should be reported, how to report effectively, the use that should and can be made of such data in planning next steps with students, the kinds of cumulative student records that represent a realistic undertaking.

Along with descriptive records of student behavior there is a place for examinations. *New types of examinations* need to be developed and designed to evaluate the particular factors of concern to the professional educator. What cannot be measured through examinations must be clearly recognized and identified, and there must be included the evaluation that can only be made through watching the citizen-educator as he works in practical situations.

In the area of examinations, attention must be given to opportunity for *equivalency examinations* so that students may wisely use their time in advancing from where they are rather than unnecessarily duplicating previous experiences. The need for such examinations is created both by the wide range of nonschool educative opportunities afforded many youth today and by the developments on the secondary-school level to provide work of collegiate caliber for the most able students. When the focus is on maximum development of the individual, provision must be made for those students with rich backgrounds or special competences to pursue work in new areas, to use their time in study of an area in greater depth or in broadening study. Here, again, the same limitations and the same needs for appropriate examinations apply. One of the cautions is expressed in the following statement:

It is unfortunate that we use tests almost exclusively to judge whether students measure up to some well-defined and quite restricted standard of expectancy, rather than to discover what students are like, what they want to do and can do, and the barriers which stand in the way of their developing into self-directing and self-respecting individuals. It is not the conformist, whether he conforms as a result of pressure to adjust to the group or whether he conforms to a prescribed mold, who has brought about the great revolutions in man's history. The real innovators have been those who dared to be themselves in spite of these conformity pressures. Yes, we need more tests and better tests, the results of which will be understood and used by teachers . . . and students *to discover more accurately what each individual is like in terms of his capacities and developmental patterns.*[15]

Equivalency examinations in some areas may appropriately provide exemption from certain work. No such written or oral examination, however, can be used as a substitute for student teaching and other forms of demonstration of ability to use knowledge in practical performance.

Demonstration of competence will be an integral part of the program of professional preparation. When it is recognized that individuals may differ widely in the constellations of personal and professional factors which they possess and still be ready to carry out their professional functions effectively, colleges must find new ways of evaluating competence. As already noted, the usual checks in terms of credit hours and examinations no longer suffice when individual uniqueness is recognized and cherished. Nor can the responsibility for the students' meeting the imperatives of professional education be delegated to state and national accrediting and certifying groups. On the new horizon, the college must include demonstration of competence as an integral part of the program of professional preparation. Evaluation of the quality of performance, theoretically and behaviorally, must be a part of all aspects of the program. Three aspects of this continuing performance-evaluation process in preservice education merit special attention.

The first aspect relates to *early direct experiences,* including the first period of close association with a group of learners, as a screening process through which the student and his advisers co-operatively arrive at judgments regarding his teaching potential. For the student whose performance indicates promise of becoming a highly competent teacher, both this and a later period of student teaching offer

---

[15] Roy M. Hall, "Needed Research in Teacher Education," *Thirteenth Yearbook* (Washington, D.C.: American Association of Colleges for Teacher Education, a department of the National Education Association, 1960), p. 23.

guides for further work to increase strengths, overcome weaknesses, and develop qualities unique to the individual student.

The second aspect has a different purpose, is focused on theoretical controls, and comes toward the close of the first four years of the teacher education program. It is the development and use by the college of *comprehensive examinations* designed to demonstrate the prospective teacher's control of knowledge in general education, in the teaching field specialization, and in professional education. Two major goals would be (1) further evidence of the student's readiness to enter the profession as an intern, and (2) institutional self-evaluation.

Several factors need to be kept clearly in focus in the development and use of such examinations. When the emphasis is on control of knowledge in action, quite different kinds of examinations from those often used today must be developed. Evidence gathered cannot be limited to the ability to state and identify conceptual matters. The examination must deal with the factors important in being a teaching scholar: value judgments, using intellectual concepts in a variety of concrete situations, attitudes toward learning, relating ideas and the self to people in the process of learning. As noted in an earlier reference to examinations, institutional representatives in the various areas of the teacher education program must work with specialists in evaluation in developing the needed instruments. There is need to explore the use not only of the written paper-pencil type of examination question, but of the oral conference, special written or practical assignments, and other means which will emerge from the creativity of staff groups.

Implied in the foregoing is the intimate relation of the comprehensive examination(s) to the program designed by the college for the preparation of teachers. The examination ordinarily should not be administered by an outside agency. Any needed control should come from careful study of the institutional program, including its examination program, as a part of accreditation. Further, it should be kept clearly in mind that such an examination is for the purpose of evaluating progress in a particular program.

The third aspect relates to performance in the behavioral sense. In addition to student teaching, there is need for proficiency demonstration through an *internship and the first year of full teaching responsibility.* Upon satisfactory demonstration of competence through the internship, as determined by representatives of the college and the local school, the teacher candidate would be given a provisional license to teach by the designated certifying body. The granting of the license would be contingent upon recommendation of the college and based upon:

Satisfactory completion of the accredited program.

General background as determined by total work in college and satisfactory passing of the comprehensive examination.

Demonstrated competency to begin to teach as determined by the student's total record, with particular emphasis on the internship.

So recommended, the young teacher enters upon his first year of full teaching responsibility, and satisfactory performance leads to recommendation for a standard license.

The same three aspects might well be applied to continuing study in service as educators prepare to enter upon other functions and areas of specialization. Early contact with the new role might be less intensive and perhaps in the nature of participation activities, but the use of comprehensive examinations and provision of an appropriate internship would be equally important as a part of graduate programs designed to prepare college teachers, administrators, and other professional personnel having other specialized functions.

Each of the above proposals is offered as a means of safeguarding the imperatives of professional preparation within the many combinations of knowledge, attitudes, and skills which make up the uniqueness of each individual.

Pre- and Inservice Education a Continuous Process

Teaching scholarship requires continuing education through inservice and graduate study. High-quality education in American schools and colleges is possible only when every member of the team—teacher, supervisor, superintendent or college president, principal or department head—is effectively served by and participates in comprehensive inservice education.

Inservice Education Should Naturally Link With Preservice Education

Preservice preparation, as discussed in this report, is designed to produce a person ready to *begin* to teach or carry out a special service function. In this view, *basic* preparation for service to the profession is not considered to be complete until study is combined with experience. Provision is made for gradual induction into full teaching responsibility through the internship. This first teaching experience is considered a part of the preservice program of professional preparation, but it is required that the preparing college and the school work closely together as the student starts inservice education as a part of his internship. By school and college working together, the beginner's competence and limitations can be interpreted as those reasonably expected of the educator at this stage of his development. Inservice education continues beyond the probationary period years and is "developmental" in nature. The needs of individuals, as persons and as educators, change with years of experience and further education.

The "developmental" concept can best be implemented as colleges and school systems accept mutual responsibility for professional preparation and effect a transition from preservice to inservice which not only avoids disruptions of and dislocations in teacher education, but insightfully and systematically organizes and implements preservice and inservice programs as a continuum. Systematically they would seek to develop co-operatively the inservice program within the school and the graduate offerings of the college.

Another aspect of continuity is found in the basic similarity of new horizons in preservice and inservice education. Such proposals as the following, already discussed in this chapter, apply equally as needed new dimensions in inservice work. Applied they would mean:

That inservice education should include provision for general education, study in depth in the field of specialization, and professional education.

That work in each area should lead to acquisition and control of knowledge in terms of significance for decision-making.

That unnecessary and artificial dividing lines between general and professional education and specialization should be erased in providing inservice opportunities.

That inservice education should be planned with reference to the individual and designed to value his uniqueness and potential competency.

That provision should be made for doing more than helping the educator keep abreast of developments in his field and in education; inservice education should be equally concerned with continuing growth in intellectual curiosity, in creativity and imagination, in seeking new insights and relationships, and in willingness and ablity to explore the unknown.

Seeing these horizons as pertinent to work in preservice and inservice education suggests that activities in service would be designed to build on previous experiences to widen their scope and to develop competence at a more advanced level.

A Wide Range of Inservice Opportunities Should Be Available to Help Individuals Achieve Their Goals

A range of opportunities must be provided to offer work in the many and different aspects of personal and professional development and to insure for each individual the program which meets his needs. Some educators will profit most from organized course work, others from staff conferences and workshops. Some needs can best be met through independent study, others through action research in the immediate teaching situation. The inservice education of some individuals should include time and opportunity to carry out a planned program of reading current materials, studying at a distance, observing and working with another teacher on a project, engaging in educational travel, participating actively in learned societies or professional organizations. The range of possibilities is almost infinite. The need is for greater insight and more refined ways of evaluating the growth to which such opportunities may lead different individuals.

While, on the new horizon, the chief motive power for continuing growth should come from the individual, school systems should provide leadership in counseling the individual and in co-ordinating the inservice program. Inservice education is both a matter of providing planned offerings and a process of capitalizing upon individual opportunities.

Such individualized planning of inservice education calls for a re-evaluation of supervisory programs and teacher evaluation procedures as presently conceived in many school systems. Supervision as it relates to teacher-supervisor, teacher-principal, superintendent-principal, or any other combination of professionals should be viewed:

As being a team of peers working together on problems important in providing better educational experiences for learners.

As bringing the special competence of two or more persons to the solution of problems. The teacher brings to the co-operative effort the intimate knowledge of the teaching-learning situation while the supervisor brings the breadth of experience which comes from less intimate but very real association with a wide range of situations.

As being initiated by any member of the team, with sensitive leadership by those especially prepared to carry out the supervisory function.

As placing the locus of evaluation in the progress made in providing more effective learning opportunities. Evaluation is seen as an integral part of inservice education and is focused on growth in self-evaluation.

As requiring continuing education for those engaged in the supervisory function.

Separately and at times concurrently, educators will be involved in supervisory and other inservice activities of the local school system and in work at a college or university.

As school systems reappraise the essentials of adequate inservice opportunities, they should consider such basic responsibilities as:

Encouraging self-study by every professional person and providing sound guidance and counseling.

Making available a wide range of opportunities—conferences, workshops, independent study, action research in the immediate situation, educational travel, and active participation in learned societies or professional organizations.

Providing released time, and for some activities partial compensatory arrangements, for planned inservice education.

Making needed educational resources and instructional materials easily accessible.

Maintaining effective working relationships with the state department of education, with colleges in the community and those which serve the school group, and with professional organizations to keep pace with developments and to utilize the resources afforded.

The totality of inservice education will be realized only as colleges, too, study their role: the offerings they should provide as a part of degree programs and those which should be designed for nondegree candidates; the values of moving a course or other college activity to the local school situation, of assisting an individual or a group with an action-research project, and of participating in discussion groups or workshops.

Not All Continuing Education Should Apply to Advanced College Degrees

The quality of work proposed for the three aspects of the preservice program of professional preparation should be adequate preparation for graduate study as a part of continuing education. It is expected that most elementary- and secondary-school teachers would engage in graduate study toward a master's degree prior to receiving the standard license. College teachers, principals, supervisors, and superintendents would be expected to take advanced work leading to a doctorate. Not all continuing education, however, should apply to advanced college degrees. Some students may find through their teaching activities that some of their needs can better be met through courses which cannot rightly be a part of the master's or other advanced degree. For them work on the degree will be delayed, but their experiences will enrich the background they bring to their work in college and should modify it accordingly.

It is of the utmost importance that appropriate recognition be given to collegiate work which does not lead to a graduate degree. It is easily possible to think of collegiate activities which would mean much for the educator in filling gaps or pursuing special interests in general education, work in the field of specialization, and professional education, which would be "graduate" only in the sense that they are undertaken subsequent to the conferring of the bachelor's degree. They are important for the particular student but not appropriately a part of a planned program of graduate study. Pressure to translate all college work into degree credits is unwise. Sound continuing education and sound advanced-degree education both suffer when this is done.

This applies to the teacher as a beginner and throughout his professional career. The teacher or administrator who has an earned doctorate may well wish to include noncredit college work as a part of continuing education.

College Teachers and Special Service Personnel: Prepared Professional Educators

Special service personnel (administrators, supervisors, materials specialists, guidance workers, and those concerned with psychological services) have always viewed themselves as members of the teaching profession. Not so in the case of the college teacher, who often considers himself a historian or physicist rather than a teacher.

College Teachers Are Professional Educators and Should Identify With the Teaching Profession

On the new horizon, the college teacher of prospective teachers, of students of the arts and sciences who have no vocational orientation at the time, and of students whose professional goals are in such fields as law, medicine, and engineering, will identify with the teaching profession. All college teachers are part of the teaching profession. This does not mean less regard for the field of specialization and for mastery of a discipline. It does mean that the college teacher will be a *teaching* scholar whose work has two interrelated focuses: his role as an effective and productive teacher and his interest in his subjects(s). It means that instruction will be recognized as of first importance on the college level. It means that effective teaching on this level will be governed by the same basic learning principles as is teaching in the elementary or secondary school. While the implementation of these principles may be different at times with the more mature learner, teaching in college is more than lecturing and giving assignments. Teaching college youth is a creative art and science.

The Program Should Be Planned With Reference to the College Teacher's Role

The question is often asked whether there should be special programs for college teachers. Such programs are now rather rare. On the new horizon, the prospective college teacher's program should be planned with reference to his goal orientation. This means three things: (1) that aspects of the program, especially in general education and at the graduate level in the field of specialization, may be the same as for students with other goal-orientation; (2) that work in professional education will deal with the same areas as those provided in programs for prospective elementary- or secondary-school teachers; and (3) that still other parts will be unique to the advanced level of teaching in which the college teacher will be involved.

The program designed for college teachers will have many of the same dimensions as those already suggested as new horizons for the preparation of other educators. The college teacher's program of study, like other professional programs, will be characterized:

By content selected with reference to the dimensions of the teaching field and the college teacher's other functions as a counselor, a member of a college faculty, a participant in professional organizations and learned societies.

By continuing general education, specialization, and professional education as a part of both graduate and undergraduate study.

By erasing artificial lines dividing the three aspects of the program of professional preparation.

By emphasis in all areas on key ideas and basic concepts and principles, on intellectual curiosity and ability to go on learning.

By help in understanding learners and the nature of learning, the critical study of teaching practices at the college level, a vision of the role of higher education in American culture—all, in this instance, in relation to college youth and their guidance in achieving the functions of higher education.

By opportunity to use knowledge in practical situations, providing a program of direct laboratory experiences.

By provision for the uniqueness and maximum development of each prospective college teacher.

For the prospective college teacher who begins his preparation at the undergraduate level, these characteristics will be a part of both his undergraduate work and his continuing graduate study. Graduate work will build upon previous experiences and provide for widening and deepening understandings and skills. Other students will begin their preparation for college teaching at the graduate level and after having engaged in teaching in elementary or secondary schools. For these students graduate study will build both upon undergraduate work and upon the students' inservice experiences.

The program designed for college teachers will also have characteristics unique to the college level function. Four of these merit special consideration in relation to new horizons. The first relates to graduate work in the field of specialization. *The college teacher must have knowledge of his subject in depth to the point of being able to push knowledge ahead*—to see new relationships; to see new and different uses of knowledge; and, for some college teachers, to discover new knowledge. To this end the prospective college teacher, who in his undergraduate program has seen the relation of the content of his teaching field to his teaching activities and understands the meaning and utility of that knowledge for life situations and problems, can with profit engage in advanced work along with students who have other vocational interests. With some guidance and counsel he can make the necessary applications of the knowledge of his field to his forthcoming work as a college teacher.

Second, *teaching general education on the college level must be a respected and valued assignment.* College programs of all types suggest increased concern for the liberal elements of education. Growing attention to the broad education needed by every college student points to the need for more college teachers prepared to work in the areas of general education. This need is further amplified by predicted rapid increases in enrollments in junior and community colleges which typically give considerable attention to this area of study. There is great need for teachers who are effective in teaching general education in both the general college and the professional school. On the new horizon, teaching general education and working in broad interdisciplinary areas cannot be considered a way station enroute to more important teaching assignments.

To prepare teachers of general education who have controls in a broad field, who know from their own experience as graduate students that studying a subject in breadth does not mean superficial learning and lack of depth, who are committed to the central goal of general education to stimulate intellectual interests in a variety of problems and life situations and to develop skills of analytical thought in dealing with them, requires new and different emphases in professional preparation. Two might be mentioned: the development of wide interests along with real depth in at least one area, and concern for the total life and rounded development of college students. The teacher of general education, who might well be a general adviser working with a staff member in the student's field of specialization in counseling the student and helping him plan his educational activities, will be both sensitive to the concerns and the ideals of college youth and aware of problems and situations in contemporary life.

Third, *college teaching under supervision should be an integral part of the preparation of the college teacher* and a necessary part of each student's program prior to appointment to a college position. This applies equally to the student who has never taught and to the elementary- or secondary-school teacher who plans to enter into college work. The successful elementary-school teacher is not necessarily equally effective in guiding college youth. However, his previous teaching experience may increase his readiness for supervised teaching on the college level and may affect the length of time of this activity.

This experience, while parallel to that of student teaching for the prospective elementary- or secondary-school teacher, has certain differences because of the nature of the college teacher's activities. The following comments, relating to both similarities and differences, are suggested as guides in developing this aspect of the program.   Supervised college teaching should be undertaken at that point in the student's program, after shorter direct experiences in college classrooms as a part of other course work, when he is ready to assume considerable responsibility for working with one or more college classes.   The length of time daily and the total length of the supervised teaching period would vary for individual students.

In making decisions regarding the factor of time, several points should be kept in mind.   Provision should be made for contact with the scope of the college teacher's work: counseling students, planning co-operatively with a class group and formulating realistic objectives, selecting and guiding appropriate learning experiences, formulating examinations which are teaching instruments as well as evaluative measures, evaluating student progress, sharing in social activities and other out-of-course activities which are a part of the total college life, working as a member of a teaching team whose members have different fields of specialization, participating in faculty meetings.

Some students may best gain competence in these areas by giving full time to supervised teaching, while others may find it more advantageous to work with several undergraduate college classes while taking a limited course program.   These are matters of individual differences among students.   Whatever plan is selected, it is essential that the prospective college teacher have adequate time to analyze the learning problems of students in his field and to develop the ability to direct their energies effectively, with reasonable competence assured before he enters upon college teaching for which he alone is responsible.

The amount of work taken parallel with supervised teaching, if that is the pattern selected, should allow ample time for preparation for the teaching responsibility and for reflection on it.   It is recommended that an organized seminar be provided for study of problems met by the students in their teaching activities and in being a part of an institution of higher education.   Such a seminar is valuable not only for the added insights gained regarding college youth and teaching, but for increased understanding of the teaching fields of fellow student-college teachers.   Students gain new perspective in seeing their fields in the context of the total college curriculum.

All work related to both the teaching and the parallel seminar should be done under careful supervision.   The neophyte needs the help that can be given in preparatory conferences, the observation and assistance during teaching that gives security and safeguards against wrong behavior patterns, the critical observation of his teaching that makes possible a meaningful analysis, and the opportunity to observe a master teacher. At no time should this aspect of the program for college teachers be thought to be met through the graduate assistantship, where all too frequently the graduate student teaches without benefit of guidance. Further, he is often assigned to work with freshman groups, the groups that probably should have the most skilled teachers. It is not a plan to provide additional instructional resources for expanding colleges or to afford a subsidy for the graduate student. It is conceived as an integral part of the total college program and, as such, is subject to the same careful teacher guidance as any other course.

Another important type of direct experience for prospective college teachers of professional education is *contact with elementary and secondary schools.* Every college teacher helping to prepare teachers should maintain continuing contact with schools to be properly sensitive to program and policy changes and to follow the on-the-job progress of some of his students in order that he can better appraise his courses. It is equally important, however, for the college teacher of general education to work with high-school teachers in defining mutual responsibilities and means of articulation.

Related to this area is the question of prior contacts that college teachers of professional education and the fields of specialization should have had with schools. It is held that, on the new horizon, they should have had successful teaching experience at the level for which they are preparing teachers. This experience may not have been more than several years in length, but it would seem a necessary one for teachers of professional education and for those in particular fields of specialization who are responsible for work in teaching methodology. This earlier experience should be kept alive and vital through observation and visitation in schools. Limited direct experience may be compensated for by team teaching in areas of specialization.

The fourth area having elements of differentiation is that of research. Like all other teachers, the college teacher should become an effective consumer of educational research. But graduate study should give new dimensions to his competence in interpreting and using research data, and he should himself engage in *research which is both thorough and relevant to subsequent teaching responsibilities.* Rather than the extreme specialization and traditional research in a narrow field, on the new horizon the teaching scholar will understand the relationship between teaching and research. Good teaching and sound experimentation should be mutually supportive, a matter of confluence rather than of conflict. The graduate thesis and other research activities should be designed to bring the student's work as a productive research scholar and as a productive teacher of students into harmonious relationship. Currently this is an area of frustration for many college teachers who, as a consequence, tend to be productive in one area only or are torn by the lack of relevance of the research work that they undertake for their major responsibility of teaching. Experience with the kinds of research important to the scholar whose central role is teaching must be a part of the graduate program.

However, preparation for teaching should not preclude some prospective college teacher's engaging in research represented by the traditional degree of Doctor of Philosophy. This, of course, does not mean that the *kind* of research ability and practice to be expected of the teacher will be identical with that of the professional investigator in a field. Nor does it mean that the teacher should always be permitted to develop his disciplinary scholarship in as narrow an area as the scholar who has vocational objectives other than teaching. It does mean that any movement toward watered-down versions of either the Ed.D. or Ph.D. degree "for teachers" should be vigorously opposed.

Whichever degree and whatever the professional role of the person earning the degree, it will have failed in its purpose if it becomes an end in itself. In a very real sense the doctorate should be the beginning of a more creative experience in educational leadership, leadership which also requires continuing education.

Programs for Special Service Personnel Should Be
at the Graduate Level With Successful
Teaching Experience a Prerequisite

Special service personnel today often undertake their functions without special preparation. The topnotch teacher is asked to accept a principalship or a supervisory post; the successful superintendent is invited to become a college president. While every person who undertakes a leadership role by way of providing special school services (administration, supervision, guidance, psychological services, curriculum co-ordination) should have been a topnotch teacher, it does not follow that the abilities required for teaching are adequate for the new role.

On the new horizon, the need for teaching experience as a pre-

requisite for preparation for special service roles should be examined. From laboratory experiences to teaching experiences the principle is the same. As prospective teachers require adequate laboratory experiences to give meaning to their professional preparation, so the persons planning to give special school services must have adequate classroom experience upon which to build understanding of their professional study. The basic unit in educational organization is the class group under the guidance of the teacher. It is in the context of the classroom and individual counseling that the great majority of the influences which affect learners must be brought into relationship one with the other. The work of service personnel has its roots in the class group and in work with individuals; the goal is improved results in the learning situation. Teaching a class with all its responsibilities for bringing unity to the teaching-learning process and achieving desired goals is vital background experience for those who would profit most from advanced study in preparation for becoming service personnel. Even though direct experiences in the selected service role are a part of the professional program, and these will take the student into schools and classrooms, time does not permit sufficiently extensive and intensive contacts to build real understanding of the teacher's work and its central role.

Like all educational programs, advanced study should be planned with reference to the demands of the role to be carried out by those for whom the program is designed. As for other educators, general education has a place in this program. Its nature, whether through incourse work or noncourse activities, will be determined by the interests and needs of the individual student. The field of specialization moves to the area of special services which the student expects to enter. Professional education is closely related to the area of specialization and made up of those professional elements pertinent to the persons and situations involved. Most service personnel will need to extend their understanding of the psychology of adults, knowledge of the instructional program of the school will need to be broad, and understanding of the role of the school in society will need to be deep. The graduate program should include provision for study in depth of many of the areas which these students will have explored in their undergraduate work and their continuing inservice education. Preparation for the leadership required of special service personnel calls for disciplined study as well as practical skills learned through direct experience.

In designing the program many of the proposals already suggested as new horizons for the preparation of other personnel are equally applicable. They need not be repeated. It is sufficient at this point to note important dimensions relating to the area of specialization.

First, provision must be made for developing *technical understanding and abilities pertinent to the particular specialization* and in keeping with the changing educational scene. For example, the superintendent must know and have skills in organizing instructional programs, making budgets, projecting enrollments, developing personnel policies, and others. However, on the new horizon, his leadership role is changing in all but the very small community from knowing the details of plant management, school finance, and business practice to comprehending principles basic to these areas and working effectively with technical specialists who are his associates. It is the associate who knows and has the detailed skills.

This frees the educational leader for the development of conceptual understandings. Well-developed conceptual skills are basic to seeing the total educational enterprise and the interrelations of its parts, to developing and maintaining diversity within the needed unity of the educational organization. Continuing with the role of the superintendent as an illustration, this means deep study in such areas as human growth and development and the workings of the human mind, sociology and fields relating to education as a community institution, curriculum theory and its implementation, the services required in a program of modern education.

Two aspects of the development of conceptual skills need to be pulled out for special attention: *understanding of the specialist's role in the changing educational scene* and *attitude and value-commitments basic to decision-making.* These form the second and third areas of emphasis. The importance of the latter for all educators has been noted frequently throughout the chapter. For those preparing to be special school personnel, there is need for more intensive exploration of the processes of decision-making and the rationale underlying a wide variety of decisions and decision-making. For those who are to carry this type of leadership function there is also need to extend and test the student's own value system and educational philosophy. An important part of such a developing philosophy is a theory of educational administration and supervision.

The fourth area, building *human relations skills,* is another aspect of importance to all educators. The student planning to engage in special school services must, through his program of preparation, grow in his understanding of people and how they live and work together—human motivations of the adult and the environmental factors that stimulate and challenge the individual's best efforts. He must understand the significance of individual perceptions and how to weld widely variant individuals into a working group. Success in working with people is central in almost every special service role. And skill in human relations must be effectively used both in face-to-face relations and in long-range communication. Special attention needs to be given on the new horizon to speaking and writing for the public and for the profession. Dull and uninteresting educational writing, which has long characterized the teaching profession, must be corrected if educators are to be effective in carrying out their roles involving communication.

Fifth, work in the area of *research,* like that for the college teacher, needs to be developed with reference to its functional use. Many in school service roles need to be able to function at a high level in designing and conducting investigations of school problems and in using the research findings of others in dealing with problems. More uniquely than the college teacher, school service personnel need competence in carrying on team investigations and co-operative research.

Finally, work in all areas should be grounded in practical situations. In the program of advanced study of all special service personnel, provision must be made for the work to be *realistically and meaningfully based in practical situations and provision made for testing competence.* It cannot be assumed, for example, that a successful classroom teacher will be equally competent or find the needed satisfactions in working as a specialist and serving as a resource to other teachers. There is need for early observation and participation to test the individual's aptitude for the new function. An internship is recommended as a part of each program to demonstrate competence in carrying out the function.

Advanced Preparation for College Teachers and Special Service Personnel Should Include Periods of Full-time Study

Each individual planning to work as a college teacher or in one of the school's special service areas should give one or more periods of full-time study to preparation for this work. These periods should be sufficiently long to realize the values that accrue from being a full-time student: high-level scholarship, freedom to engage in the opportunities afforded by the total college environment, and necessary sequential completion of the program that is important and appropriate to the individual.

Whether the goal is to become a college teacher or a special service worker in school or college, each must be a teaching scholar in carrying out his particular function. For each, advanced specialized preparation should be part of a continuing program of study begun in preservice undergraduate work.

Professional Preparation a Shared Responsibility

To provide high-level preservice and continuing education of teachers requires the co-operative efforts of the entire profession. Individual educators, colleges and universities, schools and school systems, professional organizations and learned societies, laymen— all are interested in and need to share in the preparation of educational personnel, each according to his special competence.

Repeatedly in this chapter mention has been made of the need for shared responsibility and the kinds of co-operative action required. Among those mentioned are:

The interlocking relationships in the work in general education, specialization, and professional education that require mutual understanding and co-operation, both in teaching and in planning the educational program.

Built-in co-operation in providing professional laboratory experiences such as student teaching and the internship at the elementary-school, secondary-school, and college levels.

The joint responsibility of college and school system for assignment of teachers to work for which they are prepared.

The work of the field and the collegiate institution in providing needed continuing education for all professional personnel.

These shared responsibilities require the co-operative effort of individuals and organized groups in the areas of policy-making, program-planning, and implementation of the program developed.

General Policies Governing Professional Preparation Are the Responsibility of the Entire Profession

General policies governing the preparation of professional personnel, which are the responsibility of the entire profession, focus primarily on the study and definition of goals and the qualities of the educator and of his functioning basic to achieving the broad purposes of education in American society. The entire profession of teaching has an important role in prescribing the results to be achieved through preservice and inservice teacher education. The profession has the further responsibility for evaluating the results obtained and for setting up policies in the nature of professional standards.

While these policies must eventually be sanctioned by the public through its legislatures, boards of trustees, and boards of education, it is the profession itself which must be the active leader in determining policies, for lay action invariably reflects the kind of information that has been made available to the public. Presenting the needed data for sound decision-making is the responsibility of the profession.

In each of these areas, each segment of the total profession has a unique function and contribution to make. To accomplish the ultimate aim of developing a teaching scholar, there must be a meeting of minds having the special background and understanding represented by each of these groups, and false status lines must be erased to achieve genuine co-operation. Each sees the work of the scholar-teacher from the intimacy of his own efforts and contacts; by working together there is derived a more comprehensive picture of the educator in American society.

Another value can result from co-operative efforts involving the entire profession. One of the essentials for the development of standards for the teaching profession is that educators themselves respect policies adopted for professional preparation and for professional conduct. Such understanding should rule out irresponsible criticism and the subverting of respect for aspects of the educational program or for certain departments of a college or university. In fact, the very policies developed should foster continuous constructive criticism, experimentation, and constant evaluation of the products of programs of professional preparation.

On the new horizon, machinery must be developed at the local, state, and national levels by which there is real, not token, co-operative discussion and formulation of policies. For a further consideration of this point the reader is referred to Chapter 8, which deals with the Professional Standards Movement. Suffice here to say that too long have the various groups dissipated energy by working separately on similar problems. In addition, many problems of policy have not been touched because they could not be solved adequately by persons of a single point of view and perspective, or because a particular group had responsibility for only one aspect of professional preparation.

Sound policies governing teacher education are of prime importance in maintaining high standards of education at all levels. They set sights and give direction to the planning of the educational program which is the proper responsibility of the teacher preparing institution.

Development of the Educational Program
Is the Responsibility of the Total Institution

Having in mind the needs and standards of the organized profession that it serves, the actual development of the college program becomes the work of persons who by responsibility and professional equipment are best fitted for the task. In an early section of the chapter the reasons were given why all departments of a college, to the extent that they participate in preparing members of the teaching profession, must share in the development of the program. Attention was also called to the leadership and co-ordinating function that should be taken by members of the school or department of education. At this point it should be added that while the segment of the profession engaged in professional preparation has responsibility for designing the educational program, other members of the profession have an important contribution to make as resource persons.

By working with their counterparts on the college level, high-school teachers of general education can make a significant contribution to continuity in high-school and college work in general education. A committee of classroom teachers, administrators, laymen, and state officials may well serve as an advisory body if desired by a particular college. Some colleges will find it helpful to have special conferences in which laymen, teachers, and administrators exchange ideas about professional preparation. Such *ad hoc* groups can also make an important contribution in evaluating the product of the program as they know and see educators at work in a variety of situations.

With the autonomy given the college to plan its program with regard for the standards set by the profession as a whole, there is the responsibility of accounting for the results of its efforts. Do the products of these programs demonstrate the performance standards set by the profession? Periodic evaluation of teacher education programs is a responsibility of the entire profession. This evaluation and accounting take place through several channels. Among them are central organizations, such as the National Council for Accreditation of Teacher Education which represents the profession and which calls upon the profession to share in its work. Another channel is teacher certification, a state function which focuses on approved institutional programs rather than individual credentials.

Continuous contact and exchange of ideas between college and

school personnel are essential if the preparation of professional personnel is to develop realistically with reference to the problems and
findings of educators in working with elementary-school children and
secondary-school and college youth.

College and School Personnel Work Together in Implementing the Program of Professional Preparation

Many of the suggestions for the educational program and for its
modification will emerge as school and college personnel work
together in implementing aspects of that program.

*Schools provide the direct experience laboratory for the prospective
teacher and those who work with him.* The unique and distinctive
contribution which only the schools can make to the preparation of
teachers is to provide a direct experience learning laboratory as a
continuous and integral part of the entire teacher education program.
Earlier reference was made to the significance of professional laboratory experiences, including student teaching and an internship.   So
vital a part of the teacher education program can only be implemented
through work in schools and other community educational agencies.
For the prospective college teacher, the undergraduate college functions in the same co-operative relationship in providing practice
teaching and other experiences in the college environment which are
significant in helping the prospective college teacher to more clearly
see his work and to test his performance ability.

The schools also can contribute the practical experience needed by
teachers who are preparing for such special functions as those of the
principalship, superintendency, supervision, or guidance and personnel work.

Another important function of the schools is to provide a laboratory
for college staff members who prepare educators.   To participate
intelligently in making decisions about the program of professional
preparation, to provide needed illustrations for class work, to keep
informed of changing educational practices in the schools, college
teachers need to visit schools to observe, to talk with teachers and
other educational personnel, and possibly to participate in ongoing
activities with learners.   For some college teachers the schools will
be an important resource for experimentation and research.

*The college has responsibility for contributing to the preparation
of school personnel in their roles as teacher educators.* School personnel working with prospective teachers and college staff, like college
teachers engaged in the preparation of professional personnel, must

be thoroughly prepared for this function.   Being a master teacher does not by itself qualify one for leadership in the field of teacher education.   To work with the prospective teacher as a colleague in guiding learners calls for special competence, no small element of which is the ability to teach "through" another person.   Many a master teacher finds it very difficult, if not impossible, to share his skills with the novice, to recognize and appreciate ways of guiding learning other than his own, to safeguard the interests of learners while at the same time giving the teacher-to-be freedom to "try his wings."   These and other competences required of the supervisor of student teachers call for special preparation of those who have the needed personal qualities.   On the new horizon the college must assume responsibility for preparing school personnel for their co-operative supervisory role and for carrying out this role.

This means offering (1) an organized program for initial preparation in which the work of the co-operating teacher is studied; (2) parallel seminars to discuss problems and concerns while working with student teachers (not only for the teacher having a first experience with a college student, but for experienced co-operating teachers); and (3) joint supervision of the college student in the laboratory situation by a representative of the college and the co-operating teacher.

The college can further carry out its responsibilities by making recent literature available to co-operating teachers; helping to make it possible for school personnel to attend professional meetings in which the focus is on problems of teacher education; working out with the school system ways in which the co-operating teacher's load can be adjusted to meet the extra demands of working with college students; planning with the co-operating teacher for the enrichment of laboratory experiences; involving the co-operating teacher in the full process of assignment and induction of the student into the laboratory situation.

The significance of supervision is clearly noted in the following statement in which the term "apprentice teaching" is used to refer to student teaching:

> Under a poor supervisor, apprentice teaching represents little more than an opportunity to pick up a few *ad hoc* classroom procedures and tricks-of-the-trade.   Under a first-rate supervisor it can be a liberal education in the meaning of great teaching.[16]

---

[16] National Council of Independent Schools, Committee on Teacher Training, *Preparation of Teachers for Secondary Schools* (Boston: the Council, 1958), p. 25.

This applies to the supervision given by the co-operating teacher and to that of the college supervisor who also must be a highly competent person especially prepared for the supervisory role. Competence in this work is critical not only for the prospective teacher but for the learners with whom he works. Able college students, with competent guidance, can be a positive asset and bring new dimensions to the school situation.

Induction of the novice is an important responsibility of the educator as a professional. Probably no other single experience is more important for the preservice teacher who plans to work at the elementary-school, secondary-school, or college level than to work with a great teacher in a vital school or college situation. It is a great waste, indeed, if the very best teachers do not participate in the development of new teachers. In fact, one of the essential characteristics of a profession is the induction of the young by members of the profession. To meet the growing demand for a broader and more complete program of professional laboratory experiences, school personnel must assume greater responsibility in teacher education.

Since this is a professional responsibility of competent teachers, recognition by the college and school system of the co-operating teacher's services should be other than monetary in nature. Rather than a direct payment to individual teachers, monies should be provided by the college to develop the program, making needed materials available, securing for co-operating teachers the help of requested consultants, adjusting teaching responsibilities to allow time to carry out the teaching-guiding function with the teacher candidate, making available special study opportunities relating to teacher education. Adjustments to the professional function of teacher education should be carefully and co-operatively worked out and agreed upon by co-operating teachers, administrators, and college representatives.

Experimentation Basic to New Horizons

Two factors make thoughtful and systematic experimentation a necessary part of new horizons in professional preparation. One is the need for proposals to be based on evidence and knowledge beyond that provided by philosophical, sociological, and psychological concepts. As this report shows all too clearly, substantial research data are few. Conversely, the factor of achieving standards through varied operational patterns becomes critical in a field where many of the most significant elements are not subject to currently available research tools. Within a framework of the imperatives or standards for the preparation of professional educators, there should be opportunity for variety in programs and for adjustments to meet the advances in knowledge and the uniqueness and creativity of the staffs of particular colleges.   Cottrell points to the need for trying and testing new insights as a part of determining new horizons:

> The best teacher education programs are constantly studded with new features, new ways of doing the basic job. With all that we have learned in a hundred years of experience with teacher education, we can scarcely contend that any existing program is good enough or that defects of its product are solely attributable to defects of the raw material and not of the processing we give it. Since the educative process itself is so basically experimental, our educational programs should demonstrate year by year the infinite variety of possible ways of arousing curiosity, extending horizons of perception and vision, and of forming taste. Monotony in curricula or in teaching is a danger sign of complacency in the staff and of deterioration in the program. Freshness of thought is engendered by novelty of educative approach and such novelty sponsored by disciplined faculty minds is a sign of growth.[17]

Different patterns are needed not only to implement more fully new vision and new research findings, but to provide for the uniqueness of each college and its special educational problems.   The college that has a commuting student body, and one in which most of the students are engaged in part-time work, must design its program to deal with a quite different problem than the residential college in which a wide variety of campus influences are a part of the students' living and thinking.   While different patterns are important to meet the needs of a particular student body and different faculties bring competence that suggests different ways of achieving agreed-upon goals, each college should do only that which it can do well.   No college should continue to prepare teachers which cannot provide a planned educational program that meets the recognized imperatives of professional preparation and develops highly qualified educators.

The profession as a whole should maintain an open mind toward all sincere and genuine experimentation, no matter what traditions seem to be threatened by it.   The critical factor and the point of concentration on the part of the profession, should be on seeing that every experiment has built-in provisions for careful evaluation of the product, and that the welfare of children and youth is jealously safeguarded during the experimental period.

Further, the profession itself should take the initiative in suggesting

---

[17] Donald P. Cottrell, "Some Clues to Quality," a presentation to a group session at the annual convention of the American Association of School Administrators, February 1960.

and supporting experimentation. Only when this is done will the potential of education in American society be more fully realized through the leadership given by professionally prepared educators.

*   *   *

Throughout this chapter, the report of the New Horizons Committee on Preparation of Professional Personnel, many specific proposals have been made regarding standards in preservice and inservice education. On first reading, some of the recommendations may appear to be reiterations of proposals made not infrequently before the present report. On closer scrutiny, however, the individual who is familiar with current practices in preservice and inservice programs of professional preparation will discover that implementation of the recommendations made here would demand substantial modification in the basic rationale undergirding current forms of pre- and inservice education. To emphasize this point and to summarize the key ideas of the foregoing report, major features of professional preparation as envisaged by those involved in the New Horizons Project are here presented in broad outline:

I. *Competence required of professional educators is achieved through a distinctive organization of learning experiences; it is not a by-product of becoming a well-educated person.*

II. *For the professional educator, "control" of knowledge has value in the power it provides for mature quality of action. This means:*

A. Selection and organization of content in terms of its relevance for the decisions an educator must make and implement as a person and as a professional.

B. Relating knowledge of the teaching field, and understanding of learners, the learning process, and the role of education in the twentieth century. This competence is needed equally by college teachers, elementary- and secondary-school teachers, administrators, supervisors, curriculum co-ordinators.

C. Direct experience as an integral part of work in all areas, including a period of full-time student teaching *and* an internship.

III. *The interrelatedness of general (or liberal) education, specialization in the teaching field, and professional education is recognized and the program designed to erase unnatural and unnecessary dividing lines. Balance without compartmentalization is required in a unified program.*

*IV. Human variation and individual creativity are deliberately pre-
served; each student pursues an individually designed program
in which:*

    A. Agreed-upon goals are achieved in widely different ways.
Students are encouraged to proceed at differing rates, with
differing ranges of penetration into areas of intellectual endeavor, with differing order and sequence of courses and
other activities.

    B. The student has considerable responsibility, under guidance,
for his own learning; opportunity for independent study is a
built-in part of every student's program.

    C. Evaluation of student progress is qualitative rather than only
quantitative. Primary focus of student and staff is on the
work of the professional educator, not on the degree to be
awarded.

    D. Length of a program is not an arbitrary figure. In general,
the preservice program for most elementary- and secondary-
school teachers will be five years in length; for most college
teachers and those preparing for work in administration,
supervision, and other school services, the preservice program
will be three years beyond the baccalaureate degree.

*V. Pre- and inservice education is a continuous process. Inservice
education under the aegis of the school system, as well as graduate
study, is characterized by the same principles as preservice preparation, with emphasis:*

    A. Upon continuing liberal education.

    B. Upon work in the field of specialization, and in professional
education, that goes beyond keeping abreast of developments
to concern for new insights and relationships, to willingness
and ability to explore the unknown.

*VI. College teachers and special service personnel are professionally
prepared for their roles, with graduate work including a period
of full-time study and direct experience in roles which the educator is preparing to perform (e.g., college teaching under supervision). Teaching experience in elementary or secondary schools
is a prerequisite for admission to graduate programs preparing
college teachers of professional education and special service
personnel for schools.*

VII. The preparing institution is held accountable for the graduate's competence to begin to teach or to perform other services for which his program was designed. Evidence of competence is provided through qualitative reports of the student's total college program, including satisfactorily passing a comprehensive examination and demonstration of competence in an internship.

VIII. Preparation of professional personnel is the responsibility of the total teaching profession, with delegation of leadership to those especially qualified.

We now turn our attention to the aspect of the profession's responsibility as indicated in the final statement above. If the profession is responsible for the quality of preparation of its members, how can such responsibility be met by the total profession? A substantial step has already been taken toward a process ensuring that programs to prepare professional educators do meet high standards. This step is the process of accreditation. The next chapter will examine this process as applied to the teaching profession.

CHAPTER 5

Accreditation of Professional Preparatory Programs

ONE HARD FACT about the relationships that exist between the professional practitioner and the public is that the public is ultimately dependent upon the professional to protect it from incompetent practitioners. Only the surgeon can say with any certainty whether a complex operation has or has not been competently performed. Only the doctor can say whether the man with the "cure for cancer" is a charlatan or a scientist who has made a major breakthrough in the battle against disease. Thus, although there is always much discussion about who shall evaluate the performance of professionals, the argument is at the end empty; only the professional can set the standards of competence and enforce them.

Given this power the professional is called upon by society, by his brother practitioners, and by his conscience to protect the public from abuse. Because the professions deal with the most complex affairs of humanity, they cannot set up a simple, precise, "litmus-paper" test of competence. On the contrary, the guarantees of competent service are set up as a long sequence of safeguards starting with selective recruitment, admission and retention in preparatory programs and continuing throughout the career of the professional practitioner. One of these crucial safeguards of competent service to the public is accreditation of institutions that prepare candidates for practice. What this means for the teaching profession is the subject of this chapter.

State and Regional Accreditation Agencies

In most states the legislature delegates the responsibility for the regulatory and leadership roles in teacher education and teacher certification to a state education agency. This agency indicates colleges and universities within the state which are approved or accredited to offer specified teacher education programs. The state agency is legally responsible for the protection of the public from unqualified and undesirable school personnel and is also responsible for the continuous revision and upgrading of teacher education programs. In addition, each state approves (or accredits) local school systems. One of the major steps in this process is the specific requirement that every professional worker in each school system must hold a certificate legally qualifying him to be employed for a specific task.

The regional accrediting agencies, six in number, are extralegal voluntary organizations which develop and apply standards in the over-all evaluation of colleges and universities.[1] These organizations annually list those institutions of higher education within their respective regions which are accredited. In addition, the regional accrediting agencies for many years have evaluated and identified secondary schools which are worthy of accreditation. Qualifications of teachers and other school personnel constitute one of the major criteria for accreditation. Some of the regional accrediting agencies have established standards and are now evaluating elementary schools, and some are accrediting specified programs in teacher education, particularly at the graduate level.

Professional Accreditation of Teacher Education: The National Council for Accreditation of Teacher Education

The National Commission on Accrediting, composed of representatives of six national organizations of institutions of higher education, identifies and designates appropriate agencies or councils to carry on the accrediting program in the respective professional areas.[2] The National Council for Accreditation of Teacher Education has been designated as the official agency for accreditation of teacher education.

The stage of development of a profession largely determines the functions which accreditation should perform in improving the pro-

---

[1] These agencies are the Middle States Association of Colleges and Secondary Schools, the New England Association of Colleges and Secondary Schools, the North Central Association of Colleges and Secondary Schools, the Northwest Association of Secondary and Higher Schools, the Southern Association of Colleges and Secondary Schools, and the Western College Association.

[2] The national organizations represented are the American Association of Junior Colleges, the American Association of Land-Grant Colleges and State Universities, the Association of American Colleges, the Association of American Universities, the Association of State Colleges and Universities, the Association of Urban Universities, and the National Association of State Universities.

fession.   If all or practically all of the institutions in which members of a profession are prepared meet the established standards, the major function of the accrediting body should be to *stimulate* the institutions by various means such as self-study and intervisitation.   If, on the other hand, many of the institutions that prepare persons for the profession operate programs below standards, the primary function should be to *regulate* to the extent of placing on the accredited list only those institutions that meet standards.   Historically, accrediting bodies for most professions have moved from regulatory bodies to bodies for stimulating progress through persuasion.

Accreditation of Teacher Education
Prior to July 1, 1954

Accreditation for the field of teacher education has had quite a different history from accreditation for the other professions.   It began with some emphasis on stimulation, moved in the direction of greater reliance on stimulation, and then more positively toward regulation.

Prior to 1927 there were no standards for the accreditation of teacher education, nor was there a list of institutions with accredited programs.   At that time, the American Association of Teachers Colleges began to issue annual membership lists.   One of the requirements for membership was that an institution pass an inspection based on standards adopted by the Association.   The standards were designed for single-purpose institutions (teachers colleges) and at first only they were eligible for membership.   As a consequence, only a small fraction of the total number of institutions in which teachers were then prepared were accredited and a smaller fraction of the teachers prepared each year, especially secondary-school teachers, were coming from these institutions.

It was not until 1948 that universities and liberal arts colleges began to be accredited for teacher education in any appreciable numbers.   This came about, not through the application of standards to these institutions, but rather through the creation of a new organization called the American Association of Colleges for Teacher Education.   Schools of education in most of the universities and heads of departments of education in several liberal arts colleges joined with the teachers colleges to form this new association.   The AACTE made some modifications in its standards and began about 1950 to apply them to colleges and universities not included in the merger.   Soon thereafter it announced its plan to visit all institutions involved in the merger (some 275) between then and 1954. This was regarded as an intervisitation program with emphasis on *stimulation,* though there was an element of possible *regulation* in it. The intervisitation program was almost completed when the AACTE transferred its function as an accrediting body to the National Council for Accreditation of Teacher Education on July 1, 1954.

The National Council for Accreditation of Teacher Education (NCATE) was formed on November 14, 1952. It had been in the process of being organized for a little more than a year. The constituent organizations represented on the Council were the American Association of Colleges for Teacher Education, the Council of Chief State School Officers, the National Association of State Directors of Teacher Education and Certification, the National Education Association (through the National Commission on Teacher Education and Professional Standards), and the National School Boards Association.

Accreditation of Teacher Education
Since July 1, 1954

A modification in the structure of NCATE was made in 1957, and since that time the Council has consisted of nineteen representatives from the following organizations, each by the numbers of persons indicated:

3 appointed by an *ad hoc* committee designated by the National Commission on Accrediting

7 appointed by the American Association of Colleges for Teacher Education

1 appointed by the Council of Chief State School Officers

1 appointed by the National Association of State Directors of Teacher Education and Certification

6 appointed by the National Education Association on recommendation of the National Commission on Teacher Education and Professional Standards

1 appointed by the National School Boards Association

The Council began its accreditation on July 1, 1954, in accepting by transfer from the AACTE membership list 284 institutions. For various reasons nine of these have dropped off the list. Since then, sixty-eight institutions have been added to the list, making a total of 343 institutions now accredited by the NCATE. Counting the institutions that have been denied accreditation, those that have been granted accreditation, and those that have been revisited, the Council in the first six years of its existence as an accrediting body has evaluated more than 150 institutions. All the institutions accepted by transfer from the AACTE are being re-evaluated at the rate of about fifty each year. By July 1, 1964, ten years after the Council began to accredit, all the institutions on its list will have been evaluated by the Council.

Characteristic Policies and Procedures in Accreditation by the NCATE

The following statements reveal clearly the chief policies and procedures that dominate the work of the National Council for Accreditation of Teacher Education:

> The NCATE is an autonomous organization whose sole purpose is to improve teacher education through accreditation. Only those qualified institutions that apply voluntarily and are found by examination to meet established standards for the preparation of teachers are accredited by the Council. An institution may be accredited at the undergraduate or graduate levels for any or all of the following categories: (1) elementary school teachers, (2) secondary school teachers, (3) school service personnel such as administrators, supervisors, and guidance counselors.

> Institutions that meet the following criteria qualify for evaluation by the Council:

> 1. Institutions accredited by the appropriate regional accrediting association at the level for which they request Council accreditation and by the appropriate state department of education for the levels and categories requested.
> . . . .
> 3. Institutions offering four-year curricula (a) for the preparation of elementary school teachers, or (b) for the preparation of secondary school teachers, or (c) institutions offering only graduate or advanced professional programs for school personnel when such institutions provide graduate work in other fields necessary to support these programs.

> . . . As rapidly as possible, therefore, the Council will cooperate with the regional and professional accrediting bodies and state departments of education in the collection of information from institutions, in the evaluation of institutions, and in reports to institutions.

> The Council regards accreditation by a regional accrediting association as adequate insurance of the general financial stability of the institution, the effectiveness of the administration, the adequacy of the general facilities, the quality of the student personnel program, the appropriateness of the overall program including general education and subject-

matter majors, the general strength of the faculty, the faculty personnel policies of the institution, and the quality of instruction. The Council, therefore, evaluates the teacher education program within this setting, including the teacher education objectives, the organization for teacher education, the student personnel program for teacher education, the faculty for professional education, the patterns of academic and professional courses and experiences offered in the various teacher education curricula, the facilities for the teacher education curricula offered, and the program of professional laboratory experiences. . . .

. . . .

In establishing these Standards, the Council recognizes that teacher education is and can be effectively carried on in different types of colleges and universities and in a variety of patterns. In applying the Standards, therefore, due consideration is given to differences in the nature of the institution, its internal organization, and its curriculum pattern. The essential requirement is that the institution have a program for the preparation of teachers, supported by a well-qualified faculty and adequate facilities.[3]

The National Council for Accreditation of Teacher Education is a powerful agent for professional improvement and its task is complex and challenging. It is recognized that NCATE is in its infancy and that it will change. It may change in administrative organization, and surely it will revise standards and criteria, adopt new processes and procedures, and provide expanding service, both in regulatory and leadership roles.

The Profession's Goal With Respect to Accreditation

The ultimate goal in accreditation of preparatory programs by the teaching profession is expressed as follows: To enter teaching or any other area of professional service the educator shall have completed an approved program of preparation in an institution of higher education accredited by the NCATE.

Significance of This Goal for the Profession

Primarily, the significance of reaching this goal resides in its promise as a means whereby the profession may ensure the public that those who render service as educators are qualified to do so. When the profession can provide such assurance to the public, it may be assumed that public confidence in the profession's standards of

---

[3] National Council for Accreditation of Teacher Education, *Standards & Guide for Accreditation of Teacher Education* (Washington, D. C.: the Council, 1960), p. 1-2.

preparation will increase. This increase in confidence may very well find expression in two major processes. First, licensure of teachers and other professional educators may be based, even more widely than it is at present, on institutional recommendation of the graduate of an NCATE-accredited program. Second, employing officials may consider for appointment only those candidates who are graduated from professionally accredited programs.

Evidence of the public's increased confidence in the profession's accrediting of preparatory programs is beginning to accumulate. A major achievement has been made in the free flow of teachers across state lines. Within the past four years twenty state departments or boards of education have accepted policies which assure the certification of out-of-state applicants if they have completed regular teacher education programs in institutions accredited by NCATE. Some local boards of education have already established a policy of considering for appointment in teaching positions only those who have graduated from NCATE-accredited institutions.

There is still another way in which accomplishment of this goal is important. In the internal affairs of the profession there continues to be some difficulty in defining prerequisites for membership in professional organizations. It would appear that a prerequisite of graduation from an NCATE-accredited program might become the central criterion for membership, both in the National Education Association and in the various state associations, as well as in the specialized departments at both levels.

Accreditation of preparatory programs is the keystone which supports all other standards and their enforcement. It is the core of the Professional Standards Movement. If accreditation is so significant, and few would disagree, then it is of great importance that standards and procedures employed in accreditation have the highest possible quality and validity.

Complexity of the Task in Achieving the Goal

The task of accreditation in the teaching profession is enormous in size when compared with other professions. Merely to compare the number of new teachers needed each year in the United States with the number of new doctors or lawyers or engineers causes an awareness of the magnitude of the task. To realize the further complexities of the professional accrediting program, one has only briefly to consider that there are fifty different state teacher education accrediting and certificating agencies, six regional accrediting agencies, more than eleven hundred institutions of higher education purporting to conduct teacher education programs, and approximately 120,000 elementary and secondary schools employing those who complete the varying types of teacher preparing curricula.

Complexity is not the result of size alone, however. Structure of the American school system and services rendered by it demand an unusually wide distribution of specialized functions and, therefore, specialized preparation. Definition of qualifications of persons to perform various functions, both qualifications that should be common to all educators and those that should be distinctive in terms of role, are not easily agreed upon. Furthermore, the profession possesses only limited data on questions, the answers to which are basic to making decisions about preservice and continuing selection and preparation of personnel.

Add to these complexities in accrediting preparatory programs for elementary- and secondary-school teachers the clear implications of the definition of the total profession, as presented in Chapter 2. Immediately it can be seen that present practices in accreditation encompass only part of the profession. What about those who serve elementary and secondary schools as administrators, supervisors, curriculum co-ordinators, and the like? Further, what about those who serve in institutions of higher education? In state departments? In professional organizations? Should the profession's accreditation include policies, standards, and enforcement with regard to programs to prepare these professional educators?

When size and complexity of the job are considered against the profession's brief experience with accreditation, it is not surprising to discover that much needs to be done to improve this important aspect of the Professional Standards Movement.

Professional Responsibility for Accreditation of Preparatory Programs

Responsibility for increasing the effectiveness of accreditation falls squarely on the shoulders of the entire teaching profession, both individual members and organized groups. Analyses of this responsibility have been made by two classroom teachers, one at the elementary-school level and one at the university level; by a representative of a state professional association; and by a staff member of a state department of education. These analyses are presented here as suggestive of the kinds of action appropriate to various members and groups making up the profession. Following these statements by the designated representatives, we shall turn attention to some of the persisting problems and fears that accompany professional accreditation and finally to a summary of characteristics of accreditation as seen on the horizon.

The Elementary-School or Secondary-School Classroom Teacher and Accreditation

A thorough understanding of the accrediting process and its significance for the total educational program is a necessary concomitant of the professional classroom teacher. Basic to the development of such understanding is recognition by each teacher of the interdependence of all educators in improving the learning of students and of his own efforts as but one small segment of the total educational pattern.

Development of a personal philosophy of life, in harmony with democratic principles, is mandatory for each teacher. From this, development of a personal code of ethics and performance, as well as understanding of, acceptance of, and adherence to the professional codes follow naturally. If the basic assumption that all educators are interdependent in striving for improved student learning is valid, it becomes the individual responsibility of each classroom teacher either to concur with or to take action toward the improvement of existing standards of professional practice.

Concern with teacher preparation and, more specifically, with accreditation—the process designed to evaluate programs of formal teacher preparation—*is clearly and incontrovertibly a professional responsibility shared by every classroom teacher.* This is especially true in the present and continuing period of dynamic change in our world and our way of life. It is difficult, if not impossible, to make a reasonably accurate forecast of the world in which today's and tomorrow's students will function as adults. The necessity of providing them with competent, creative teachers, prepared to stimulate learning of the processes of wise decision-making and purposeful self-direction in the uncharted years ahead, cannot be ignored by any of today's teachers.

Responsibility for developing teacher understanding of accreditation is shared by the teacher preparing institutions, the professional associations at all levels, and the individual teacher. Formal course work in professional ethics, standards, and practice might well form one facet of preservice teacher education. Local, state, and national associations of both student and professional teachers have grave responsibilities in this area of promoting their members' individual understanding of the accrediting process and its significance for both pupil and teacher welfare. Study groups, panel discussions, speakers, reports of developments, clarification and promulgation of standards are among the many types of both preservice and inservice activities which can be channels of communication for these professional groups. It seems unnecessary to delineate the responsibility of the individual who professes to be or become a teacher in accepting such opportunities, whether ones of contribution or of personal benefit. This responsibility cannot be ignored.

Another fact becomes equally obvious as understanding of the accrediting process deepens. *Membership in the professional education organizations at the local, state, and national levels must be considered in terms of the completion of preparation in accredited institutions.* Serious study of the entire membership problem becomes essential. The questions of various categories of membership and of due provision for unusual preparation or competences are but two of the many which must be carefully investigated and reviewed if these organizations are to be truly professional, offering genuine assistance to all educators and assurance of quality to the students and to the public.

The ultimate success of the accrediting process in teacher education depends in no small measure upon the co-operation and the contributions of the classroom teacher. *Valid, scientifically sound improvement of teacher preparation and performance clearly requires constructive, positively oriented feedback to the preparing institutions by the classroom practitioner, both individually and in association.* Education associations must seek new channels of communication between the public-school classrooms and the preparing institutions, as well as strive to free and enlarge existing routes. It is a logical expectation that many suggestions for the continuing development of both standards and procedures for the accreditation of teacher preparing programs will originate with classroom teachers. Alertness to opportunities for making such contributions and willingness to do so in a co-operative and constructive manner are characteristics of the professional teacher.

Effective service on actual accrediting teams can and should be rendered by classroom teachers. Orientation and background in the accrediting process for such service is the shared responsibility of the teacher in service, the professional associations, and the accrediting agency. Development of a continuing supply of professional teachers familiar with the accrediting function and ready for effective service as evaluation team members is an important responsibility of the education associations. Opportunity to participate in such professional service should be freely granted by an employing school system.

Still another responsibility of the classroom teacher in the accrediting process is that of upholding and maintaining standards that have been established. Operating within the accepted code of ethics and the legal framework, the individual teacher, through the professional group, must investigate apparent deviations from standards in preparation for specific teaching assignments. Moreover, distasteful though it may be, responsibility for disciplining members who fail to promote and maintain existing standards must be accepted by the professional association if it is to merit public confidence.

Interpretation of the accrediting process, through both individual contacts and association activities, is a continuing public relations duty of every professional classroom teacher. At every opportunity he must clarify and promulgate the necessity for professional accreditation, its ultimate value to the individual pupil, its fundamental relationship to the quality of education available in any school. General clarification of the need for accredited specialized preparation for specific teaching assignments is the task of all teachers. Those charged with the guidance of students have special responsibilities for emphasizing to prospective teachers and their parents the importance of seeking teacher preparation only at institutions offering accredited programs.

Through the professional associations the classroom teacher can make known to all teacher education institutions his approval and endorsement of the National Council for Accreditation of Teacher Education. Information about it, as well as encouragement to seek its approval, should be freely offered by the associations.

It is in the classroom that the success or failure of the accrediting process is manifest. It is the teacher who must continually verify the validity of the total accreditation process.

The College or University Teacher and Accreditation

In the accreditation of institutions of higher education for teacher education at all levels, the college teacher is called upon to fulfill an important role. The college teacher is obliged to define his role in the accrediting processes of a vocation intent upon charting its course of professional development for the next decade. In order to clarify the field of his responsibilities he needs to give thought to both the general and the special demands made upon him.

Like other professionals, the college teacher must respond to the large general responsibilities that devolve upon all practitioners. In the accreditation of higher education this would comprise the requirements to support the entire accreditation endeavor at all educational levels and among the related associations, agencies, and institutions. In a sense this is to say that the college teacher of prospective teachers at all levels and in every department or division of the college or university shares the general obligations of affiliation and membership. This concept of direct responsibility for accreditation and for general associational duties is not at present highly developed among college and university personnel. A source of alienation may evolve from the college teacher's doubts as to whether an agency of accreditation or any other agency commands the resources necessary to make even the minimal judgments of competence of the teacher, of the program of preparation, or of the performance of the candidates for teaching. This deep current of doubt runs strongly through all the levels of teaching. Is any satisfactory resolution of the problem possible?

In sum, the college teacher is called upon to establish, support, regulate, and improve an agency whose operations and judgments may touch upon his own competence and upon the status of his college. Moreover, the very processes by which these judgments are made are not themselves unquestionably reliable and valid. Why then is the college teacher called upon to enlist himself in this precarious endeavor? The answer to this question is that the welfare of the client is at stake and that the teacher is called upon, if he seeks to protect the client, either to rely on the fallible operations of an agency which may stumble into error or to disavow the agency and leave the field open to the certain abuses that arise in the absence of intra-professional regulation. This constitutes the minimal, hard-reality view of the value of accreditation. It is only fair to note that many persuasive arguments are also made that accreditation intelligently and competently performed goes far beyond this minimum function and contributes constructively to the advancement of the total professional endeavor.

The college teacher of education has special responsibilities in the accreditation of higher education. These derive from several sources. They are related to his special role in the organization of the college or university, his special role as a scholar, his special role as a teacher, his special responsibilities as a professional in the actual processes of accreditation, and his special relationship to the public. In dealing with each of these categories an effort will be made to indicate what warrant the college teacher has for his actions and toward what person and institutions he directs his efforts.

The Institutional Role. The college teacher has a double affiliation: he is a member of the institution *to be accredited* and of the profession *requiring accreditation.* He is called upon, therefore, to meet obligations within each sphere of action and to relate each to the other. He acts in these capacities not because he happens to be available but because he exercises power both in the college and in the agency of accreditation. He is, of course, further obliged to act because he possesses certain special competences required for the operation of accreditation.

Relating the College to Accreditation. The college teacher is in a position to work within the institution for the adoption of objectives and policies that are congruent with the principles and codes enunciated by the accreditation agency. This internal guardianship is one of the guarantees that the spirit rather than the letter of accreditation will be observed. Where accrediting teams may be competent to make broad observations, only the resident teacher knows the true nature of the strengths and weaknesses of the college. Only the resident teacher can carry on the continuing effort to raise the level of the program of teacher education.

College and university teachers have the opportunity to describe and interpret the objectives and the processes of accreditation to their colleagues in other departments. This may be an especially important contribution to efforts to achieve for education a parity of esteem in the college.

The obverse of the college teacher's responsibility to relate the institution to accreditation is his responsibility to safeguard the college against mechanical and literalistic application of accreditation codes. The maintenance of valuable idiosyncratic features of the college and the protection of appropriate experimental and research programs must be the province of the college teacher. This task will be especially important in an era of bold experimentation and radical new departures in programs for the education of teachers. Too often the tendency of bureaucracies and complex agencies devoted to review and evaluation is to encourage conformity in the affiliated institutions. The college teacher is especially well placed to protect and encourage research and development, to insist upon accreditation codes that not only recognize the need for such work, but also reward it as one of the marks of institutional excellence.

The whole process of evaluation and improvement of the organizational and administrative operations of the college is related to accreditation. College self-study, a necessary first step in accreditation procedures, is the institutional equivalent of the scholar's attempt to improve his own work, to examine himself and his work objectively. It is apparent that the scholar in the college is uniquely placed and especially competent to make the self-study an important part of the process by which the community of scholars examines and improves itself.

Certainly the college teacher is in an especially favored position to work toward the adoption of recommended practices in collegiate instruction. He is called on to be vigilant in the protection of academic freedom, to improve personnel policies and other conditions of employment. He knows better than anyone else whether the conditions of teaching and learning are up to required standards.

Evaluation and improvement of programs of teacher education are uppermost among the college teacher's responsibilities. In a very real sense, these programs represent one of the principal justifications for the existence of the professional school. Serious questions about professional programs must be answered by the faculty: What is the proper balance of general, special, and professional work? Is this balance readjusted to take into account the variations of maturity, previous experience and education, and personal qualifications among candidates for teaching? Are professional policies and practices in the recruitment, selection, and retention of students matched by differentiations in the programs of the candidates so carefully chosen? The accredited school is called upon to meet and surpass accreditation standards in the quality of instruction offered to its candidates.

It is the tendency of agencies and institutions alike to develop a sort of cultural lag. Primary objectives become dim; purposeful activities become ritualized. The college teacher, versed in the foibles and history of institutions, must act to insure that accreditation processes serve to stimulate improvement and to see that they do not become mere rituals of inspection. He will therefore work to promote review and revision of criteria and procedures of accreditation, striving to keep them flexible and sensitive to change, but not spineless. Evaluators themselves must refine their practice, develop the special skills and the special instruments needed in their tasks.

The college teacher must work to promote accreditation practices and policies that will maintain in force the institutional autonomy of the colleges and universities. He must oppose any tendency of the accreditation officials to over-legislate, a tendency of regulating agencies. Colleges must retain their special strengths. The agency must remain sensitive and responsive to the legitimate claims of the college to interinstitutional differences; it must avoid imposing conformities for the sake of administrative economy or other second-order considerations. New colleges must have avenues open to them by which they may realistically hope to qualify themselves and become accredited.

In sum, the college teacher must work to make the operation of the accrediting agency a force for experimentation, development, and variety, not conformity, vested interest, or stale tradition.

The college teacher, by force of his special competences, is called upon to fulfill certain functions vis-à-vis the accreditation movement. The first of these is to make a critical examination of the foundations upon which accreditation rests. This task includes the examination of the rationale undergirding it: Is accreditation a necessary and beneficial process, or does it simply repeat functions already performed by colleges themselves? What are the effects of accreditation upon the programs of colleges? How far may educators expect to follow the analogy with medicine? Have strong accrediting procedures acted to suppress experimentation with new programs in medical education?

Answers to these questions and many others like them must be supplied by the scholars who can plan, carry out, and evaluate research designed to provide the evidence needed. Scholars can examine and refine the theoretical and conceptual framework set up in order to facilitate the systematic development of knowledge about accreditation.

In addition to carrying out their examination of the rationale and procedures of the accrediting agency, college teachers have responsibility to publish results of their work. In this way public consideration of issues arising in connection with accreditation may be based on systematic thinking of scholars and evidence they have provided.

Responsibility to Students. Only a little research is available to tell us how and when and where the student enters into and commits himself to the traditions, the ethics, and the lore of his profession. In medicine it seems likely that students' commitment to their work is deeply influenced by the example of honored teachers, as well as by formal instruction in the meaning of "profession." The lesson for the college teacher of prospective teachers is clear: he informs his students about the significance of accreditation and its place in professionalization, and by force of his own example he helps to induct them into their professional responsibilities.

Responsibility to Accreditation Processes. Like other professionals, the college teacher of education is called upon to join in the action phases of accreditation. This implies his willingness to become a member of working committees needed to carry on the work. It also includes participation in the selection and training of evaluators and in efforts to improve the instruments, the methods, and the organization of the processes of accreditation.

Responsibility to the Public. The responsibility of the college teacher is ultimately to the public. All other duties derive from this. The public must depend in large part upon the specialists, the practitioners, to inform them about issues that arise, about possible abuses and advantages of accreditation.

The college teacher must protect the public against unwarranted restrictions on entry into the profession, restrictions which may create an artificial shortage of practitioners. But above all the college teacher must safeguard the public interest in every phase of accreditation by making the agency and the profession constantly aware of the expressed and implicit needs and demands of the community at large. To do this is to guarantee professional modesty, sanity, and service; to fail in this is to guarantee professional arrogance and the alienation of practitioner from the public.

The State Professional Association and Accreditation

The state professional association can and should be involved in the improvement of teacher preparatory programs. Some specific ways of involvement in an action program might include:

> Forming state-wide study groups to consider the standards which should be included in a teacher education program in an institution accredited by the professional accrediting agency, and developing of specific recommendations as an outgrowth of the work of such study groups.

> Studying standards included in preparatory programs of other professions to discover parallels between them and teacher education; developing co-operative activities with other professional groups in order to share experiences and utilize knowledge of others in the historical development of standards for preparation in their fields.

> Providing for the establishment of a continuing, official body, under the organizational structure, to carry on studies of changing patterns of teacher preparation standards as related to other professions and to the world in which we live.

Publishing findings from studies and resulting recommendations for improving standards so that the growing body of information can be shared by the profession and with others.

Co-operating with teacher preparing institutions, to obtain the acceptance of co-operatively developed standards by the organization and the institutions, and establishing lines of communication for a continuing flow of ideas, issues, problems, and recommendations between secondary schools supplying candidates for teaching and teacher preparatory institutions.

Participating in evaluation to determine the validity of the standards developed, established, and administered by the institutions. (Joint committees with the professional organization and the institutions make this an ongoing relationship of mutual benefit to the children being taught.)

Planning for periodic revisions in the light of new knowledge, new experience, new demands upon the schools. (Infrequent and reluctant unilateral approaches to the consideration of revisions have been most frequently the history of this function and cannot be permitted to continue. Revisions can be effectively approached and achieved only on the basis of co-operatively developed criteria. There must be sharing, not telling, with all parties concerned.)

The professional organization cannot escape its responsibility in this entire area. *Continuous development and revision of accreditation standards is shared by the professional organization, the individual member, and the legal agency.* Joint consideration of these matters provides that by a system of checks and balances the program moves ahead without loss of time and effort. Teacher preparing institutions must keep those outside the institution informed of developments which tend to make reconsideration of these mutually accepted standards necessary.

The professional organization must include among its goals in the teacher education area those particular objectives which it feels will be necessary in the immediate future and in the more remote time ahead. An effective professional organization has defined its purposes and made plans as to how purposes may be realized. The foremost purpose of most such organizations is the improvement of education. The application here is the improvement of teacher education programs so that school personnel may more effectively teach.

Realization of purposes must be more than statements. Purposes must be undergirded with strong foundations of improved financial support of education at all levels. The New Jersey Education Association has recently demonstrated its concern with the total educational program in that state. By a massive support program of legislation to provide very much needed increases in financial support for higher education, teacher education, as well as other programs of higher education, was moved forward significantly.

The Michigan Education Association has given effective leadership in securing additional funds for operation and for new construction of the various tax-supported institutions of higher education. The California and Florida associations, among others, have followed similar programs of action in their states.

Seven states have now developed qualifications for membership in their professional organizations which will give them new prestige. Colorado, Connecticut, Kansas, Maine, Maryland, Michigan, and Washington require that all new members must be graduates of four-year programs of teacher preparation and must be properly certificated when necessary. This is a significant development and is a part of a growing understanding of the professional responsibility of a state association.

Further steps being considered by some states include a requirement that the candidate for membership in the association be a graduate of a teacher preparing institution which is accredited by the National Council for Accreditation of Teacher Education. Elimination of retroactive clauses and applicability to new members only will not work a hardship on present members. However, also under consideration is a requirement that present members with less than four years of preparation and with substandard certification complete their education in NCATE-accredited institutions. These later qualifications are feasible now or will be shortly as the number of NCATE-accredited institutions increases. This may be interpreted as a pressure upon non-NCATE-accredited institutions to become accredited. Yet, it would appear that this is an ethical and professional exercise of responsibility well within the province of a professional association.

Financial support is secured for tax-supported institutions by legislative appropriations. Non-tax-supported institutions derive their funds from other sources. *The professional association must dedicate its efforts to the matter of total support from all sources for accredited teacher preparing institutions.* This is the broad responsibility of the association. This also provides an opportunity to the association to direct attention to the comprehensive need for adequate financial support for all qualified institutions and to encourage and hasten the accreditation of other institutions.

The professional association has responsibilities in the area of development and revision of certification codes. Participation with the agencies or agency in the states in reviewing and improving the certification structure affords a real opportunity for an action program by the state professional association. Enforcement of certification requirements is not within the province of the state association in a direct manner. However, it is an association responsibility to direct attention of the legal agency and its own members to violations of the code. Implementation of the code is a state function. Poorly qualified teachers cannot provide a quality program for children.

Improvement of employment practices is an ongoing responsibility of the professional association. Such improvement will result in better educational programs for children, youth, and adults. School officials, in selecting personnel, should take into account their program of preparation. There is reason to believe that employing officials will put greater confidence in NCATE accreditation as a single basis for accepting the preparation of a candidate when high standards are rigorously enforced by the profession through its accrediting agency (NCATE).

State professional associations must remember that giving information once will not be sufficient. *The story of the accreditation movement must be told to the teachers new to the profession. It must be repeated for those who have forgotten it.* Those who do recall the movement need to be reminded of the reasons for concern that all institutions be fully accredited.

There is an opportunity for the state professional organization to provide information to its members about the Professional Standards Movement through the publications of the association, its many committees and commissions, and its many conferences and workshops. Participation of representatives of the organization in evaluation and visitation teams gives mutual benefit to the organization and to the institution.

The state professional organization has three legislative functions: to initiate legislation, to support good legislation proposed by others, and to oppose harmful and detrimental proposals. Close liaison between the institutions of higher education, particularly those preparing teachers, the state department of public instruction, and the state professional organization must be established. Gulfs between them must be narrowed, where they exist, rapidly and effectively. These legislative efforts are not, and must not be, competitive efforts to secure legislative advantages for elementary and secondary schools as opposed to higher education institutions. Co-ordination of these groups can very well be a role to be played by the state professional organization. This is true because of the recognition of the comprehensive nature of education from elementary school through the graduate institution.

The association has among its staff and membership many who may be well qualified to serve on evaluation teams, either on initial visitations or during re-evaluations. *One of the obligations of the association would seem to be that of identification of potential visitation team members.*

The magnitude of the initial evaluations to be carried out and of the re-evaluations of the institutions "blanketed in" in 1954 pose greater obligations than present funds and staff permit NCATE to accomplish in a reasonably short time. An adequate reserve of trained personnel would present possibilities for expediting visitations. The state association's TEPS commission should undertake, in communication with other state TEPS commissions and with the National Commission, the development of adequate standards of selection of such personnel. States which have relatively large numbers of teacher preparation institutions will find this an ongoing responsibility, for the number of visitations will be larger than in some other states. A periodic review of the criteria of selection would be essential.

Experience in teaching and in teacher education, educational background, service in related areas (such as regional accreditation review panels), interest in the NCATE, published work, contributions to professional associations, and other related items should be included in criteria for the selection of visitation team members. The professional association has a responsibility to indicate competent people available for the study and revision of the NCATE standards for accreditation. The professional association should budget funds to make possible the performance of its important role in accreditation.

The State Legal Agency and Accreditation

State departments of education are organized under the provisions of state constitutions, state laws, or regulations of the state boards of education. Their operation must be consistent with such laws and regulations. Thus, it is possible that state departments will have many similarities and yet be very unlike in specific organization and function. Acceptable practices in one state department may not be approved in another state department. From time to time regional organizations have been unable to accomplish their desired goals of closer co-operation between state departments of education because of these specific legal difficulties.

State departments of education can implement the work of accrediting agencies, particularly the NCATE. Operating under the leadership role a state department of education becomes the leader, the consultant, or the adviser in providing quality teacher education at the institutional level and in providing bases for the selection of teachers who are to be employed in the schools of the state. Under the regulatory role the department becomes the agency for issuing standards of teacher preparation and selection and for policing local schools to see that the standards are met.

Under either or both of these roles one of the most important functions of a state department of education is that of improving the schools of the state. This function is accomplished in some measure by providing information by use of which local school authorities may select well-qualified teachers.

At the present time there is a general demand for improvement of our schools. Since the instructional program cannot be better than the classroom teachers, parents and school officials must seek better-qualified teachers. Institutions of higher learning must assume responsibility for improving the quality of educational programs for prospective and inservice teachers. State certification patterns change from state to state and may not provide the excellent teachers needed today. When states accept the work done in institutions of neighboring states, there is a question as to the quality and pattern of this work. Accreditation of higher institutions by regional and national agencies insures the quality of the work.

Teacher education, perhaps more than any other professional program, is the product of the institution as a whole. The teacher education program can be no better than the institution in which it is offered. On the other hand, the teacher education program is not necessarily strong simply because it is offered in a strong institution.

Regional and national organizations require schools to request an evaluation by the accrediting agency. Such evaluations may or may not result in accreditation. Many state departments accept the evaluation of the regional agencies in which the state is located. Accreditation by national agencies is being accepted by many states at the present time as a basis for certification of qualified teachers.

State departments, although political in origin, are quite professional in function. Many of the department personnel who deal with the certification of teachers have had experience as teachers and administrators. Thus, statements relative to teachers or the teaching profession are accepted as being applicable to certification personnel. The quality of teachers, the free exchange of teachers between states, and better standards of certification are concerns of state departments of education. They can exercise their responsibility:

By working with institutions in an effort to improve their programs of teacher education.

By recommending to NCATE for accreditation only those institutions whose programs are of such excellence that they apparently meet the standards of NCATE.

By accepting for certification purposes the graduates of teacher education programs in NCATE-approved schools throughout the nation.

By proposing to local boards that their best assurance of high-quality teaching will probably come from employing the graduates of institutions accredited by NCATE.

By working closely with local boards of education and other state departments of education in the development of state and national proposals which would allow for the certification of teachers from NCATE-approved schools only.

The roles of state departments of education should not be overlooked nor purposely omitted from plans for the improvement of teacher education at state and national levels. It is most probable that state standards for certification and approval of programs of education have been and will continue to be patterns for institutions in their development of teacher education programs.

Both the regulatory and leadership roles are operative in the development and application of state accreditation of teacher education institutions. Groups (representatives of institutions of higher learning, local school officials and teachers, representatives of academic disciplines and other professional agencies) work co-operatively with state department of education representatives in developing and recommending standards for state accreditation of teacher education institutions and in approving specific programs of education and standards for certification of teachers.

When such accreditation standards are adopted one of the following procedures is usually followed:

1. Institutions develop programs of teacher education and then

submit a proper description of that program to the state department of education for approval. If the program meets the standards, the institution is accredited and its program is approved for some definite period of time.

2. Institutions develop programs of teacher education, present them to the state department of education, and request a committee visitation to the school for the purpose of examining the program. Usually such a committee is selected co-operatively by the institution and the state department. If the visiting committee is convinced that the institution and its program meet the standards, then accreditation is recommended. Acceptance of the recommendation by the department grants accreditation of the institution and approval of its program for some definite period of time.

State departments of education surrender neither their leadership role nor their regulatory role when they recognize the standards of other accrediting agencies as acceptable to the state department and use such standards in accrediting institutions for teacher education.

Since all states must accede to the demands to certificate teachers from other states, additional plans and procedures of accreditation of institutions and acceptance of teacher education programs must be provided. It is in this area that states must look to the national professional accrediting agency for specific help.

It is assumed that the state accrediting agencies for teacher education will administer their leadership and regulatory programs in such ways that in the foreseeable future all state-accredited institutions which prepare teachers will meet the minimum threshold criteria established by NCATE, and all will then become nationally accredited. The state agency will continue to exert leadership to provide increasingly better programs (some much higher than achievement of minimum standards) and will encourage experimentation and research. The state agency will also discourage certain institutions of higher education because of inappropriate or inadequate programs, personnel, and facilities so that they withdraw from teacher education.

*   *   *

From the preceding statements by representatives of several segments of the total teaching profession it is clear that some responsibilities for steady improvement in the standards and processes of accreditation of teacher education are shared by all. Note the emphasis in all the statements on these suggestions:

Understanding the purposes, policies, standards, and procedures of professional accreditation is an obligation of individuals; organized groups should help individuals build such understanding through dissemination of information and provision of study opportunities at both preservice and inservice levels.

It is the obligation of all to abide by standards of accreditation; further, where violation of standards occurs, individuals and groups are obliged to take action toward correction of violations.

Both formal and informal methods should be employed in assisting the public in understanding the nature and purposes of professional accreditation.

Both moral and financial support of the profession's accrediting agency, NCATE, should be forthcoming in substantive ways.

Interrelationships among accreditation, certification, professional association membership, and employment practices should be examined by individuals and groups.

Individually and collectively, members of organized professional groups are responsible for active participation in the continuous development and enforcement of standards.

Other such responsibilities that are common to all professionals are referred to in the statements. Notice, too, that some specialized obligations are suggested. Examples of these are as follows:

Classroom teachers can provide some of the best feedback in appraisal of the effectiveness of accreditation standards and their enforcement.

College and university teachers, with special competences and resources available, can provide much needed research and experimentation, both in the development of standards and in appraisal of the effectiveness of the accreditation processes.

Members of the state legal agency can exercise leadership in stimulating institutions to prepare for accreditation, assisting in the process of accreditation, and encouraging institutions to improve programs beyond the minimum standards; they can as well provide information to the professional agency (NCATE) about institutional programs during the interim between evaluations by the NCATE.

State professional associations have unique opportunity to guard the checks and balances so that accreditation plays its appropriate role in relation to the entire program of professional standards and the central purpose of increasing the quality of education in schools and colleges.

Fears Related to Professional Accreditation

A regulatory process conducted by a profession has within it potentials for both good and evil. For example, sometimes there is little distance between regulation by standards and regimentation toward conformity. Effort to enforce minimum standards may unintentionally bring about on the part of some individuals and groups satisfaction with the minimum rather than a drive to achieve the maximum. Where it is necessary and desirable for procedures of regulation to depend largely on judgments of quality rather than on analysis of quantitative data alone, effectiveness of standards and procedures of regulation are inextricably bound up with the adequacy or inadequacy of evaluators and their judgments.

Concern for human welfare is the basic motivation in the establishment of regulations. Such concern prompted child labor laws, compulsory school attendance, stipulations on the use of allocated funds, fair employment practices acts, and so on. Regulatory processes may be instituted by legal agencies; they may be established by formal business or industrial groups; or they may be employed by professional groups. The agreed-upon regulations may be intended to discipline the activities of the entire population of a nation, a state, a municipality; on the other hand, they may be pertinent to a limited group of persons, as is the case with regulations on licensing of service personnel.

Accreditation of teacher education programs, as a regulatory process, was established out of a concern for the educational welfare of citizens. Like other procedures of regulation, accreditation has potential for good and for evil. *It must be assumed, at the outset, that the purpose of accreditation is to improve the quality of educational opportunity through guaranteeing the public that professional educators are fully prepared.* Holding this purpose uppermost in mind, the profession must take whatever steps are necessary to see to it that its standards and processes of accreditation actually accomplish the central purpose. Similarly, vigilance must be exercised to see to it that professional regulations do not bring about undesirable conformity; that they do not fail to stimulate creativity, experimentation, and innovation; that they do not become a vehicle for the exercise of bias by any group.

Because regulatory processes, though intended to function in increasing the welfare of all, have dangers within them, it is quite natural that there should be deep concern about them. It is natural that those to be affected by them should have some fear lest they result in unfortunate controls rather than in sound regulations, intelligently administered. Such fear is observable on the present scene.

Some institutions of higher education seem to fear loss of enrollment (or dollars) if high standards in the preparation of teachers are enforced. There appears to be some concern that teacher education will become more difficult to obtain. That accreditation will make it less possible for new and experimental colleges and programs to evolve is a frequently expressed fear. Among personnel in higher education institutions there is considerable concern about the loss of cherished autonomy. Many aspects of these fears disappear when one views realistically current developments in higher education.

First, the vastly increasing number of college students will make it possible for many colleges that wish to do so to limit enrollments and, as a consequence, to delimit curriculum offerings. In fact, in most states discussion indicates the need for expansion of present facilities and the starting of new junior or community colleges, and in some instances new four-year colleges. Such a situation makes it possible for a large number of colleges, which now offer teacher education programs only to attract numbers or to balance budgets, to withdraw from the program. Some liberal arts colleges may wish to return to their primary function, and other colleges and technical institutes may abandon the teacher education function as a means of using their available dollars for their more appropriate purposes. This trend of greatly increased enrollment somewhat alleviates the fear that new colleges cannot be organized and become accredited for teacher education.

The second trend, the teacher education program becoming a five-year curriculum for initial certification, makes it almost mandatory that the four-year colleges rethink the undergraduate program. Many believe that it is impossible to include in a four-year undergraduate program all the general education that is necessary and desirable. The need for more knowledge is felt by doctors, lawyers, teachers, businessmen, housewives, and everyone else. This trend is related to that of extending professional programs to five, six, and seven years.

The question of the validity of any judgment of competence in teaching is brusquely and inevitably pushed to the forefront of discussions about merit salary plans, programs of supervision, evaluation of teacher performance, or the accreditation of teacher education. The honest truth of the matter is that judgments often do differ, even among carefully trained evaluators. And, say many teachers, if the reliability of judgments is questionable, what use is it to speak of validity? Watertight judgments probably cannot now be made as to the rank order of individual or institutional competences. The reply to this must take into account two other hard realities: First, neither can other professions make watertight judgments, yet these others do make judgments about minimal competence and about the minimal requirements for accreditation. The second point relates to the first, that is, accreditation seeks to set up only the threshold, the minimal criteria for the accreditation of programs, and it may well be possible to secure reliable judgments by qualified evaluators as to this minimum point, this danger line. These minimal precautionary judgments must be made, or else both the public and the profession are hopelessly adrift, liable to be victimized by any institution that is entitled to offer courses and issue transcripts, as is now being done occasionally and will be done increasingly as the demand for teachers makes diploma mills more and more financially rewarding.

The existence of a national professional accrediting agency and the actual administration of national standards produce fears that some of the self-direction or autonomy of institutions of higher education will be affected. In all accreditation, and especially professional accreditation, the question of institutional autonomy arises. Some people argue that professional accreditation makes it impossible for boards of control and administrators to determine policies and develop programs for their institutions in line with their best judgments. On the other hand, professional accrediting bodies say that if institutions are to prepare persons for their professions they should offer those professions assurance that reasonable standards are being maintained. This difference in point of view has resulted in an attitude ranging from resistance to tolerance on the part of many college administrators to all professional accrediting. It should be granted at once that a minimum of interference with institutional policy, consistent with reasonable professional standards, should be exercised by professional accrediting bodies. But this is not the fundamental issue. It is whether there is any such thing as absolute institutional autonomy. Some analysis of this issue may be useful in clarifying the position of professional accrediting bodies.

Absolute autonomy would mean that a faculty or board would be completely unhampered by outside influences in developing its policies and plans. Everyone knows that no such state of autonomy exists in this practical world of social, economic, political, and educational pressures. To begin with, a most subtle influence on institutional policy—public opinion as to whether a program should be expanded in a particular direction or not—is likely to weigh heavily in the decision. The pressure of public opinion to establish a medical school has been known in at least one case to cause a president to resign on the ground that such a unit would create an unbearable financial burden. No one thought to call this a violation of institutional autonomy, yet it was an outside pressure too strong to be resisted by constituted authority.

The influence of alumni on institutional policy is so common as to be overlooked. What is being done in athletics, in fraternities and sororities, in priority of buildings, and even in the sacred trees to be cut or saved is often determined largely by alumni sentiment. Research and foundation grants, as well as bequests from corporations and estates, tend to modify institutional policies and plans. The National Defense Education Act pointed some institutions in directions in which they would not have gone on their own initiative. These are all outside influences much like professional accrediting but with one factor missing: they do not always carry the threat of specific sanctions.

Obviously, therefore, institutional autonomy in the absolute sense is a myth. It simply does not exist in our kind of society. The wise board and administrator will not assume that all outside pressure is bad. Instead such forces will be taken into account in formulating policies. The wise board or president will balance them and develop the best policies and plans possible under existing circumstances. And the wise professional accrediting body will state its standards in such a way as to allow maximum flexibility in meeting them. When standards are clearly not being met the wise professional accrediting body will make clear to the institution concerned *what* must be done in order to be accredited, but it will not tell the institution *how* it must do it.

Challenges for the Future in Accreditation of Teacher Education

Conclusions reached at a recent national conference on accreditation are basic to future developments:

1. The recognized accrediting agencies not only should continue to be concerned with the maintenance of minimum standards of educational practice and performance in colleges and universities but also should assume greater responsibility for assisting institutions in their self-improvement.

2. In the process of aiding institutional self-improvement, accrediting

agencies should encourage and assist in the collection of important comparative data for institutions to employ in their self-studies. Accrediting agencies also should aid in providing "bench-marks" against which individual institutions may compare their own performance.

. . . .

5. Great care must be exercised by accrediting agencies to assure that the use of comparative data, the standards for evaluation, and the means of assisting institutions in self-improvement do not hamper well-conceived experimentation and innovation.

. . . .

9. Continued research on the criteria, instruments, methods and techniques employed in the accreditation and evaluation of institutions should be encouraged. Constant attention should be given on the part of all accrediting agencies to the maintenance of high and appropriate standards of evaluating educational practices.[4]

What these conclusions mean for accreditation of teacher education is suggested by the recommendations of the New Horizons Committee on Accreditation. They commend to the profession careful consideration and appropriate action on such ideas as the following:

1. Local, state, and national groups, professional personnel at all levels in elementary and secondary schools and in colleges and universities, must be provided with more adequate information concerning purposes, procedures, and desired outcomes in accreditation of teacher education. The National Council for Accreditation of Teacher Education should provide for a free flow of ideas, research findings, and concepts related to the development of standards and procedures from all points of view. It is suggested that the NCATE develop and expand *ad hoc* or co-operative groups, in an advisory or consultative capacity, so that significant contributions from all with a stake in teacher education might be forcefully utilized in development of standards. Groups such as the Modern Language Association of America, National Science Teachers Association, and others, should be encouraged to work with the NCATE in determining appropriate standards in the preparation of personnel for positions in elementary schools, in secondary schools, and in colleges and universities. Through a series of conferences, or by other means, results of deliberations by such groups should be understood and utilized by the fifty state accrediting agencies, by the regional accrediting groups, and by the National Council for Accreditation of Teacher Education.

---

[4] Dewey B. Stint (ed.), *Accrediting of Colleges and Universities in the Coming Decade* (Washington, D. C.: National Commission on Accrediting, 1959), p. 29-30.

2. Future changes in standards and procedures should be achieved through the co-operative efforts of the total teaching profession; revisions and expansions should be based on careful research, study, and evaluation. The accreditation policies, programs, and procedures should be sufficiently flexible so that all groups, agencies, organizations, and institutions have opportunities to make contributions. NCATE must receive adequate support to conduct the needed research to determine best practices, to clarify standards and criteria, to develop new standards, and to validate evaluating and measuring procedures for accreditation.

3. Accrediting is not merely meeting minimum standards or crossing a threshold. After initial accreditation an institution must continue to take steps and move toward new horizons to meet the needs of a changing society and changing professional demands. Now and in the immediate future provisions must be made for more manpower, more staff in the central office to carry on the work of accrediting by the NCATE. Pressure for initial and periodic visitation and revisitation of teacher preparing institutions cannot be met by present efforts and funds. There is at present a challenging need for additional evaluators and a critical need for more skilled evaluators, examiners, or visitors. The expanding demands are self-evident.

4. The NCATE can meet expanding demands for visitation and evaluation of teacher education institutions only by increasing the number of better-qualified evaluators. Evaluators need to have seminars, institutes, and a series of training experiences under the direct supervision of qualified examiners. Representative elementary- and secondary-school teachers, other public-school personnel, college and university faculty members from various disciplines, administrative staff members from institutions of higher education, representatives of learned societies, state education officials, and professional association officers must be carefully selected and provided adequate information, time, and finances for these training experiences.

5. The task is of such magnitude that a minimum of fifty to a hundred persons should be selected and trained each year for the next five years. Funds for such a program must be provided by the profession or obtained from some foundation immediately, or the whole process of national accrediting of teacher education will be irreparably damaged. A pattern for training evaluators and consultants similar to that organized and administered by the North Central Association of Colleges and Universities would be suggestive.

6. Could and should each state teachers association, each year for the next five years, provide funds of a "scholarship" type to pay an

appropriate registration fee and all expenses for carefully selected members of the profession from within the state to attend institutes to prepare NCATE examiners? Could and should each or most of the learned societies (or subject-matter organizations) provide such funds on a national basis so that ten or twelve persons each year for the next five years could participate in these same experiences? Could and should each college and university nominate and volunteer to provide funds for a different selected faculty or staff member to participate each year for the next five years? From these lists, when combined, could and should a national committee select approximately one hundred potentially able people to become additional qualified examiners?

7. Many institutions that apply for accreditation misjudge their readiness for evaluation by the NCATE. The standards are stated in terms of broad principles, so much so that officials in institutions need help in relating them to their own teacher education programs. The present NCATE staff is too small (two professional persons) to permit much help to officials of such institutions beyond that which can be provided by correspondence. The need is for one more person to assist presidents and deans in the interpretation of standards and in their preparation for evaluations. Doubtless, fewer institutions would fail to achieve accreditation if officials understood better the crucial factors in accreditation. Within the past two years, approximately one in four of the new applicants has been unable to qualify for accreditation. The Council feels that it has an obligation to do everything possible, consistent with high standards, to reduce this proportion.

Conclusions

A most important step toward effective enforcement of standards in the preparation of professional personnel has been made with significant success in the establishment of a national professional accrediting agency, the National Council for Accreditation of Teacher Education. Constituent membership in this agency is a matter that must engage careful study by the profession to ensure that its representativeness is most appropriate to achievement of the task assigned to it and that it provides adequately for contributions by all groups who have a stake in professional standards.

Standards employed by this agency must be co-operatively developed by the total teaching profession and based on sound theory and practical data. Once adopted, standards must be under constant review through research and analysis. Standards themselves must promote research and experimentation.   Individuality of institutions and programs must be protected; indeed, individuality must be encouraged.   If standards are to stimulate improvement in preparatory programs, they must be set beyond present practice and provide a challenge to institutional personnel.

Procedures employed by the NCATE should (1) make maximum use of institutional motivation for self-improvement; (2) include preparation of evaluators and limit membership on accrediting teams to those who have been prepared for the job; (3) involve all segments of the total profession; (4) provide maximum service to institutions in minimum time; (5) require regular interim reports from institutions; (6) include periodic re-evaluation of accredited programs; and (7) apply standards rigorously, approving only programs of high quality.

It is crystal clear that if the professional accrediting agency is to perform its service effectively, the profession must assume, far more than it does at present, responsibility for the moral and financial support of the NCATE.

CHAPTER 6

A License to Teach

EACH OF THE STATES has developed a system of education which requires those who teach in its schools to have a license. This requirement was established in the public interest to protect children from being taught by persons who did not meet appropriate standards of preparation, health, and character.

The states have followed a similar system of granting licenses in other fields such as architecture, dentistry, law, and medicine, for example, which are vital to the public welfare. It is a system which has grown up, also, in other parts of the world. The policy of the state to require a license to practice a profession is so widespread in the world today that it is reasonable to presume it springs from a fundamental persistent need in society and is not of fleeting importance.

Since the license is a means to identify those who shall be permitted by virtue of qualifications to teach, and hence is not issued indiscriminantly to all who make application, it is not surprising to find that it is a subject of controversy and discussion. Who shall be eligible to apply? What shall be the standards for granting the license? How does one determine which of the applicants are qualified?

In the critical discussion of American education over the last decade, during a period of severe teacher shortages, there have been many challenges and attempts to subvert reasonable standards for licensure as teachers. In addition, however, there is a substantial body of criticism coming from within and without the profession which maintains that the system of licensing teachers has serious weaknesses which require remedy. Among the more urgent problems are these:

The wide variation in licensing requirements among states, making transfer difficult.

The practice of counting credits and courses as a basis for granting licenses.

A questionable relationship between requirements for licensure (certificate or credential) and competence to teach.

The failure to place responsibility for teacher education upon the preparing institutions.

An excessive number of different licenses.

The use of the license to perform functions which are inappropriate.

Members of the profession are invited to consider, in an open-minded spirit of impartial and critical inquiry, a few suggested new directions on the horizons of educational advancement in the field of teacher licensure.

A Preview of Recommendations

It is important for us to be reminded at the outset that licensing is a small, albeit important, part of the whole of teacher education. The licensing system can be a valuable and important adjunct and support for desirable standards. The license cannot adequately assure the proper assignment of teachers, for this rests upon a proper personal, administrative, and organizational responsibility in the local school, backed by strong accreditation. Furthermore, the license cannot be effective unless it is backed by a program of preservice education which genuinely prepares teachers who are competent to practice. Properly conceived, the license is a capstone, a visible indication that all of the basic segments of teacher education are strong. For proper perspective the licensing system needs to be considered in relation to and as an integral part of the total program of teacher education. Reforms in the licensing system will be dependent for their success upon developments in all of the other parts of the total program.

In order to overcome the weaknesses of present licensing practices, advances along several fronts are proposed in the following outline:

1. Present standards for issuing a license to teach should be simplified and improved.

    A. Standards for licensure should be formulated by representative groups of leaders in the profession and subjected to a comprehensive long-term program of research for their validation. These standards should be based upon the principle of placing responsibility for preparation upon teacher education institutions and they should require evidence of competence to teach.

B. Questions of duration and revocation of the licenses to teach need resolution. For example:

1. Should the standards be sufficiently high for the granting of an initial license to warrant permanent validity, except where the evidence shows that the holder has become incompetent (as in other professions), or should the continuance in force of a license be predicated upon continued practice and prescribed additional study?

2. Should responsibility for the revocation of a license be largely assumed by the profession itself through its organizations, where expert testimony is used, or should we continue to rely primarily upon the public through boards and courts of law when charges of incompetence are made?

C. The number of licenses issued by the state should be reduced to a minimum. It is proposed that a state should issue one basic initial entering license with standards high enough to ensure competence. Other specialized licenses beyond this basic one might well be developed and administered by the profession itself, through its various associations, as particular specialties within the profession are identified for which highly specialized preparation is required.

II. Clarification should be sought as to who should and who should not be required to have a license. Such questions as these need resolution:

A. Should teachers at all, or only at some, grade levels be required to have licenses?

B. Should teachers in all types of institutions, public and private, or only those in public schools be required to have licenses?

C. Should professional workers from other fields such as medicine, nursing, psychology, and social work be required to have licenses other than those of their own profession when they work in schools?

III. The burden of formulating and enforcing standards and administration of the licensing system should be carried less by laymen and the state and more by the profession and the preparing institutions.

Standards for Issuing a License to Teach

It is proposed that the purpose of the license should be to assure the public that the holder is competent to teach. To realize this purpose will require a substantial improvement in programs of teacher preparation and in our capacity to evaluate teaching competence. It should not be necessary to labor the point that at present the license too often means only that the holder has completed certain prescribed college courses. It is assumed rather than demonstrated that he is competent to teach. The basis for issuance of the teacher's license should be demonstrated competence. How may this be accomplished?

The preparing institution should provide assurance that the person to be licensed has demonstrated teaching competence. The preparation program should be of such depth and comprehensiveness that those who complete it will have shown evidence of competence to teach. The initial judgment of a teacher's competence by the preparing institution should be followed by evaluation of his first teaching experience as a final basis for issuance of his teacher's license. This evaluation should be made by the new teacher's professional colleagues under the auspices of appropriate professional organizations. Thus, the bases proposed for issuance of the teacher's license are:

Completion of an accredited college program of preparation.

Recommendation by the preparing institution on the basis of demonstrated competency as a beginning teacher.

Recommendation in terms of teaching competence by the appropriate organization of teachers.

An Independent Measure of Background Knowledge

A measure of the candidate's background knowledge in broad liberal education, in his field of specialization, and in education as a profession should be one of the bases used for evaluating a candidate's readiness to begin teaching. Adequacy of this background knowledge, however, should not be equated with teaching proficiency, nor should a candidate be recommended for a license solely on the basis of such background knowledge. It is proposed that the institution should measure the teacher candidate's background knowledge independently of his achievement in the various parts of the course of study. The institution's standards and procedures for such measurement should be subject to appraisal in connection with institutional accreditation.

This proposal for a supplementary check on the teacher candidate's background knowledge is made because experience shows that persons who complete courses of study in these areas range widely in the degree and depth of knowledge they acquire. The evaluation obtained, supplementing that from courses completed, should be of invaluable assistance to preparing institutions in determining if a teacher candidate should be recommended for a license.

This "independent measure" should be conducted by the preparing institution rather than by a separate agency, such as a state licensing office. This approach is desirable chiefly because of the importance of insuring genuine institutional responsibility for the character of its program and the quality of its product. The quality of teacher preparation programs should be improved by substantially increasing institutional responsibility and by providing for evaluation of their standards, programs, and performance by a strong professional accreditation association as well as by the state education agency. Also, placing this responsibility with institutions should insure the desired benefits without the risk of undue conformity of preparation programs or overemphasis on one aspect of teacher education.

Recommendation of Teaching Competence by Appropriate Organization of Teachers

Once the teacher candidate has completed his preparation and assumes a fully responsible role as a teacher he is in fact a professional teacher. Responsibility for his competence and professional growth should rest upon him, his professional colleagues, and appropriate professional organizations. Since he is a novice in the profession it is essential that his early teaching experience be guided professionally and that his competence to continue in the profession on a career basis be established firmly. For this purpose, and as a basis for licensure, a thorough process of evaluation should be provided. It is at this stage in the teacher's development that the profession should assume a direct role in evaluation of his competence and promotion of his professional growth.

Considerable planning, organization, and experimentation undoubtedly will be needed to accomplish this evaluation. The process of evaluation should involve the teacher's colleagues, including the administrators in his school system. It also should involve qualified professional persons from outside the school system, including those from preparing institutions and state education agencies. The decision on recommendation for licensure should be the responsibility of the profession and should take the form of official action by a properly constituted group.

The difficulties encountered in evaluation of teacher competence need not be detailed here. The problems to be resolved in developing satisfactory processes for assumption of organized professional responsibility in this area are complex. We do not suggest a model plan but rather propose that progress toward this objective will be furthered by experimentation that recognizes the role of school administration, the responsibility of professional organizations, and the professional integrity of all participants in the evaluation. We see no genuine basis for assuming that professional organizations will usurp the prerogatives of school administration in this area. Rather, the role of the profession should be supportive of administration policy and should clearly abjure administrative functions. Properly, we should conceive of committees and individuals having clearly defined roles in the evaluation. In time this function should include evaluation not only of novice teachers, but also of experienced teachers.

Duration and Revocation of Licenses

In recent years the states have largely discontinued the practice of issuing permanent or "life" teaching certificates. One reason for such action has been the desire to raise standards for licenses. A higher and more uniform level of preparation of all teachers has resulted from requiring those to continue study who had received licenses at an earlier time when standards were lower. Other reasons for requiring additional study to maintain a license have been the rapid increases in knowledge in all teaching fields and the need for "refresher" study by those who leave teaching and desire to return some years later.

License Renewal

The question is not whether there is value in continued study and other efforts to be abreast of one's field and otherwise to be sensitive and knowledgable professionally, but how most efficiently, economically, and soundly these objectives can be achieved. Should a system of license renewal be a part of the program to keep the profession "up to date"?

A primary consideration should be the general level of standards for teaching. If these standards are high, the basis is laid for a high level of individual responsibility for professional growth and there is less justification for across-the-board renewal requirements for those who are continuously in educational service. There would seem to be some reason, however, for those who have left teaching for a period of time, such as five or ten years, to present evidence of professional growth.

A secondary but important consideration is the nature of license renewal requirements and their administration. To serve the purposes intended, the requirements should be broad and individually applied rather than narrow and rigidly applied. Administration of such a program of license renewal at the state level would be difficult. The natural tendency is for the administration of such requirements to become increasingly inflexible and less closely related to the desired objectives.

Next, the question may properly be raised whether the license renewal approach to promoting professional alertness and growth is consistent with sound principles of professionalism. These principles call for a high level of professional responsibility by the individual and his professional organizations. They call, also, for school personnel policies which provide for a high standard of faculty qualification and performance. It would seem that the highest sense of professional responsibility on the part of individuals, school administrations, and professional organizations would be promoted by assigning the task of appraisal of experienced teachers to the local level. Practically, both from the standpoint of determination of desirable requirements for remaining in teaching and the administration of the requirements, it seems clear that the responsibility should be placed at the local level once the basic standards for licensure are sufficiently high.

Revocation of Licenses

Similar problems are encountered in connection with standards and procedures for revocation of the license. In most states adequate laws and procedures presently exist for the revocation of the teacher's license. Too generally, however, there is inadequate assumption of responsibility by individual professional persons, school administrations, and organized professional groups. Professional responsibility needs to be expressed through evaluation and documentation of competence in its various aspects and through initiation and support of the actions necessary to revocatory proceedings. Granted that the state laws on such matters are not all ideal, the major need is for the assumption of a high degree of professional responsibility by individuals and by their professional organizations. An important part of this responsibility is an active assisting role in an effort to rehabilitate any teacher prior to action which would lead to revocation of his license.

Professional organizations need to develop operating procedures for the discharge of their responsibility in these areas. These processes should support official school agencies in meeting their responsibilities. Professional self-discipline of the individual should be supported in the local, state, and national spheres by professional organizations. Improvement in this area will be furthered by legal provision for recognition of teaching as a professional area of expertness. This is generally provided for in "professional practices acts," a subject which is discussed in Chapter 8.

Reduction in Number of Licenses and Simplification of Licensing Processes

There are several reasons why the licensing system for teachers needs to be simplified:

1. Higher institutions in most states prepare many teachers who plan to secure teaching certificates in adjacent states or even states in another section of the country. Although there is some similarity in standards and in kinds of certificates, there are considerable differences in these respects among the states and often a high degree of specificity in certificate requirements. This situation complicates the efforts of teacher education institutions to plan well-conceived programs applicable generally to all their teacher candidates. In most states certificates are issued for teaching different subjects or age levels of students. This practice puts emphasis on differences in preparation of teachers and tends to obscure the fact that much of each teacher's preparation is similar. Since each state makes its own distinctions in this matter, the variety of teaching certificates in the nation is considerable.

2. Many states require applicants prepared in institutions in other states to meet particular, and sometimes provincial, requirements despite the fact that the applicant has completed a generally comparable teacher education program approved by a sister state. Progress is being made toward elimination of this problem through adoption by states of policies which permit acceptance of graduates of institutions whose programs are accredited by the National Council for Accreditation of Teacher Education.

3. Perhaps the most important reason for simplifying the licensing system is that too much dependence is placed upon the license to regulate the operation of the schools with respect to the use of teachers and other professional personnel. On the whole, the educational system has been developed to a stage that makes possible and desirable a different, more differentiated allocation of the control functions for which licensure has been utilized. This should permit the license to be used only for its primary function, namely, the designation of a person who is prepared and competent to teach.

Licensure and Utilization of Teachers

Why should not the license be used to control the use of teachers? In addition to the obvious administrative difficulties inherent in doing this through state-level licensure, the attempt to do so detracts from our effort to develop other more desirable controls. Licensure for specific fields and school grades encourages artificial distinctions in preparation programs and between teachers in school systems. Such licensure also tends to hold back the development of sound programs of evaluation of teacher competence in relation to the specific teaching needs in a school system. Once a teacher has become experienced much more should be considered in determining the teaching role in which he will be most effective than the specific nature of his basic preparation.

Simplifying the licensure system so that the control of teacher assignments is placed in the hands of school administrations and professional organizations not only will be consistent with sound principles of educational management, but should promote the best use of teachers. School systems need to be in the best possible position to be soundly experimental and to meet the ever-growing and ever-changing educational needs of our society. It should be noted that aside from licensure most states have an operating system for control over local school programs in the form of state accreditation.

Three developments in recent years are bringing about new conditions in educational service. They make it possible to reduce substantially the amount of control exercised by the state through licensure. The first of these is the establishment of professional accreditation for teacher education. This development has been accompanied by the growing practice of replacing specific certification requirements with state guidelines for teacher education programs. The second development is the steady reorganization of school districts throughout the nation, resulting in a substantial decrease in small educational units. Generally this has been accompanied by improvement in the quality of educational programs, in school faculties, and in their administration. The third development is the growth of strong and responsible professional organizations of teachers, both of large all-inclusive groups and of specialized groups. As these developments mature it seems reasonable to assume that one license for teaching should suffice. The need for control of assignments of teachers by means of the license should be eliminated as the quality of the administration and faculties of larger educational units improves and professional organizations assume much greater responsibility.

Because of the all-important nature of the teacher, in his central role in education, certification *as a teacher* should be restricted to the teacher himself and to those whose administrative, supervisory, or consultative function bears directly on the performance of the teacher. Conversely, no one whose function bears directly upon the performance of the teacher should be permitted to serve without certification as a teacher.

Whether administrative, supervisory, or consultative personnel should have a license in addition to that required of the teacher is a question which may call for examination and debate. In last analysis, the controlling factor may be the function of the ultimate professional supervisor of the teacher—the superintendent of schools. As the executive agent of the citizens charged with the responsibility for conducting the schools of the community he has a primary responsibility for upholding professional standards. His is the final decision which recommends employment of a teacher, his the final decision where the teacher shall be assigned if employed, his the final decision to recommend whether or not to retain the teacher in the system. The executive and professional leadership responsibilities of the superintendent could be detailed further. Indeed, it seems clear that he needs specialized training in addition to (but not instead of) that required of the teacher. Whether the superintendent and other administrative and supervisory personnel should be required to qualify for a special license should be considered carefully in light of principles for a sound system of licensure. Possibly some intermediate step is indicated. Possibly designation of qualified personnel in specialized fields of all kinds within the teaching profession should be made by the professional organizations of these specialists.

If the professional tone of the system is established at the administrative and supervisory level, the stage is set for infinitely more flexible management at all other levels. Assignment of all professional personnel can thus be assured on a professional basis, unhampered by fragmentary, unduly divisive certification regulations, and designed to insure the most effective use of every staff member in furtherance of the effectiveness of each teacher in each classroom.

The goal is a highly qualified profession of teachers with the status of the teacher established at a much higher level than is true generally at present. One license based on a strong program of preparation and demonstration of teaching competence will provide the necessary legal foundation for protection of the public. Desirable differentiation of preparation and of performance will be controlled, not by the license, but by the teaching profession itself, including school, college, and state administrations.

This approach to licensure of professional school personnel will result in a greatly simplified licensing system. It will not preclude but rather it will encourage desirable differentiation of functions within the ranks of teaching and specialized personnel. The setting will be provided for sound differentiation in functions to develop in response to teaching needs. This should occur when needed to provide new and different as well as old and tried ways of teaching and of organization for learning. With highly qualified teachers and with organized professional participation in the maintenance and improvement of program standards, there should be no danger of a chaotic situation developing in the utilization of either professional or nonprofessional personnel in the school program. Rather, an adaptable situation should exist with the teacher as the responsible center of the program, functioning in relation to students and other teachers in the ways in which he can be most effective.

Licensure for Whom?

The basic prospect for the license to teach consists of making the requirements, and the administration of them, correspond so economically to the needed *competence* that professional qualifications will be assured without the waste motion and the actual deterring of excellent students from school teaching, which have rightly been objected to in present practices.

Assuming that this can be achieved, there follows the further prospect of applying the standard everywhere that it will benefit the quality of American education. What will this mean? Should licenses be mandatory for teachers in private schools and in higher education? Should the teacher's license be required for professional persons from other fields who serve the schools?

Licensure and Private Schools

Whether a state should require private schools to employ only licensed teachers is a question which has to be answered by reconciling principles which tend to conflict.[1]

On the one hand, the state has the collective responsibility assumed by the people in a democracy to see that each person, and hence the Republic, is adequate to play a successful part (as far as humanly possible) in the task of maintaining our precarious civilization. This responsibility of the state clearly entails the obligation to see that all children and youth living within its boundaries are taught only by teachers who are competent according to the best professional judgment obtainable.

On the other hand, church-related schools can argue that the principle of separation between church and state is violated if a state imposes its definition of teacher competence upon such a school. A church-related school may hold that qualifications of character and doctrine are the only essentials for its purposes; and it may show that its supporting religious group cannot afford to compete for licensed teachers, with the result that the requirement of licenses would close the school and deny the freedom to practice its religion.

It seems a reasonable answer on the state's part, however—in fact, the only answer consistent with its responsibility—that it must protect the public, and hence all children and youth, from being taught by persons of substandard qualifications. One might draw an analogy to the field of building regulations: a minimum standard is set by the state on the advice of the publicly recognized organizations of specialists, and the local school authorities can add any further safety precautions they wish.

Religious groups must be free to give the instruction they want in place of public education, or at least as a supplement to it, but without sacrificing such secular instruction as the appropriate organizations of specialists consider essential for the welfare of all.

Among private institutions the independent schools, particularly, have fought for freedom of decision in order to reach higher standards. Their spokesmen have often claimed, indeed, that their freedom benefited all education by giving leadership in the pursuit of excellence.

---

[1] For a summary of present practices, see Fred F. Beach and Robert F. Will, *The State and Nonpublic Schools*, U. S. Department of Health, Education, and Welfare, Office of Education, Misc. No. 28 (Washington, D. C.: Superintendent of Documents, Government Printing Office, 1958).

Any curtailment of this freedom would violate the principle of free enterprise and thwart educational progress.

One must grant this contention, but it would be a weak case to argue that the freedom to set higher standards of teaching requires the freedom to hire teachers ineligible for a license, *unless* the requirements for obtaining one fail to signify true competence or actually deter potential superior teachers from preparing for positions that require a license. If the licensing system thus fails in its purpose, the logical concern of a professional spirit, and of the leadership toward excellence, is certainly not just to build a private freedom from the license but to reform it for the good of all. The independent schools have demonstrated their concern to share in the national responsibility for the quality of teaching;[2] and the nonpublic schools should have a share in the defining of any standards that will be applied to them.

Once the license represents a valid standard of competence, and once the granting of licenses is based on demonstrated competence, there remains no valid argument against its application to both public and private schools—church-related, independent, and proprietary. Indeed it then becomes the moral obligation of the state to apply the standard throughout its jurisdiction.

Higher Education and Licensure

Do the reasons for licensing teachers apply to those who teach in college and graduate school? Several differences bear on the question.

The freedom of the student at these levels to choose his school and to choose whether to go to school at all has bearing only insofar as the protection of the individual is concerned; it has no bearing on the state's obligation to the rest of the society.

A second, more important difference is that college and graduate students should be expected to study on their own initiative, to depend relatively little on the teacher to show them how to learn what he has to offer. Yet adults still learn more rapidly and more thoroughly from a wise and skillful teacher. And as added knowledge and techniques have to be mastered by modern specialists, the efficiency with which they learn has become vitally important for their

---

[2] See, for example, National Council of Independent Schools, Committee on Teacher Training, *Preparation of Teachers for Secondary Schools* (Boston: the Council, 1958). The recommendations of this constructive report, pages 40-42, look toward co-operation of the secondary schools, faculties of liberal arts and sciences, and professional educators to improve both preservice and inservice education.

lives and the lives entrusted to them.   It may be necessary to waive the requirement of teaching qualifications for various temporary functions as lecturer, consultant, clinical demonstrator, and so on, in order to get a person with other qualifications essential for the position. Such positions, however, are the exception, and they are used to best advantage in an institution whose policy-making staff has the full range of qualifications.

Third, the candidates for full-time college and university positions can usually be chosen from a world-wide roster of experts.   But this is no reason to condone the choice of a person who is below standard in any qualification requisite for the responsibility offered to him.

Fourth, the choice of personnel can be made in first-rate colleges or universities by expert judges since they are the source of the best available judgment in their fields of specialization.   Yet the expertness that can be counted on is limited to one field.   It does not necessarily encompass all the essential elements of competence as a teacher.

Fifth, college and university departments have a responsibility, which is far less marked in the schools, to advance human knowledge beyond what may be believed or appreciated in the surrounding society.   The institution of higher education needs all the freedom necessary for this peculiar and sometimes unpopular service.   But the necessary freedom does not include the freedom for inept and unskilled teaching.

Consequently, an increasing number of college and university teachers and administrators are of the opinion that somehow a minimum level of professional teaching competence should be assured throughout higher education.   This opinion was reflected in a conference on "The Preparation of College Teachers," called by the American Council on Education in 1949,[3] and in a sequel conference nine years later at which Chairman O. Meredith Wilson, then president of the University of Oregon, observed that:

> In a sense, higher education since much earlier than 1949, but certainly since 1949, has continuously felt the urgency to re-examine the preparation of college teachers and to re-examine the methods by which, once prepared, they are inducted into their offices.[4]

[3] See Theodore C. Blegen and Russell M. Cooper (eds.), *The Preparation of College Teachers* (Washington, D. C.: American Council on Education, 1949).

[4] "The Invitation to Re-examine the Preparation of College Teachers," *Graduate Study for Future College Teachers,* edited by Joseph Axelrod (Washington, D. C.: American Council on Education, 1959), p. 4.   The chief relevant conclusions are summarized on pages 88-89: "2. *Should Ph.D. programs include training for pedagogic competence?*   There was clear agreement that some provision be made for such training.   But there was disagreement on how much or what kind of

Professor W. H. Cowley traces the concern back to 1922.[5]   In more recent years, Earl James McGrath, Karl Bigelow, and other leading minds in American higher education have contributed to a growing consensus among thoughtful teachers and administrators on the need for a more systematic solution of the problem.

The emerging consensus has to do with objectives, not with means. It does not suggest the required courses or otherwise prescribe the means.   It does select the areas in which qualifications ought to be required: the field to be taught; general education; skill as an instructor; and professional conscience, not alone as a scientist or scholar but also as a teacher, concerned to strengthen the good influence of education upon society and informed as to how to take part in organized, effectual efforts toward that end.   In the last three of these four areas it is generally admitted that too much of our higher education now falls short of an adequate standard.

But here stand two practical difficulties, one in adopting and the other in administering a standard.

The qualifications essential for college and university teaching may not be subject to as general agreement as are those for high-school teaching, or for university teaching in other countries where a candidate may be judged largely on his delivery of a lecture in his field. Before a standard can be adopted which will win assent, the elements of it will have to be hammered out by groups of specialists who have the respect of university teachers and administrators.   A basic recommendation, therefore, is that such groups be brought together to define and propose the qualifications which they believe ought to be required. Only on the basis of such a proposal can there be useful talk of a license requirement in higher education.

The administrative difficulty arises from the fact that the university must be separate from the government in order to fulfill its role as critic of the local society and culture.   The public interest would be endangered—even national survival under present conditions— if the state were to assume a control over the hiring of professors or, for that matter, elementary- and secondary-school teachers, which could spread into matters of ideology and of conscience.   Settlement

---

training should be provided; on whether it should actually be required; if required, on whether it should be required of all students or only of prospective teachers; and on whether it should be handled by experts in the subject matter, or experts in pedagogy, or a combination of these."

[5] "Recruiting Talent for College Teaching," *Expanding Resources for College Teaching*, edited by Charles G. Dobbins (Washington, D. C.: American Council on Education, 1956), p. 5-7.

of the question of how to enforce a standard can be taken up when the needed standard has been acceptably defined. A basis upon which the licensing authority in higher education should be delegated should be evident when professional associations and the voluntary organizations of colleges and universities develop the interest and the means to discharge this responsibility.

Nonteaching Personnel and Licensure

There is serious question whether many persons now under the shelter of the license (certification) "umbrella" truly belong there. In many states financial aid to local communities is based on the number of certified personnel employed. This fact has often seemed to result in the inclusion under teacher licensure of persons who really have only the most obscure connection with the actual instructional process. The solution to the financial argument is simple: offer state aid on a different basis, pupils in attendance for instance, as do some states.

Another factor tending to increase the number of categories of school personnel under teacher certification has been the retirement plans available to teachers in many states. Certification is sometimes the criterion of eligibility for membership, and loud are the claims of the instructional value of the work of such personnel as the school physician, the school dentist, the school nurse, the school dental hygienist, the school social worker, and the school psychologist.

Many of these valuable servants of the public schools are or could be licensed by state agencies having special jurisdiction over the special areas involved. There seems little point in requiring also that they be licensed as teachers. Their services are valuable to teachers and children alike, as are the services of similarly trained people performed in contexts other than the schools.

Much has been written and said about the noninstructional duties with which the teacher is saddled day in and day out. Especially during the past decade, interesting experiments, some under careful control, have been conducted in an effort to determine to what extent these duties can profitably be assumed by noninstructional personnel, often referred to as teacher aides. The professional conduct of the classroom under the guidance of the kind of teacher envisioned in this report, supported by professional administrative, supervisory, and consultative services designed to enhance professional effectiveness, should be insurance enough that services assigned to teacher aides will be noninstructional in nature and that the persons to whom these duties are entrusted will be selected for qualities which will redound to the best interests of the children. In the professional climate contemplated there should be no need for licensure for teacher aides.

Placement of Responsibility for
Standards in Licensure

In considering the relationship of the public and the profession in the determination of standards for the teacher's license, the basic responsibility and authority of the state is the starting point. When it is stated that the profession should determine these standards it should be understood that this can only be in the sense of performance of a delegated role. The state cannot relinquish its responsibility. Accordingly, the role of the profession must be consistent with the general responsibility of the state for the direction of the educational system.

For several reasons a clear delineation of the roles of the public and the profession has not as yet been achieved in this country. A long background of public control of education by lay bodies has been paralleled by an equally long period of lack of strength and unity of professional organizations of teachers. In recent years there has been a proper recognition by professional educators of the need for widespread public knowledge and support of the educational program. Desirable lay involvement in study of educational problems often has been extended so as to put laymen into positions of judgment on matters which should be entirely within the province of the professional. The confusion which has resulted is compounded by the fact that "the teaching profession" is represented by many voices in the form of many organizations. These organizations have yet to develop effective means of communication and co-ordination, such as might foster the formulation of professional opinion that is truly representative. Also, there exists a fear that professional organizations, when granted extensive responsibility, would put the selfish interest of their members ahead of the public interest.

Undoubtedly, a crucial test of the professional in any field is his capacity to place the fulfillment of his public trust in the first position in all his actions. An essential characteristic of a professional person and of professional organizations is a wholehearted devotion to the public interest. Most certainly this should be true for the teaching profession. In view of the fact of ultimate public control, those matters in education which require professional knowledge and judgment should be made a professional responsibility. Responsibility has a sobering effect, and especially so when subject to regular review by the delegating authority. Further, the maturing of a profession and its capacity to achieve its ideals should be fostered by increased responsibility.

In actual fact, the public must work through and depend upon the specialized knowledge of the profession to improve the quality of education. While the public can detect the grossest forms of incompetence, the more subtle, pervasive, and important factors reveal themselves almost exclusively to those within the profession itself, to those whose knowledge and skill permit critical evaluations. It is in the inner recesses where the professional person daily practices his art that his conduct and competence reveal themselves. Here he is judged by his professional fellows according to the known standards and accepted facts of his profession. Hence, the public is substantially dependent upon the good will and co-operation of the profession itself. Especially is this true in the day-by-day intimate supervision so necessary for maintenance of the highest standards of professional performance.

Thus, in the public interest it is proposed that standards for teacher licensure should be determined by the appropriate organizations and agencies of the teaching profession. More than one set of working relationships and processes may achieve the needed professional responsibility in this area. In general, at the present time, state education agencies provide for some distinction between the role of the lay governing body and the profession in the determination of licensure standards. Usually, a state board of education or agency sets up procedures for securing the recommendations of various professional groups and of groups in society that take an especial interest in education. These procedures may or may not provide for formal recommendation from professional organizations. Commonly, the state agency attempts to crystallize recommendations through an advisory committee which is representative of professional groups and interests and possibly also of some lay groups that have taken an active interest in educational policies.

In this process the major professional leadership which co-ordinates the effort to make recommendations representative of professional judgment and usually of lay groups as well is normally provided by the professional staff of a state education agency. There would seem to be no sound reasons why the important professional services of these agencies should be decreased as a result of greater professional organization responsibility for determination of standards for teacher licensure. In fact, the role of state education agencies is evolving as one of leadership in improving educational programs. Through the exercise of professional leadership and the co-ordination of the services of official agencies, the state agency might well become the most satisfactory avenue through which the decisions of the profession achieve official sanction.

There is need for improved techniques for bringing informed professional judgment into focus and expressing it through recommendations of professional organizations. There is need correspondingly to limit the actions of official lay agencies to the acceptance or the rejection of these recommendations. In this development it is important that the positive characteristics of the unique relationship in this country between laymen and professionals in the planning for education should be retained. This relationship at its best is exemplified in the working climate and procedures achieved by some of our state education agencies, professional organizations, and state and local lay governing boards.

CHAPTER 7

Identification, Selective Admission and Retention in Teacher Education

THE TEACHING PROFESSION has its challenge for new horizons, not only from within the profession, but from without among citizens who have concern for the children and youth of this nation and for preservation and improvement of the democratic society. At the 1960 Golden Anniversary White House Conference on Children and Youth, various conference forums urged maintenance of high standards of personnel selection to protect children from incompetent persons and recommended "that criteria for selection include: mastery of subject matter; sympathetic understanding of students and willingness to confer freely with them; effective classroom presentation; recognition of the partnership nature of the learning process; and teaching methods which will inspire love of learning, stimulate civic responsibility and instill democratic ideals."[1] In addition to emphasis on the need for favorable working conditions, recognition, and adequate salaries, stress was laid on the importance of providing "opportunities for continued study, professional growth and advancement . . . to insure the highest possible quality of instruction."[2] The faculties of institutions of higher learning were urged systematically to study ways of improving the use of all facilities so as to extend teaching resources to greatly increased numbers of students, and were challenged to "develop bold and imaginative approaches to improving curricula and instruction. . . ."[3]

Youth attending the Golden Anniversary Conference placed "quality education" third on their list of nine priorities for the decade ahead, developed from the more than sixteen hundred recommendations produced by conference forums. Said the youth delegates:

---

[1] *Conference Proceedings,* © 1960 by the Golden Anniversary White House Conference on Children and Youth, Washington, D. C., p. 341.

[2] *Ibid.,* p. 342.

[3] *Ibid.,* p. 335.

Education is the main basis for the broad political participation and individual mobility essential for a free society. To fulfill these needs, we must provide varied educational opportunities to challenge each individual to realize his full abilities. It should be recognized that all institutions and programs designed to meet individual needs can and should maintain high standards. To do this, local, State, and Federal Governments, as well as individuals, businesses, and nonprofit bodies must greatly increase their support for education on all levels. Further, the teacher must be more adequately honored as an individual and recompensed as a skilled professional.[4]

The profession itself must take up this challenge. The profession must assume responsibility for identifying qualities that can be measured accurately enough to provide bases for evaluation. Instruments and procedures must be set up to ensure evaluation of each prospective teacher by competent personnel, self-evaluation by each student, and continuous analysis of the evaluation processes themselves.

Assumptions Regarding Identification and Selection for Teacher Education

The *right* of institutions and the profession to select persons admitted to preparation for teaching and to its practice is seldom questioned today. However, assumptions regarding the *ability* to select, with reasonable assurance of success, those persons who will discharge effectively their responsibilities in the increasingly diverse roles of schools and colleges are frequently questioned. Assumptions regarding the responsibility in the selective process at various stages are perhaps generally acknowledged. Responsibility certainly is not generally discharged by the profession as a whole, nor do the various segments having major responsibility for the processes at various stages in the selective sequence consistently assume leadership in these roles. Here is a real horizon for the profession.

Similarly, many reasons for selection are acknowledged by various groups within the profession and with varying degrees of conviction. The horizon is not so much in deciding what should be done as in assumption of responsibility by all segments of the profession for unified professional action.

Assumptions Regarding Reasons for Selection

Teachers must help develop not only an educated citizenry, but sufficient trained manpower for all other professions and occupations essential to our culture. Much has been done in the development

---

[4] *Ibid.*, p. 293-94.

and revision of curricula designed to prepare teachers and to increase the standards of preparation both quantitatively and qualitatively. Much more needs to be done in these areas. But full value cannot be derived even from present developments until programs of selecting candidates for teacher education are also more adequately developed. Teaching must become a profession worthy of its high responsibilities and must attract to it enough capable young people to staff the schools as the American goal of education for all is approached.

Manpower shortages, the long period of preparation required, the inadequate remuneration, the changing demands in terms of the changing complexion and size of collegiate student bodies—all make more imperative intensified concern and action to increase the supply of qualified college teachers. But perhaps the paramount reason for concern and action at this level lies in the unique role of higher education in advancing the frontiers of knowledge. A real challenge is the staffing of colleges and universities quantitatively and qualitatively so that the members of this segment of the teaching profession can, more effectively than ever before, discharge their unique responsibility as intellectual frontiersmen, and so they also can assume more effectively their expanding role in the general education sequence and the teaching-learning process for the increased numbers and ability ranges of persons requiring education beyond the high school.

Quality. An increasingly complex society is extending the responsibility of the school and college. The more complex the society and the higher its educational level, the greater the need and demand for a lengthening span of formal education for succeeding generations. Increased birthrates and the improved ability of the schools to keep a greater proportion of a given age group in school have set up a rapidly paced increase in school population which is unlikely to decelerate significantly in the foreseeable future.

These factors combine to result in an ever greater and more diverse school and college population, in terms of abilities, backgrounds, and needs, to require increasingly varied teaching skills and knowledge, and thus to require more and better-prepared personnel. These teachers need to be selected not only for their ability to become prepared for the profession of teaching, but for specific responsibilities in what has actually become a constellation of highly specialized professional roles.

An overriding assumption supporting selection in the teaching profession is that the quality of teaching in our schools is of first importance to preservation and growth of a democratic society. This has been called a time for greatness, a time to pursue excellence. Quality must be the keynote in teacher education, in certification standards, in performance, and in services of all professional personnel, from those responsible for the planned program for nursery- and kindergarten-age children through those responsible for education in the graduate schools in all fields of endeavor. But quality in all these aspects and areas is dependent upon rigorous application of standards in identifying and selecting prospective teachers and in retaining them in programs of preparation and in the profession.

The selective process must function so effectively that both the public and the profession can be sure those who enter the teaching profession are qualified to assume the responsibility of experts in their fields. Only when this happens will the profession as a whole be exercising professional autonomy that is not only its right but its obligation.

Additional important assumptions that make selection a necessity are:

Members of a profession must themselves be well qualified in order to determine standards and develop processes for achieving the goals of education.

The profession has a right to expect its new members to be well qualified.

New members of the profession have a right to expect that acceptance indicates they are well qualified as persons and by preparation, that they have not been victims of poor guidance.

Each state is responsible for *official recognition* that there are bases for selection of competent teachers.

A competent teacher is a reasonable expectation for every pupil.

The teacher is an important influence on the learning process and on what is learned.

Teaching demands specific abilities and qualities of personality not possessed in sufficient degree by all people.

Although there may be some few characteristics required for persons in all specialties, different characteristics will be needed in different kinds of educational work.

Quantity and Cost. The need for diversified and high-quality personnel and the increase in scope and responsibility are of primary importance. However, the sheer practicality of the need for increased numbers and the wisdom of reaping benefits from monies invested provide additional valid reasons for extending the horizon of selective practices in the teaching profession to the point that the program of evaluation and selection is operative consistently from initial identification and selection through the teaching career.

A reasonable assumption, from the economic as well as the qualitative standpoint, is that those persons should be selected who can profit most from preparation and for whom success in teaching can be predicted, rather than to spend limited educational resources of staff, facilities, and finance on persons whose predictions for success are doubtful. The high cost of misfits, of transients, and of those prepared for teaching but who never teach deserves serious consideration and positive remedial and preventive action.

It may be assumed teaching will truly become a profession only when those who prepare for it plan to make it their lifetime career, or at least to give ten or fifteen years of professional service along with a career of family-rearing and homemaking. Teaching will truly become a profession only when it no longer has within its ranks a sizeable number of persons who look upon their preparation primarily as "insurance," or who use teaching primarily as a "meal ticket," a "stepping-stone," a "time-marking" occupation, or an escape from boredom.

A former assumption now supported by fact is the positive effect of higher standards on supply. There is accumulating evidence that higher certification standards and definitive operating programs for selective admission and retention in teacher education increase rather than decrease the supply at the same time these procedures improve the quality of teaching personnel.

State-by-state studies have for several years indicated that wherever certification standards are advanced (or even announced prior to enforcement), enrollments in teacher education jump disproportionately to the increase in the over-all college population. Increased enrollments in teacher education and increased supplies of teachers appear to be positively correlated with the raising of certification standards. The number of states (including the District of Columbia) requiring the minimum of a baccalaureate degree for elementary-school teachers has moved from 16 in 1946 to 42 in 1960. In the same period, the number of degree teachers prepared increased from 41,000 to 129,000. The differences in rate of increase of supply have been particularly noticeable in areas where concerted efforts are resulting in higher certification standards.

Now we also have statistically significant evidence that institutions having definitive selective programs for teacher education are distinctly better producers than institutions with less selective programs, both in terms of the percentages of initially admitted persons who complete the program and in terms of percentages of their graduates initially placed in teaching positions.[5]

The Right to Select

The right of institutions and of the profession in the selective process is acknowledged by most colleges preparing teachers. It is seldom questioned by practitioners in the field who have real concern that teaching become a quality profession. Nor is it questioned by laymen who respect persons charged with a major responsibility for developing "the minds of men."

Selection of those most fitted for professional service to society can be justified at all times. Though acceptable practice in most professions for some years, selection for professional preparation has only recently become an acknowledged right and responsibility in teacher education. Yet effectiveness of preparation and performance for practitioners in all other professions is directly dependent, in significant degree, upon the effective performance of teachers.

In a study of 785 regionally accredited, baccalaureate-degree-granting institutions that are engaged in preparing teachers (91 per cent of all such institutions throughout the country), respondents for 83 per cent expressed the belief there should be selective admission to teacher education. Only one-tenth opposed selective admission, and some of these rejected such a program only on the basis that it appeared unworkable or inexpedient in terms of administration or teacher supply at the time of the study (1953).[6]

The Ability to Select

Criteria of identification and selection are many. In total, they present a mosaic of the individual personality, ability, preparation, and the teaching situation. Recent research having implications for selective processes may be classified into four categories: (1) efforts to identify good teachers and thus to identify qualities which may be predictive of effective teaching as these findings may apply to pre-preparation selection and retention in the preparation program; (2)

---

[5] Ruth A. Stout, *A Study of Admissions and Retention Practices in College and University Programs of Teacher Education* (Unpublished doctoral dissertation, University of Minnesota, 1957).

[6] *Ibid.*

identification of characteristics which, when fostered or developed, may be supposed to result in the preparation of effective teachers; (3) elements, procedures, and apparent effects of selective admission and rentention programs in specific institutions; and (4) general studies of selective admission and retention practices.

Assumptions dealing not only with the right to select for a profession, but also with the ability, responsibility, and criteria for selection and the selective process itself are basic. Assumptions on which identification and selection for teacher education and retention in the teaching profession operate concern the goals of instruction, the setting in which learning takes place, the teaching process, the nature of the learner, the learning process, the colleges preparing teachers, the persons being prepared, and the profession-society relationship.

The need for selection has been recognized for at least the last half century. Ben Blewett, in addressing the 1913 convention of the National Education Association, saw the need but also thought the process simple, for he said that "the qualities which distinguish successful teachers from tyros or misfits stand out in bold relief and cannot be overlooked or mistaken by one who is an experienced educator."[7] Articles and reports of studies until about 1940 reflect continued interest and increasing concern with the matter of selection for teacher preparation and entrance into the profession. They also indicate increasing recognition of the complexity of the procedure which Blewett thought so simple. Comparisons of studies reported in the 1940 and 1950 editions of the *Encyclopedia of Educational Research* indicate rapid acceleration of efforts. Since 1950, studies and research have bourgeoned in both quantity and extent. Bagley, in 1939, issued a clarion call for accelerated action, but its significance is only now really being recognized. He stated:

> I do not hesitate to say that, if three-fourths of the time, energy and money spent during the past fifteen years in carrying through elaborate programs of curriculum-revision had been spent in a determined effort to raise the standards of selecting and training teachers, a far more significant contribution would have been made to the improvement of American Education.[8]

As early as 1947, Cook and Leeds reported it is possible to measure "teaching personality" with as high a validity as that for academic aptitude, if by teaching personality is meant "those characteristics

---

[7] *NEA Addresses and Proceedings* (Washington, D. C.: National Education Association, 1913), p. 291.

[8] William C. Bagley, "An Essentialist Looks at the Foreign Languages," *Educational Administration and Supervision* 25: 250; April 1939.

of the teacher's behavior related to the emotional responses of pupils and the ability to establish intimate and harmonious working relationships with them."[9]

The number of programs which have a substantial history and consistent pattern in selection are conspicuous because of their scarcity, but they are also conspicuous because of their evident effectiveness.

The assumption is therefore made that the ability to select for teacher preparation does exist with some reasonable assurance of success. Any program of selection is subject to human fallibility; subjective judgment may result in exclusion of some individuals who would make good teachers and inclusion of others who would not.

The Responsibility

Responsibility to select is fourfold. It is to the pupils who will be taught by the selected teachers, and through these pupils to society. Responsibility is also to the students preparing for teaching and to the profession itself. In turn, all segments of the profession— elementary- and secondary-school teachers, college teachers and administrators, and others—have responsibility for elevating standards of the profession and for selecting those persons who will be prepared for the profession and accepted and retained in it. One of the hallmarks of a profession is that its members accept responsibility for defining and maintaining high standards of selection and preparation of potential members and equally high standards of selection during service.

A college is responsible for the competence of its staff and of its graduates. But the entire profession is responsible for identification and guidance of pupils into whatever further educational pursuits will best fit them to develop their aptitudes and interests to the maximum. The institution preparing teachers has responsibility to its own students and also initial responsibility to the pupils who are to be taught by its graduates. The entire profession has responsibility for continued evaluation throughout the careers of its members.

The community, as represented by the administrative staff through its board, is responsible for attracting and retaining qualified personnel in the schools and colleges as one important means of achieving a sound educational program and continuous effective learning. In communities and colleges where effective teaching is respected, more

---

[9] Walter W. Cook and C. H. Leeds, "Measuring the Teaching Personality," *Educational and Psychological Measurement* 7: 409; No. 3, 1947.

capable young people become interested in becoming teachers, and capable teachers remain to discharge their teaching and professional responsibilities with merit.

Early identification of able youth, selective admission and retention during preparation for the profession (whatever profession it may be), placement in appropriate settings, and desirable school-community climate and program do much to maximize the likelihood of securing in greater numbers and increasing the average years of service of those persons most able to conduct the educational program of the nation.

Assumptions Concerning the Selective Processes

If the result of the selective process is to be continued competent performance, identification of potential teachers should begin whenever teachers themselves note in their pupils characteristics, aptitudes, and interests suitable to teaching personalities. The process may well begin in the elementary school. It should continue through formal preparation and throughout the teaching career. Selection for teacher education is a two-way process. The student must select the profession or occupation as indicated by his interests and aptitudes and also, to some extent, the college or colleges he wishes to attend; the profession, through the college, must select the student.

Identification and Initial Selection. At the precollege level selection is largely on the part of the student. But identification and encouragement of prospective teachers can be carried on effectively in each school where there is a strong guidance program to help students evaluate themselves in reference to careers; where a planned program for identification and selection of potential educators at the precollege level, either curricular or cocurricular, is operative; and where every teacher on the staff (1) embodies high standards in his own teaching and in his professional and personal life, (2) fosters within the pupils in his classroom an interest in learning, (3) instills in them a respect for the place education and the schools and colleges play in maintaining a free society, and (4) fosters within each pupil respect for others and a desire to work with other people.

Education in the United States is built on the worth of the individual, but it must be the individual teacher as well as the individual child. Only when the teacher understands himself and accepts himself in an honest light can he have faith in himself as an individual, a teacher, and a member of a profession, and thus be able to identify and interest others capable of joining the professional ranks.

The Selective Process at the College Level. If the college is to attest to the academic ability, the health, the personal characteristics, and the professional competence of the individual seeking recommendation for a teaching position, it must be assumed (1) that abilities and characteristics desirable in teachers can be stated; (2) that a sufficient number of the abilities and characteristics desirable in teachers can be measured or identified accurately enough to provide a basis for evaluation; (3) that the college has a unique and essential part in the selection of teachers because it can provide a sequence of selection points, adequate control of the program by means of degree requirements, and a continuing knowledge about the student; and (4) that the college can and should make provision for its evaluation of each student preparing to teach and also provide for self-evaluation by each student.

The critical importance of placement and follow-up in the improvement of teacher education indicates that college staff members dealing with these functions need to be competent in evaluation, in guidance, in administrative activities, and in interpersonal relations. After preparing and graduating its students and recommending them for certification as teachers in elementary or secondary schools or in colleges, an institution is responsible for helping candidates secure initial teaching positions in which they will be most likely to have success that is satisfying to them and productive of the desired learning experiences for their pupils. These situations should help the new teacher to grow on the job. Further, an institution has responsibility for extended follow-up to the end that, insofar as possible, at all times, each teacher is placed in the position where his ability and experience can be applied to exert optimum influence on all with whom he is associated, both in the classroom and in the community. Moreover, an institution has responsibility for follow-up of its graduates in terms of evaluating adequacy, deficiency, and developing needs for additional formal or informal study; for stimulating self-evaluation; and for co-operating with employing agents and the profession in maintaining performance standards.

Throughout the period of professional service, assignment of staff in terms of persons, situations, and task performance, if based on continuous evaluation, should produce an educational program of high quality. A continuous evaluation process to determine retention in the profession and effective utilization of teacher talent and time must be the shared responsibility of individual teachers, the administrative staff, and the *total* profession, including the staff of the institutions providing initial and inservice preparation.

Such a process of placement, follow-up, mutual evaluation, and growth implies greatly increased support in terms of finance, professional staff time, supportive services, and facilities.

Assumptions Concerning Criteria for Selection

For some time it has been evident that the teaching profession is actually a constellation of professions within a profession, with different kinds of people being required for performance of different kinds of services (or even different kinds of people required for performance of the same kinds of services under different circumstances). Considerable evidence indicates validity of the assumption that a mature profession is strong, not only because of the characteristics and goals common to all its members, but also because of its diversity, provided people with differing personalities and skills have been selected in terms of the work to be done and in terms of the situations in which effort will be made to achieve both the common and the unique goals.

Although there is no single "teaching personality," there are personality characteristics which, along with certain knowledge and skills, maximize the likelihood of success in teaching, and other personality characteristics whose existence, under most circumstances and as part of most constellations of knowledge and ability, may preclude effective teaching.

Minimum criteria which may be assumed as essential in the selection of all persons for teaching are:

Keen intellectual ability.

Interests, abilities, and values that give some assurance to the individual that he will find satisfaction in a teaching career. This satisfaction can rarely be derived unless the teacher is more concerned for others than for himself.

Character, attitudes, and action worthy of emulation by pupils, because one of the ways children and youth learn is by example. The teacher's habits of thought, attitudes, and values should be expressed in ways that fall within an acceptable range of human behavior.

Ability to carry on work throughout the day each day. The teacher's physical and mental health must be sufficient to permit regular and effective teaching.

Possession of ability, interests, and self-direction appropriate to success in college and continuing development as a scholar, as a person, and as a teacher.

Evidence of being (or having the probability of becoming) broadly educated and of having (or having the desire and ability to secure) a comprehensive knowledge of that which he would teach.

Ability to guide learning, to respond to the intellectual and affective state of pupils, and to control and give direction to learning activities.

The student characteristics, which, when examined, should provide means for evaluating these criteria, are discussed in a later section on the selection program (see page 184 ff).

Processes of Identification, Selection and Retention

Just when a child or youth decides he wants to teach depends on many factors. Studies show there is no one time when students decide on their future occupations. A typical child changes his mind periodically; any time between early childhood and maturity he may select the work he will actually do. Identification and selection for teaching, therefore, must not be a process planned for one year; it must be a continuous process, with all teachers alert to their responsibilities in helping students make wise choices.

Selective admission and retention imply a series of choices on the part of the college. Less often is it recognized that selective admission and retention also imply a series of choices on the part of the student. Although selection is usually looked upon as an institutional function, the character of the student body may be more directly affected by the kinds of students who select the college. Choices are made by a decision process. The kind of institution is often determined more by the students who select the institution than by the institution's selecting the students. Hence, the ethics of identification of students, their interests, and guidance are of paramount importance. If we would modify or alter by means of identification and selection the kinds of people who become teachers, it is important to look at the processes of identification and selective recruitment and at the processes by which institutional and individual decisions are made.

The Precollege Processes

In the elementary school, encouragement of an interest in the profession is usually quite incidental. Though the influence of the individual teacher remains important during the junior-high-school years, other factors begin to affect vocational interest. It is usually here that the pupil receives his first formal introduction to occupations and begins to explore for himself reasons for accepting or rejecting them. A view of the profession of teaching is usually presented with views of other vocations and professions, often as part of social science work. The teacher needs to give a true picture, not only through presentation of materials and information, but through attitudes and example. Even when not manifested by overt action, his attitudes may negate his verbal explanations of the career in which he is himself personally involved. Teachers have a responsibility to foster within the pupils in their classrooms an interest in learning and to develop attitudes of future citizens that include respect for the place of education and the schools in maintaining a free society.

The teacher must open doors of understanding and means for self-evaluation by pupils of their own characteristics and interests in terms of the demands and rewards of the various vocational choices. The skilled teacher imparts to the child not only something of his own diligence, his love of learning, his respect for excellence, but his satisfaction in his own work. Teachers, like members of other professions, need to portray their own profession accurately. They can be ethical and work consciously to place teaching in its rightful value position. They need to be aware that the less-observed, less-understood professions may have an aura of glamor and that the pupil's constant association with teachers may prevent his viewing a teaching career in the same light. The assumption that participation in the teaching-learning situation as a pupil provides understanding of the career of teaching is probably erroneous. Exploitation must also be avoided, however.

Programs and Patterns. The manner of giving pupils opportunity to learn about the profession and to evaluate themselves in relation to what they learn will not be the same in all schools. The beginning of the process of identification and selection of students as potential teacher candidates lies in the identification of capable young people in the elementary and secondary schools. Administrators and teachers interested in promoting high standards of selection and professional performance should assess conditions existing in the individual school, determine the basic philosophy and purposes, and develop a plan of action accordingly.

In some communities elementary-school children have become "TOTS," or "Teachers of Tomorrow." In such activities the emphasis usually is on developing understanding of the satisfactions of teaching and realization that teaching requires above-average ability. In the upper grades, whether through Future Teachers of America clubs or credit courses, professional attitudes and interests can be encouraged among potential teachers and awareness of certain needed skills can be fostered.   Credit courses designed to provide pupils with facts and bases for making vocational decisions may also provide experience and observation.   Care must be taken that the student is not exploited in the observation-experience activity, that his own opportunities for learning in his own classroom are not sacrificed, and that no teenager is given complete classroom responsibility for other children and youth.

Full-credit courses are offered in a few high schools and are enthusiastically endorsed by both students and teachers.   For many years high schools have accepted as a part of their responsibility the giving of vocational information and guidance.   Courses related to this purpose have been accepted as worthy of credit, but only in recent years have school people begun teaching about the vocation which they themselves follow.   Such courses, then, are really a new horizon, just coming into view.

To date, courses follow two general patterns.   In some cases the guidance of the student and the responsibility for clarifying advantages, opportunities, and challenges are given to the elementary-school personnel with whom the high-school student as a prospective teacher works.   In other cases the high school retains this responsibility.   The need that teachers have for a strong basic education indicates that any course given as an introduction to teaching be for one semester only and be organized so as to "hold its own" as an academic offering.   Though basic information will be related to the profession, the manner of presentation can make the course valuable for college preparation.   Ease and effectiveness in both oral and written communication, improvement of study habits, acquisition of techniques of note-taking and research are valuable for any high-school student, and particularly for students who are taking a look at teacher education.

Anyone interested in learning about a profession wants to know about the advantages and disadvantages of his selection for his life's work, the opportunities, the qualifications, and the education needed. Students may also take a long look at their local school system, its organization, support, problems, and plans.

An introduction to child study can be made in such a course and can be of value not only to future teachers, but to future parents as well.

Problems in setting up such a course are multitple.   At present there are no well-recognized objectives, no organized support, no prepared plans, no texts.   Preparation of reading lists, compilation of materials, evaluation of results must be the job of the individual teacher.   Though the programs of diversified occupations and distributive education have strong state and national support, similar endorsement and support have not yet been given any program related to a career in teaching.   One essential element also is co-operation between the elementary and secondary school, along with teachers who can enthusiastically present the profession to students.

Schools that have developed strong selective recruitment programs report an increased respect for the profession on the part of many students, not just those enrolled in the course or the club.   There is recognition that just as important as encouraging the fit is redirecting those who are interested but apparently unfit for a teaching career. Whatever the type of high-school program related to a study of the profession, the general purpose is to interest more potentially effective youth in the profession of teaching.   A by-product can be the fostering of support for high standards of education, increased prestige for the profession, and improvement of schools, staff, and school finance.

Professional groups should support the principle of including some type of exploratory work in teaching as a part of the curricular offerings of the secondary school.   Support should be active and should include the preparation of materials and leadership planning and promotion.   Because each community is unique, the actual setting up of philosophy and purposes may best be done at the local level.

Guidance.   It is the teacher's responsibility to do everything he can to help each individual be his own best self.   This involves guidance, and by the very nature of his role every teacher has a guidance responsibility.   Truly effective guidance, however, extends beyond the work of individual teachers.   High schools of today need well-developed guidance and personnel services dedicated to helping students toward self-understanding, self-determination, and self-direction. Study of cumulative records, use of various standardized tests and inventories, individual and group counseling—all can help in identification of the potentially effective teacher candidate.   Foremost at all times must be the well-being of the student.   The teacher and the counselor may help the student understand himself and the demands, opportunities, and challenges of given professions, but the picture must be an honest one and the final decision must be left to the student.

Though the college can weigh a candidate's qualifications and accept or reject him for teacher preparation, the college can achieve high standards of selection only when students with high qualifications apply for admission to the program. It therefore becomes imperative that teachers themselves encourage potentially effective teacher candidates to consider teaching among the professions from which they may choose to prepare for a career. It also becomes incumbent upon secondary-school staffs that they develop cumulative records which will relay to the colleges information about students that will be meaningful in determining their selection for professional preparation. Not only previous academic records, test and inventory data, but evidences on the student's emotional stability, specific information regarding his physical fitness, English proficiency, speech and voice, performance in extraclass activities, and ratings and recommendations on his personal, social, and ethical fitness should be relayed to the college admissions officers.

If students enter college with some understanding of themselves and their abilities and of the professions they may wish to consider, in all probability their work at the college will become more meaningful and problems of selection will be greatly clarified and perhaps simplified.

A case is sometimes made for the acceptance into teacher education programs of interested students even if they are weak in some of the desirable qualifications. The "democracy" of an open door to opportunity, indications of some "late blooming," and theories on compensation are often referred to. However, able students are best attracted by high professional standards; they are uninterested in a profession that admits to its ranks those who are not well qualified personally, intellectually, or emotionally. Fairness to the student whose qualifications apparently do not merit his admission to a teacher education program requires that he be counseled to consider another vocation, rather than to plan his college years on the assumption that he can prepare himself for a career in which his chances of success are slight. Fairness to the children to be taught also points to the quest for quality through the setting of high standards in identification and selection and high standards for retention in the program.

Co-ordination of Effort. When one speaks of selective recruitment, the general reaction is that *more* needs to be done. The result has been that many groups have spasmodically taken action they hoped would prove valuable. Much has been valuable not only in itself, but as a stimulus to more far-reaching and better-organized programs. On the other hand, well-meaning groups have sometimes created schemes which have proved academically and professionally unsound. It would appear that not more work but better articulated and professionally oriented work needs to be done.

Many organizations that are giving at least lip service to a program of selective recruitment for teaching have headquarters in Washington. If representatives of these groups would meet in a small work conference, a step might be taken toward better co-ordination. The conference could consider what each group proposes to do, what needs to be done, and how best to co-ordinate or delineate efforts to accomplish mutual or unique goals. Studies of the relation of supply-demand data to expressed interest and evident aptitude among high-school students could promote a realistic and meaningful concerted action.

Selective Processes at the College Level

The trend has been away from a search for single traits or a single constellation of factors, away from single measures or the seeking for a certain type of person for teaching. Nevertheless, there is now general agreement on the importance of high-level achievement, emotional stability, and the characteristics generally found in excellence of professional achievement in any field. There is considerable advocacy that the presence of these characteristics may be more important in teachers than in members of some of the other professions.

The more extensive programs for selective admission and retention described in the literature appear to be designed to achieve the objective of securing for teacher preparation individuals who possess these characteristics and abilities, or the potential for acquiring them. Programs appear further to be designed to retain and improve the effectiveness of these teacher-candidates. But such programs are not numerous, and evidence is accumulating to the effect that the positive results of selectivity in one program are being nullified by the absence of admission policies in some other institutions. Here, then, lies not a new horizon but a broadened one.

Increased and more effective effort also needs to be made in co-curricular programs for prospective teachers to develop awareness of professional responsibility. Once a student has shown interest in the teaching profession, either in terms of determination of goal or merely concern for more knowledge of the profession as a basis for vocational decision, there should be opportunity for him to have uninterrupted participation in cocurricular, preprofessional organizations throughout the period of formal initial education. A voluntary autonomous professional organization, particularly when it is the largest in the world, must choose its members so as to secure persons who can effectively bring about professional cohesion and self-direction, who can counteract the likely inertia of large bodies by having clear-thinking leadership for significant action. By its nature, to some extent, because a sizeable part of its membership must combine family rearing with professional service, the teaching profession has a larger turnover than other professions. This fact also has import for selection of persons, whether their careers will be continuous or intermittent. Members can be effective only when the significance of professional membership with its attendant responsibilities is not only recognized but accepted.

The Student's Cocurricular, Preprofessional Activities. At the college level, active participation in a preprofessional group such as the Student National Education Association is essential for students who would become teachers. Such an organization should provide students with opportunity to improve and demonstrate ability to participate effectively as members of a group, to understand and adhere to a student professional code of ethics, to increase their knowledge of professional problems in education, to appreciate the responsibilities to society of professional membership, to understand the opportunities for effective leadership in the organized profession and in the community, and to assume the obligations of full professional status at such time as they become teachers.

The Student NEA in accredited institutions provides opportunity also for study of the history and program of the profession at state and national levels. With restriction of Student NEA chapters primarily to the campuses of institutions accredited by the National Council for Accreditation of Teacher Education, these groups increasingly will be structured in such a way as to meet the needs of students already individually committed to preparation for teaching and assumption of professional responsibility.

The need is therefore emerging for a similar organization which, where necessary, will bridge the gap between the Future Teachers of America and Student NEA, or which will meet the needs of students interested in teacher education or already personally committed to teacher preparation but not yet formally enrolled in the curricular program. Such an organization conceivably can provide students with opportunities to evaluate themselves in terms of their fitness for the profession and can provide the colleges with additional evidence of value in the selective process.

Student organizations will reach maximum effectiveness only when their support and program are closely meshed with the activities of local and state as well as national professional groups. Though a clear distinction should be maintained between preprofessional participation and professional responsibility, the extent to which prospective teachers-in-preparation are provided opportunity to learn and participate in the work of the profession should be limitless.

At the college level nationally organized prospective teacher groups also are active in several specialized areas. Clarification of the similar and diverse purposes of these organizations is needed. A horizon in the preprofessional organization program would be the co-ordination of similar efforts among these groups and thus avoidance of duplication and competition for student time. The result could also be intensifying of effort in pursuit of those purposes unique to each organization and understanding of the difference between professional responsibility, individual and organized, as related to improved knowledge and skill in a specific teaching field; and professional responsibility of all teachers, kindergarten through graduate school, art through zoology, for the development of a truly professional body that can promote and maintain high-quality education for children, youth, and adults. The Student NEA, with its broad concern for professional ethics and responsibility, may well become the "tent" organization, with students holding dual membership—in the general professional area and in the subject-area or level organization. Such a structure, with careful programming, should provide prospective teachers with understandings not now generally possessed by teachers.

Cocurricular programs are closely related to curricular programs. They have responsibility for serving the students of the various professional education programs offered by the various campuses on which the student organizations are located. Close liaison between FTA and other preprofessional secondary-school groups and the Student NEA or other preprofessional groups at the college level could be a means for helping the student select the college and the college select the student. Prior contacts and orientation programs in which the secondary schools and colleges co-operate are becoming an increasingly important part of the identification and selective recruitment programs of schools and colleges. About half the institutions preparing teachers in 1953 reported making initial contacts with prospective teacher education candidates during their senior year in high school. More than half the institutions entered into individual correspondence with applicants.[10]

---

[10] Stout, *op. cit.*, p. 61.

As one evaluates evidence in making a decision, whether it be the student selecting his career and the institution in which he will get preparation or the institution selecting its students, the judgment is made in terms of a model. Probably the greatest single deterrent to better selection for teacher education is failure to define the model. For teaching there may be several models that are appropriate.

The Institution's Decisions. The desire to select those most likely to become teachers is an institutional value based upon the goals of the institution and the teacher education program, and the desire and need to maximize the effective use of staff, physical plant, community resources, and budget.

Admission and selection decisions of the college are based upon rules. These rules, usually stated as requirements, should be developed from a clear statement of the institution's goals and values. So far as student selection is concerned, decisions should be based on information collected about applicants. The rules should state what the persons who make decisions will do in any possible contingency when presented with information.

The college may set up a series of rules to be applied sequentially and at specified intervals as students are continued from one level to the next in the teacher education program. Selection is then a sequential process occurring at several different points in the program.

One distinguishing characteristic of selection decisions made by the college is that the institution employs similar information, the same rules, and a constant system of values to make decisions about many people. Recognizing that some errors will be made, the college should set up its rules to lead to the greatest number of correct decisions in the series of similar decisions.

The values that guide the college may be any of a number of kinds: academic, humanitarian, social, or economic. In one college it may be important to give an opportunity to all high-school graduates who seek higher education, without concern for the fact that many will not remain to graduate; in another college it may be most important to be assured that the greatest possible number of those admitted will complete the degree program.

If the college that prepares teachers looks upon teacher education as a professional program and upon teaching as a profession, its value system may well specify that its time, money, and instruction devoted to teacher education should be expended upon those students most likely to be graduated and to teach successfully. It should then be influenced by this value as it sets up the rules by which it admits students from the student body at large to the teacher education program.

The application of the established selection rules requires that the college collect information about people. What kinds of information should be sought? Some information may be obtained because research has shown it to be helpful in identifying those applicants most likely to be successful students. Information derived from studies of the predictive efficiency of a college aptitude test or of the relationship between an attitude inventory and teachers' classroom behavior belong in this category. Such information may be classified as actuarial.

Other information sought may be based upon the college concept of the kind of individual it wishes to prepare for teaching: persons with a certain level of competence in English usage, a certain level of previous academic achievement, or with certain measurable or observable attitudes or personality traits. The latter information is descriptive and calls for a greater degree of judgment. It may be looked upon as of a clinical nature.

Institutional Evaluation. Interpreting information about an applicant or a student is an evaluative or judgmental process. On the basis of test information that has been studied in its relationship to the goal, an actuarial prediction may be possible. But with other kinds of data, such as those pertaining to health or speech or emotional adjustment, "clinical" judgment is necessary. For any one student a complex of information needs to be available. Although it may be that a student will be denied admission or prevented from continuing on the basis of a single kind of information such as college achievement, evaluation and decision can and usually should be based on several interrelated factors.

If we believe that students develop or mature in the process of learning, then the concept of the student an institution desires to admit may be quite different from the concept of the student it seeks to graduate. The concepts of the kinds of students a college may wish to include in its program may be given specific statement, and these statements then describe the models to which the college compares those who would be enrolled in the program. The model for admission should be the person who is most likely to become the kind of student the college seeks to develop. If we regard selection as being sequential, that is, a continuing process, the model midway in the program may be set up according to a concept of "satisfactory progress" for that stage of development.

The setting up of such models as guides in the selective process should be a prime objective for each teacher education program in order that student admission and student retention decisions may be made against the established models or guides. Evaluation of the students then becomes a built-in feature of the program. It should be concerned with studying the development of students within the program and with relating the characteristics of different kinds of students at one stage to their later attainment in order that appropriate models may be defined.

Just as there may be appropriate models against which to evaluate at different stages in the sequence, there may be different models appropriate to different teaching subject areas. Studies of the physical and psychological characteristics, of the interests and attitudes and abilities of teachers, have shown different patterns among teachers within each of several teaching subject areas. To some extent the differences probably result from the fact that different subjects attract different kinds of people. To some extent the differences may be developed during the college years. It is also likely that differences may be brought about by the selective effect of different expectations held for teachers in different fields. In any case, the differences may be taken into account in setting up models employed in selection.

Colleges have also established different models of the kinds of students they wish to serve. The private eastern college, the midwestern state university, the community college—each has its clientele. The curriculum, the cost of attending, the geographical area in which the college is located, or the sponsorship of the college may affect the model or models of students for an institution. A student who develops his talents in one college may find another incompatible to his learning. Colleges may define certain kinds of persons they wish to prepare for teaching and set up programs appropriate to the defined student population. In an enterprise as vast as higher education, there is need for colleges which, in their teacher education programs, serve different groups of individuals and in so doing achieve excellence as colleges.

The Individual Decision. Unlike institutional decisions, those of the individual are not based upon rules. Also, unlike the institution, the individual may not speak of being "right" on the average. Individual decision is usually made but once in a lifetime and, as a consequence, the average has no meaning. The "rightness" of the individual decision may be judged only upon the basis of the values of each person. Value systems vary from one person to another. Individuals may or may not be aware of their value systems and of the bases upon which they make decisions.

When the college assumes responsibility for helping the student in his self-evaluation, this does not imply that the college should try to persuade the student to arrive at a decision in conformity with that of the college. The college decision may be based upon a different concept and a different set of values from those of the student. Although the college should inform the student of its values, the greatest aid the college may provide to self-evaluation by the student may be helping him become fully aware of his own values. In the light of these values, the college, through its professional counselors, may then help the student explore his interests, attitudes, abilities, experiences, or achievements and supply some kind of probability statement concerning his likely success and satisfaction in one curriculum or another, or in one occupation or another. But the college cannot know whether an individual decision is "good" or "bad," because the student is the judge of his decision. He alone can decide whether to measure his success by economic standards, by college marks, by subjective satisfactions in his relationships to other people, or by his contribution to the general welfare of society.

Individual Evaluation. Although the individual may make an independent evaluation of himself and of the college, and certainly does in the majority of cases, the college that aids the student in reaching his decisions may gain in many ways as it seeks its stated goals. A guidance point of view is not incompatible with selective admission and retention on the part of the college.

Guidance associated with selection and admission should have two objectives in mind. It has already been suggested that one function is to aid the student in becoming fully aware of his own true values. It is an assumption here that as the student is more fully aware of his values he can make wiser decisions if the information at hand is appropriate. The objective is to increase the likelihood that the student will make a "right" decision, where "right" is defined by his individual values. To this end the college may not only help the student clarify values, but may also help him obtain information about himself, about teaching, and about the college.

A second objective of guidance may be to set the stage for more effective learning throughout the college years. It is assumed here that in gaining information about himself and in becoming more aware of his value system, the student gains in self-understanding that is important to learning.

If a guidance program based upon these objectives is effective, it has advantages for both the student and the college. If the guidance program has assisted in self-selection in such a way that those who enter the college are most likely to remain to graduate, and if it has set the stage for learning of a kind that makes for more competent graduates, it has realized objectives for the students and for the college.[11]

The Selection Program at the College Level

Underlying the conditions essential to a program of selection, the criteria to be used, and the sequential steps in the selective program must be a belief *that selection is essential to an adequate program of teacher preparation.* The faculty must be willing to expend the time and rather substantial amounts of money required to carry out an effective program. Most important, the staff must believe that even though they are human and subject to error they must sit in judgment over their fellow men and, on occasion, *deny admission even to academically able students who they believe should not be working with children and youth in a schoolroom.*

As those involved in selection apply rules or make judgments to arrive at decisions they become acutely aware that although errors may be reduced, they are never eliminated completely. The errors are of two types. The first type eliminates from the program those students who, had they been given an opportunity, would have succeeded in college and in teaching. It is this type of error that has most frequently argued against selective admission. The college that would completely avoid the first type of error, however, is led to make a second type. In this instance, the persons who will fail in teacher preparation or in teaching are admitted. With either kind of error both the individual and society lose something, but the loss may be particularly great in the second case, as the individual spends his college years preparing for a career that will not yield satisfaction and, for from one to thirty years, as children in his classes reap the effects of poor instruction. A well-developed program of selection based on a solid foundation of actuarial and clinical data can reduce both kinds of errors.

The Necessary Conditions for Selection

A review of studies since the Stout study of 1953 indicates little change in attitude toward the importance and recommended processes which that nationwide study revealed. The gap between belief and

---

[11] The discussion of institutional and individual decisions is based upon ideas expressed by Lee J. Cronbach and Goldine C. Gleser in *Psychological Tests and Personnel Decisions* (Urbana: University of Illinois Press, 1957).

practice is still almost as great, also. Respondents to the 1953 study, when asked to identify the most important "next steps" in selective processes for teacher education (selecting and ranking from a list, with opportunity to supply others), emphasized the following: (1) consideration of evidence in addition to grades and rank in class; (2) provision for better vocational guidance and counseling for high-school students; (3) extension of recruitment and orientation programs; (4) establishment of specific criteria for periodic review of students' progress; (5) use of more nearly objective measures of personality; and (6) use of a greater number of persons to pass on admission, retention, and recommendation of the prospective teacher.

Institutional responsibilities for selection must be clearly placed. Those persons charged with the professional preparation of teachers should have the authority and responsibility for selection. They should control the admission, the continuing selection, and the recommendation for certification of those who would be teachers.

Selection activities should be shared, as appropriate, with those who are affected by them and by those who must take action based on the decisions that are made. The persons to be consulted or to share in making decisions may be different according to the point in the student's academic career at which the decision is being made. Appropriate persons in all institutions and groups cannot be designated by a single set of titles since responsibility for different activities may be assigned variously in different colleges, but the points of view included might be those of people with titles such as faculty adviser, director of student personnel, and professor. Each has a stake in the selection program and each has a point of view and a body of information to contribute.

There should be adequate records, well-planned and diversified. They should be designed with three thoughts in mind: (1) They should contain information useful in working with individuals, that is, cumulative reports of test scores, academic program, biographical data, interview notes, notes from instructors, health and speech data, and a record of progress toward graduation. (2) They should be organized in such a fashion that they can readily be sorted, tabulated, and analyzed to answer questions about the students that have pertinence for the selection program and for the curriculum. (3) They should be located and maintained in a manner that makes them convenient for staff use in daily work with students.

One or more staff members, well prepared in the area of student personnel work, should be employed specifically to co-ordinate the selection program, to supervise records of teacher education students, to counsel with students, and to carry out other personnel functions. This should be someone with special responsibilities to teacher education rather than a person with institution-wide responsibilities.

College and community agencies to which students may be referred for special assistance as needed should be available. The optimal use of such referral agencies is probably attained if one individual, such as the student personnel director for the college or department of education, is responsible for working with these agencies and seeking their co-operation in the preparation of teachers.

The selection program should be tied to faculty and administrative structure so that those who administer it are responsible to faculty thinking on policy, utilize faculty resources in serving individual students, and keep the faculty and administration intimately aware of the problems of student selection through periodic reports and daily working relationships.

Assumptions of responsibility and systematic and sensitive application of the sequential steps in the selective process cannot be over-emphasized as to importance. Maximum effectiveness in these respects can be achieved only if the staff for the student personnel services is an integral part of the teacher education program. A conscious structure for communication among members of all faculties who share responsibility in the education of prospective teachers is vitally important. Essential also throughout these faculties are attitudes favorable to assumption of the various roles in assisting in the educative process of prospective teachers.

Student Characteristics To Be Examined
in the Selection Program

Respondents representing 785 colleges (91 per cent of all regionally accredited four-year colleges preparing teachers in the United States in 1953) were asked to identify, from a suggested list of nine, the five most important criteria for use in selective admission and retention.[12] An outstanding "first" was emotional stability. The next four in the order named were moral and ethical fitness, and general intelligence (tied for second place), demonstrated ability to work with children, and professional interest and motivation. Roughly three-fourths of the respondents reported considering satisfactory completion of course and honor-point requirements as only one of several requirements, either for admission to student teaching or for certification.

---

[12] Stout, *op. cit.*

These characteristics are among the several that would follow from the assumptions enumerated on previous pages of this discussion. In addition, numerous studies reveal that evaluation of health is commonly made for admission to the institution and retention in the higher education program. For this reason, probably, health is not listed among the most important for evaluation though it is among the top several criteria for effective teaching.

When the 785 institutions were analyzed according to extent of their admission and retention programs for teacher education, 189 were found to have extensive programs. For 182 institutions, programs were slight or nonexistent, and the remainder (414) lay somewhere between the "high" and "low" groups. Recurrent evaluation of emotional stability and communication skills appeared characteristic of the 189 institutions whose programs not only were more extensive, but in general appeared to be functioning more effectively than those of institutions in the other two groups. All 189 institutions reported evaluation of both emotional stability and communication skills at one or more points in the selective admission and retention process.

Percentages of the 785 institutions evaluating any one process at any one time may be seen in Table 1.

Table 1

Evaluation of Student Characteristics and Experiences[13]

Characteristic or Experience	Per Cent Responding		
	(1)	(2)	(3)
None of those listed below	11.1	31.0	27.0
Previous academic record	85.4	58.8	58.5
Student's record in prerequisite professional-education courses	8.0	30.6	55.7
Physical fitness	66.2	35.8	31.5
Emotional stability	32.4	37.6	44.8
Speech and voice	11.6	21.5	22.2
English proficiency	33.1	25.7	25.5
Personal-social-ethical fitness	48.8	39.6	46.1
Extraclass activities	22.9	17.8	19.9
Work experience	10.4	11.1	11.8
Others	2.5	3.8	5.6
No response	.4	.4	.4

Legend: (1) Admission to the institution
       (2) Admission to the teacher education program
       (3) Admission to student teaching.

[13] Stout, *op. cit.*, p. 66.

If one examines the reports of the 189 "high" institutions, it appears that ror purposes of admission to the teacher education program previous academic record is evaluated by 87.8 per cent; physical fitness by medical examination by 70.4 per cent; emotional stability by 81.5 per cent; speech and voice through a specific test by 47.1 per cent; English proficiency through writing sample by 60.8 per cent; personal-social-ethical fitness through multiple ratings by 79.4 per cent.[14]

Emotional maturity was ranked as of primary importance by the greatest number of institutions. It will be noted from Table 1 that the number of institutions evaluating this characteristic increases with each major step in the admissions and retention program. Daily life contains stress situations and calls for choices to be made. In the course of living, individuals learn ways of coping with their experiences. The ways in which they deal with stress or make decisions may be looked upon as evidence of emotional maturity. It is the evidence of emotional maturity in the behavior of the individual that is of interest in selection.

The question to be asked is this: Does the behavior of the individual preclude his functioning adequately as a teacher? If his anxieties lead to physical symptoms that keep him from his classes, if his self-concern makes him insensitive to the thoughts and feelings of his students, if his varying moods produce disturbing relationships with pupils, he cannot be an effective teacher. Some persons lack a sense of responsibility, are indifferent to others and lacking in empathy, are unable to maintain good personal relationships to a degree that they should not be given the responsibilities of the teacher.

Selection of students on the basis of their emotional behavior will usually be of a negative kind, in that it is easier to specify those who should not teach than to identify those who should teach. The question asked about this characteristic is pointed at identifying the unfit rather than the fit. A challenge lies in the development of means to assess degrees and kinds of emotional fitness for certain types of teaching situations with a view to maximizing affective values and minimizing tensions which, even among those emotionally fit, can temper their effectiveness.

Communication is the principal tool of the teacher. His ability to express himself effectively is of crucial importance. Assessment of effectiveness of speech includes not only questions of speech defects such as stuttering, but voice control and problems of dialect as well, and the affective elements of voice quality. Experience in those col-

---

[14] Stout, *op. cit.,* p. 326.

leges that regularly employ a speech examination for admission indicates those students with such severe speech handicaps as would eliminate them from acceptance seldom apply, but that large numbers who do apply could, with the help of a speech therapist, improve the effectiveness with which they speak.

Communication is more than speech. So far as teaching skill is concerned it includes, most importantly, ability to clarify thought in words a student can understand so that a minimum of distortion is developed between the idea in the mind of the teacher and the one in the mind of the student. It includes ability to phrase and rephrase with varying degrees of complexity and emphasis and to sense when communication is satisfactory and when it is not. It includes ability to hold interest and attention and to stimulate thought, as well as to give information. And it includes the ability to listen and read perceptively if the teacher is to understand the student as well as to communicate understandings to him.

Basic Skills. In their daily activities teachers regularly make use not only of the oral and written language arts, but of the computational skills. Acceptable English usage and arithmetic skills should be prerequisite to preparation for teaching. Assessment of these skills should be part of the selective admission program. Since a student's daily performance in these areas may not be at the level of which he is capable, as demonstrated at the time of admission, the college may well give attention to further screening in the academic program itself.

Moral and Ethical Fitness. Selection on the basis of moral and ethical fitness may again be a matter of eliminating the undesirable rather than encouraging the desirable. One evidence of maturity of a profession is its development of a sound and enforceable code of ethics. Such a code has only recently been developed for teaching and the imposing of sanctions remains a serious problem on a near horizon. Those parts of a code that pertain to students preparing to teach can be enforced in selection more easily than they presently can be enforced among teaching personnel.

Academic Aptitude or Intelligence. Certainly teachers should be selected from those well above the average of the general population in academic aptitude. If an institution in general permits students with low test scores to prepare for teaching, there is great cause for concern. College admission policy may recognize, however, that tests of intelligence and academic aptitude were developed to estimate likelihood of success in an academic setting. For the individual student the proof is in academic achievement. A few individuals in a preprofessional program at the college level will do far better than test scores may lead us to expect.   Achievement is the more important factor in dealing with the individual.

Academic Achievement.   The teacher must know that which he would teach.   Today he must also have learning in considerable breadth and depth in several fields other than his teaching field.   Only then can he assist his students in acquiring knowledge and developing understandings that relate specifically to what he teaches; furthermore, only then can he help students develop awareness of interrelatedness in an increasingly complex world and implications for a further quest for knowledge and its significance in the operational and spiritual field of living.

Since the knowledge necessary for teaching may exist in varying amounts and with varying emphases within a discipline, and since there is no standard generally accepted, the college will necessarily set its own standards.   Although there are minimum credits prescribed for a teaching major or a teaching minor in many states, even these permit wide variations.   The school may well set its own pattern of general (or liberal) education and specialization, subject to minimum requirements of the state and the accrediting association.   The fact that minimum standards are restrictive only at the base should be more obvious than practice indicates it is.

The college may control the quality of the academic performance of those recommended for certification by means of comprehensive examinations or grade-average requirements.   Frequently colleges require that those preparing to teach earn grades above the level required of persons not in teacher education programs.   It is reasonable to believe that where substantial numbers of students engaged in a liberal arts program are in the same classes with those preparing for teaching, the teacher education students should perform somewhat above the general level required for liberal arts students.   Effectively to relate and apply knowledge and understandings to themselves, to other individuals, and to society, those preparing to teach need knowledge and understandings in the liberal arts and the sciences above and beyond that required of others.

Increasingly, the academic achievement, coupled with proficiency in interpersonal relations, will be required of those persons who would teach.   They must be able to use their knowledge, their ability to work with others in their peer group as well as with students, and their skill in teaching in teaching situations which will no doubt be far different from the teacher-in-a-classroom situation prevalent today. Their knowledge of learning theory, of child growth and development, of situational effects on learning and on teaching method must stand them in good stead as teaching-learning procedures become more flexible, even fluid. Their wisdom must be such as to enable them to distinguish between the relevant and the not-so-relevant, the verity and the facts-that-change, and to provide resources for learning appropriate to the times.

Ability to Work With Others. If one defines teaching as something more than delivering a brilliant lecture, and includes in the definition the ability to encourage and promote learning in others, one may reasonably assume teachers must be able both to respond to and to influence the thoughts and feelings of others. Ability to recognize what is taking place within the individuals of a class and to respond in such a way that their thoughts and feelings are utilized in an integrative fashion to further learning are important. Ability to arrange learning opportunities so that desired thoughts and feelings develop is equally important. Such abilities should be examined at some point in the selection process. They may be difficult to assess at the point of admission, but they should be observable in the laboratory experiences of students.

Role in a Democratic Society. As indicated in Chapter 3, every single citizen, insofar as his capacity permits, needs to understand and accept his responsibility as a participating member in our democracy. It is necessary that teachers be informed about the basic principles of our country and issues confronting it, and that they show themselves willing to assume an active role in making our democracy work. As in "Ability to Work With Others" (above), these characteristics may be difficult to judge at the point of admission. But since, in reality, such awareness and willingness to act from knowledge begins in the lower grades, these traits are not impossible to pinpoint and to foster.

Health. Selection on the basis of health is difficult. In one instance a chronic health problem may yield sufficiently to medication to permit the person to function quite well; but in another instance medication may not control the problem sufficiently. It is for this reason that attempts to specify disease or physical impairment which may disqualify an individual for teaching have been somewhat unsatisfactory. There are few health problems that can be considered categorically to eliminate a person from teaching. The question is whether the health of a person permits effective teaching.

Each case requires consultation among those persons who can observe the student in his classes or in his laboratory experiences, and between them and the physician who can make a statement about the student's present health and the prognosis for him. A teacher needs to be in the classroom regularly. He needs to be physically and mentally active in order to respond to the great variety of individuals he encounters in the course of a day. Being with small children throughout a day and guiding them through varied activities which require not only careful advanced planning, but ability to alter plans suddenly, to shift and concentrate attention quickly; meeting four or five classes each day five days a week, along with preparation for each, and extraclass activities as well; preparing for and performing in college and university classes, plus attending seminars and working with individual graduate students, researching, and performing consultative service—all require a high energy level that far exceeds the apparent expenditure of energy in meeting and teaching classes.

Sequential Steps in Selection

A co-operative process of selection and evaluation must be carried on by the total profession so that a favorable climate is created for preparation, entrance into the profession, and continued effective performance in it. The profession must be concerned not only with the identification of able students and with criteria for selection, but with the processes of applying these criteria.

The total profession has responsibility for exercising the wisdom and courage to accept as its members only those persons who are graduated from accredited programs of professional preparation and who are recommended by the institutions in which they took their preparation. The processes of selective admission and retention in formal preparation are primarily the responsibility of the higher education segment of the total profession—the college staffs not only in the professional sequence, but in the various disciplines in which the prospective teachers will specialize.

Important to the institutional decision and the individual decision, however, is the first step in the college program which does require co-operative effort of the total profession. The college-initiated selective recruitment and orientation program needs to have as its central concern the identification of prospective students most suitable to the kind of student body and the institution's curricular offerings. At this point the selective recruitment and identification programs of the elementary- and secondary-school staffs should be invaluable if they have been conducted on a professional and ethical plane. The institution's initial and follow-up contacts with students prior to admission to the institution can be best effected if secondary-school teachers and counselors assist in the program.

The Precollege Identification and Orientation Program. Some elements in the program prior to admission to the institution may be (1) distribution of literature on institutional offerings, with particular reference to teacher preparation; (2) college staff conferences with the staffs of junior and senior high schools; (3) contacts with junior- and senior-high-school students for specific purposes of vocational guidance and stimulus to self-evaluation and evaluation of institutional offerings; (4) campus "open house" for high-school seniors in which the program has specific educational goals, rather than mere entertainment and institutional recruitment; (5) participation in state-wide testing programs of high-school juniors and seniors; (6) summer orientation programs; (7) individual contacts in person and by letter, other than form letter, with prospective teacher education candidates; (8) joint sponsorship, with the high-schools, of FTA or similar clubs; and (9) maintenance of close liaison between Student NEA or similar college organizations and the cocurricular activities at the secondary-school level.

Admission to the Institution and to the Preprofessional Program. In connection with the various activities generally associated with institutional admission, such as a precollege camp or orientation week, an orientation course, the administering of test and inventory batteries, physical examinations, individual or group counseling and guidance, and academic advisement, other procedures geared to the selection program for teacher education may be conducted. For example, additional standardized test and inventory batteries, a special orientation sequence for teacher education candidates, or the requirement of a special application for admission to the preprofessional program may well supplement institutional admissions practices.

The Preprofessional Program. Students who wish to become teachers should begin their college study in a preprofessional program of one or two years' duration. The length of such a program will depend, to some extent, upon local considerations such as the organization of the college and curriculum policies. Such a program should provide not only a broad curriculum base for later study, but should also be designed to strengthen the selection program.

General (or liberal) education with breadth and depth is essential to each student recommended for graduation from an institution, as well as for those preparing to teach. But for persons upon whom responsibility will lie for transmitting both knowledge and understanding of the various disciplines, their interrelatedness and the cultures from which they have evolved or toward which they are developing, it is imperative that learning be effective. Those who would become teachers may well be expected to demonstrate knowledge and understanding to a greater extent than that required of liberal arts graduates as a whole, and even to a greater extent than that required of persons in the general education curricula prerequisite to admission to the professional sequences for some other fields of endeavor.

During the preprofessional years the student should have opportunity to demonstrate not only the scholarship, skills, and personal attributes expected of those preparing to teach, but also his ability to relate and transmit knowledge and understandings and to stimulate in other persons the desire to apply these understandings to contemporary life. Further, there should be indication that the student is developing a set of values from which, if he has not already done so, he will, during the period of professional preparation, clarify his basic philosophy of life and his role in his community, state, nation, and world. Manifestations of attitude should provide some clues to the consistency of a student's set of values and his degree of commitment to them. The pooling of information from standardized inventories, from observation of performance in various curricular and extraclass activities, and from interviews can provide indication of the degree and direction of developing values.

Admission to the Teacher Education Program. Admission to the professional program of preparation should require:

That a student make formal application. He should make application according to an established procedure that is published and available within the college community.

That the candidate and the institution give careful attention to factors important in making a decision. A thorough review is important at this point in order that the student who shows little promise for teaching may learn this early and may seek a more nearly appropriate goal. One purpose of early screening is to avoid lost time for the student and for the college.

That the final decision on the part of the college rest with a committee. A committee's decision is desirable for several reasons, but two should be given specific mention: First, the college should have the benefit of many points of view in making a serious decision about a human being. Second, denying admission to an individual is too serious a responsibility for any one person to carry.

It is important that there be included within the specifications of a selection program a provision for the "second chance" or the appeal of a decision. Such a provision is needed to take care of the inevitable appeals in an orderly fashion. Much more important, however, if the nature of the second chance is specified for the purpose of reducing the errors of acceptance and the errors of rejection, the program can be strengthened. Provision for a "second chance" is also important in the retention program and will be discussed further under that heading.

Evaluation for Retention in the Program. In a process of continuous selection, questions about the advisability of permitting certain students to remain in the program may arise at any time. Periodic review of progress and reassessment of certain personality traits and attitudes, as well as of achievement, may be essential. Matters of health, speech, and mannerisms amenable to correction or improvement should also be evaluated periodically. It may be that, with thorough review, it will become evident either that the student's program should be modified or that he has little likelihood of success and should be counseled into other channels of endeavor.

It is in the borderline cases that error is mostly likely to be made and further evaluation needed. The selective retention program should be organized in such a way that further evaluation of borderline cases is obtained and errors both in acceptance and rejection are avoided. Here again, the "second chance" provision may be helpful.

An error of acceptance might be avoided, for example, in the case of a student on the borderline between passing and failing a required course. The instructor may be moved to "give the student the benefit of the doubt," unless he is aware that the student may have a second opportunity. If this were an instance in which the student was not adequately prepared, the "benefit of the doubt" would probably be harmful rather than helpful.

Similarly, it is important to avoid errors of rejection. In the finest student teaching program a student may occasionally be placed in an unfortunate assignment. At the time of a final examination he may have had to cope with outside factors that jeopardized the effectiveness of his performance. In order that a single event or a possibly erroneous decision in a borderline case may not forever exclude from teaching a person who otherwise gives promise of success, established procedures for the second chance must be known and made available. The procedure would not usually be a repetition of the first experience but should provide for the collection of new information that could increase the likelihood of a correct decision. Such provisions benefit the student immediately and the schools, and particularly the public, later.

Admission to and Retention in the Student Teaching Program. A formal application for admission to student teaching should be an established part of the screening program. Admission to student teaching should be recognition of accomplishment by a student. It should signify that each student given an assignment in student teaching has completed prerequisites providing breadth and depth in a general education program, knowledge in fields of specialization, and skill and knowledge through a professional sequence. Admission to student teaching should require comprehensive evaluation of all the factors involved in determining a student's suitability for teaching, with particular emphasis on demonstrated performance as evidence of his having met standards of quality and having achieved readiness for student teaching.

A review at this point should include each of the criteria used in selection and should call for information from all appropriate sources —e.g., instructors, adviser, physician, speech clinician, supervisors of previous laboratory experiences—and data collected through objective measures and individual and faculty committee interviews. If earlier screening has been effective and indicated remedial programs have been operative, the percentage of students failing to meet requirements at this point should be substantially less than the percentage eliminated from the program at earlier review points in the selective process.

Evaluation of Readiness to Teach. Occasionally a student may be far along in his student teaching when it becomes evident he will need extended or different laboratory experiences before he is worthy of recommendation for teaching. Evidence may even indicate the student should not be recommended for teaching. Persons should be designated and procedures established so that such matters may be dealt with according to a predetermined plan and according to known policy. Not only the director of student teaching and college faculty members who have been working with the student in connection with his student teaching, but the personnel in the school or school system providing the laboratory experience and the student himself should be involved in procedures determining readiness for teaching and subsequent programming.

Recommendation for Certification. If institutions are to be accredited for the purpose of preparing teachers, each institution should also be charged with the responsibility not only of vouching for the quantity and kind of preparation of its graduates, but also for the professional quality of the candidate for the teaching certificate. The institution's recommendation or denial of recommendation for a legal license to teach must therefore be based on careful assessment of the various measures and judgments made during the period of selection and preparation that are applicable in determining whether or not a candidate should be admitted to professional practice.

If the selection of students has been based on institutional goals and objectives, its evaluation of the "student product" should also be consistent with these goals and objectives. The primary criterion for certificate recommendation should be whether or not the selective and educative processes have resulted in a person who can achieve success and derive satisfaction in the kind of position for which his program was designed to prepare him.

It is to be expected that each institution preparing teachers would develop a program such that the curriculum, the selective processes, the staff, and the liaison with the profession in the field would, insofar as possible, produce a graduate who has made the most of his potential toward becoming the kind of person who possesses scholarship and integrity; has firm goals without rigid patterns; is patient and permissive but persevering; has appreciation of people and respect and concern for them; is critically sensitive to change, has ability to influence both people and change for the better; and is eager systematically to augment his specialized knowledge and skill so that he may utilize in practice the best that is known, and may make a contribution to the knowledge in his field and the knowledge and its use by other people. In addition, it is to be hoped each person who becomes a member of the teaching profession will exhibit not only his own proficiency in performing his teaching task, but his ability and willingness to assume responsibility as a member of the profession for development and enforcement of standards for selection, preparation, and performance.

Studies during the last decade indicate the following practices appear to characterize an institution having a consistently functioning selective admission and retention program for teacher education: (1) special application and requirements for admission to the teacher education program and continuance in it which go beyond those for institutional matriculation; (2) evaluation of emotional stability, personal-social-ethical fitness for teaching, and communication skills, at *three or more* points in the student's preparation, along with evaluation of academic ability and physical fitness; (3) review of each student's case at stated intervals, with interviews and faculty committee evaluations as elements in the review procedure; (4) consistent efforts to relate the student's interests and abilities to job opportunities; and (5) a continuing program of follow-up of graduates. This is not a new horizon, therefore, but one which must be extended. What appear to be reasonably extensive and effective practices by slightly more than one-fourth of the institutions in the nation preparing teachers must become operative in all such institutions.

Subsequent Selection

Bringing into reality three new horizons in teacher education will require additional steps or extended application of acknowledged procedures in the selective process:

1. *Requirement of the five-year program* as basic initial preparation for a teaching permit, with evaluation of internships or actual teaching of from one to three years prior to issuance of a standard certificate, would extend responsibility not only of the college and university staff, but of elementary- and secondary-school teachers and administrators who may be directly or indirectly involved in supervision of interns.

2. Issuance by state legal agencies of a *single certificate of professional competence* attesting to an individual's qualification as a *member of the teaching profession,* irrespective of the level or area he will teach, will require that institutions recommending prospective teachers for licensure assume full responsibility for attesting not only to the candidate's general professional qualifications, but also to his proficiency in the teaching field and level for which he is to be employed.

3. A recommendation that *licensure be extended to those who will teach at the higher education level,* as well as having a license requirement for those teaching at the elementary- and secondary-school levels, has far-reaching implications for the selective process and for definition by institutions of the kinds of teachers they choose to prepare. Of particular importance in this connection would be the setting up of criteria for evaluating effective college teaching, for early identification and guidance of persons apparently suited to preparation for college teaching, and for selective admission and retention processes designed to choose and prepare persons for the desired product—an effective college teacher.

Advocacy of a single certificate for the right to be a teacher apparently is based on the assumption that principles already stated regarding the selective process at the undergraduate level, and involving professional responsibility, broad participation, adequate records, committee decisions, and so on, can be applied throughout the profession. As noted above, however, advocacy of a single legal certificate also places upon the profession, and more specifically upon the institution preparing teachers, responsibility for determining fields and levels for which each teacher candidate is prepared, and for governing recommendation and placement practices accordingly.

The implication then appears to be that each teaching field and level and each specialized group or profession-within-the-profession must define its model, develop plans for recruiting outstanding candidates, and evaluate procedures and means for their application, not only during initial preparation but during the teaching career. Criteria to be used in the selection for the specialties may be expected to vary from one to another and therefore must be developed with care. Research studies and experience dealing with the best practices in selection are needed in order that appropriate steps for selective admission and retention can be specified for each area.

The real challenge lies in securing the involvement of specialized groups within the profession so that each can make a major contribution to the total procedure of effective selection, admission, and retention practices in such a way as to provide a total teaching profession that performs efficiently and effectively in a total educational program.

Advocacy of an initial permit, followed by standard certification after evidence of successful teaching experience, places institutional responsibility for this period in a "twilight zone" between the institution's selective retention program and its follow-up program after placement of teachers. It is clear, however, that the institution will have major responsibility during this period and that this responsibility will be shared with the novitiate's peers.

Placement and Follow-up for Retention in the Profession

Selection programs on the part of the preparing institutions, the employing administrators of schools and colleges, and the teachers themselves should continue throughout the period of identification, professional preparation, and professional service. Leadership in assuming this co-operative responsibility, however, shifts from one segment to another, with the institution bearing major responsibility in the preparation period and the profession as a whole assuming that responsibility during the teaching careers of its members.

The Teacher Preparing Institutions

The value of sound professional practices in selection and preparation for teaching can be realized only if procedures in initial and subsequent placement of teachers adhere assiduously to the institution's goals and objectives for its graduates and the pupils and students they will teach.　There is general agreement that one of the best ways to improve retention in the teaching profession is to bring about improvement in the conditions under which teachers are expected to guide the learning of students.　This means that if teacher education is to be effective it must focus not only upon the prospective teacher, but also upon the environment in which learning is expected. The institution's placement and follow-up staff should be aware of conditions which need to be improved and should work with the profession as a whole to bring about improvement.　For the benefit of the institution preparing teachers and the prospective teachers themselves, placement officers should analyze closely the situational factors that, when combined with the individual teacher's abilities and the aggregate ability of the teaching staff, will bring about desirable teaching-learning situations.

A process of selection and preparation, which goes beyond the initial selection of individuals for teacher preparation and is designed to assist each individual in choosing and preparing for the teaching situation for which his aptitudes and interests best suit him, must also go beyond the point of recommendation for certification and placement.　In terms not only of effectiveness of performance, but in terms of efficient use of the institution's resources and the individual's ability and energy, the program should include identification and selection of school systems and teaching situations.　To evaluation of the recommended graduate should be added evaluation of prospective teaching situations.　Only then can the prospective teacher have reasonable assurance of securing a position which will maximize his likelihood of satisfying and successful performance.

The three-way continuous selection process, carried on by the preparing institution, the employing agent, and the teacher, should provide the preparing institutions with means for discharging their responsibilities to their graduates in follow-up, placement, and inservice growth services.　A planned by-product of such services should be the securing of bases for institutional evaluation of both the undergraduate program for selective retention and the curricula for teacher preparation in terms of demand and ever-changing societal needs.

The Employing Agents

The school system or college employing teachers should have clearly defined and operative procedures for continuous analysis of the system's characteristics and needs. Selection of new teachers should be so conducted as to achieve a satisfactory melding of situational and individual characteristics. Whatever the frequency or extent of change in personnel, the selective process should maintain a balance in staff talents and responsibilities which maximizes effectiveness in achieving the educational objectives of the school and also stimulates individual and staff professional growth.

For the employing administrators of schools and colleges, the three-way continuous selection process should lead to constant improvement of processes in initial selection of staff. Equally important, it should provide well-defined and defensible bases for evaluating individual teacher performance as related to individual potential, to the teacher's role in the teaching team or total staff, and to the objectives of the educational program.

Such evaluation should lead directly to evaluation of the total program itself in relation to societal needs, and should thus feed back into the programs of institutions preparing teachers. Though most effects will be characterized by improved procedures and inservice growth, the agents specifically responsible, with the support of the total profession, must discharge their responsibility of eliminating from the profession, as well as from the formal program of preparation, those persons whom carefully designed and applied processes of selection and evaluation have shown to be unqualified for the teaching position and whose prognosis for improvement jeopardizes the effectiveness of the educational program.

The Teacher

Availability of results from evaluative and selective processes on the part of teacher preparing institutions and school systems or institutions employing teachers should enable each teacher better to evaluate his own position, performance, and needs. Hence he should have adequate bases for subsequent determination of the types of additional formal education for himself, the institution that can best provide it, and the teaching position that will afford him the best opportunity to use his abilities in the achievement of professional educational goals.

Present situations of finance and staff prevent the extent and quality of follow-up activity essential to existing programs, if investments in the preparation of teachers are to be protected. Follow-up activities will become even more important if the various new horizons are implemented. Only as the process of identification, selection, preparation, evaluation, performance, re-evaluation, and growth becomes a continuous one can the selective process function effectively enough to produce an educational program whose quality is sufficient to meet current needs of society.

Summary and Recommendations

The upward spiral of evaluative and selective processes on the part of institutions preparing teachers, employing agents, and teachers themselves should result in a constantly improving program of education at all levels through maximum achievement of staffs comprised of well-qualified and constantly growing professional persons.

Both from within the teaching profession and from the public comes emphasis on the need to select carefully those who will teach. Assumptions regarding responsibility for selection, ability to select, criteria and processes of selection are receiving not only advocacy but support and effort to validate and extend them.

By concept and by deed the profession must include all persons who, as staff members in elementary schools, secondary schools, colleges, or graduate schools, serve in an educational capacity as professional personnel. The process of selection should apply to all, beginning whenever teachers themselves note in their pupils characteristics, aptitudes, and interests suitable to the teaching personality, and continuing through formal preparation and throughout the teaching career.

The profession must develop criteria for selection and the processes of applying those criteria. Continuous improvement of teacher education programs and accreditation of these programs must be a direct concern of the profession. The profession must also have the courage and wisdom to see that the processes of selection and performance are constantly evaluated and improved and wisely and judiciously administered. This means the profession must refuse admission to whoever, in the judgment of those within the profession who are delegated responsibility for the decision, is not qualified to enter the professional ranks. It also means the profession must see that judicious means are taken to eliminate from the profession whoever is not sufficiently competent through attitude and performance to assume and discharge his share of professional responsibility. Similarly, competent members of the profession must be protected from unjust treatment and judgment by any but highly competent professional personnel. These processes require never-ending study, evaluation, and growth, and adequate financial resources as well, so that all persons possessing potential for professional performance, the desire to prepare for teaching, and the ability to continue in preparation and in teaching can do so.

It is therefore recommended:

That a co-operative process of selection and evaluation be carried on by the total profession so that a favorable climate is created for preparation, entrance into the profession, and continued effective performance in it.

That only those institutions be accredited for teacher preparation which have definable operating programs of continuous selection.

That the selective processes at least be based on evaluation of emotional maturity, moral and ethical fitness, health, demonstrated ability to work with children and youth, academic aptitude and intelligence, academic achievement, demonstrated competence in speech and basic skills, and professional interest and motivation.

That responsibilities for selection be clearly placed, that instruments and processes be well planned and diversified, and that sequential steps be sensitively applied and systematically followed.

That the staff in student personnel services be an integral part of the teacher education program, and that personnel from all faculties dealing with the education of prospective teachers be involved in the evaluative processes.

That the total profession, as defined above, accept recognition of the need and responsibility for helping develop and apply a continuing program of selection throughout the teaching careers of its members.

That programs of selection, admission, and retention for preparation and performance have as a primary goal securing qualified staffs for quality educational programs.

CHAPTER 8

The Advancement of Standards:

Policies and Procedures

To DISCUSS "advancement of standards in the teaching profession" is to imply that improvements are needed. The implication is wholeheartedly intended. In this chapter a plan of action is outlined which would facilitate bringing about professional autonomy, as well as a dependable structure through which to advance standards. In presenting certain problems as they exist it has been necessary to consider the present status of the teaching profession, what changes are desirable, why they are desirable, and what can be done to bring them about. If the proposed "advancement" takes place, it is evident that the boys and girls of the nation will be the chief beneficiaries and that the action ultimately taken by the profession will favorably influence the public welfare.

The Profession's Current Status

Unlike members of certain other groups, the American teacher does not have a clear image of his role as a professional. There are many reasons for this. Whether in public or private institutions, schools, or colleges, educators perform their responsibilities in a variety of settings, under a variety of arrangements and conditions. Educators are acutely aware of such things as local control of education, desires of donors, and the high degree of their dependence on the good will of their respective communities. It is evident that many feel "possessed by their constituency." Faced with a range of forces affecting their work, teachers have become rather fond of the cliche, "our unique relation to the public." Holding an image of themselves as preciously unique public servants, they have not yet created adequate programs, procedures, and machinery through which to exercise fully their own expertness in the interests of the larger public welfare. As a profession, educators have not developed appropriate authority to speak for education. It is a misconception of democracy and of professional responsibility to base professional decisions upon popular opinion. There is evidence that the public respects the expertness of professionals and desires to see such expertness used in dealing with professional aspects of American education.

Imperative Changes in the Public-Profession Setting

A partial reason for the slow development of teaching as a mature profession is the confusion of roles in the task of fulfilling the great historic ideal of equality of educational opportunity. Professional morality demands that the teaching profession assume *major* responsibility for the quality of education. Social morality demands that the public assume *major* responsibility for quantity. In both cases there must be mutual understanding, respect, and appropriate machinery for moving ahead.

Essential educational services in this nation need to be improved in quality and increased in scope. To ensure that the teaching profession can carry its share of the national commitment to public education for all, it is essential that the profession be able to guarantee competent performance and ethical behavior of practitioners. The profession is not now in a position to do this.

Advancing professional standards, which also means enforcing them, requires a clear delineation of the relationship between a profession and the public it serves. Although the profession must carry the major responsibility for the quality of education in our country, it cannot and should not assume total responsibility; the public must shoulder its share. A clear distinction must be made between the public's responsibility for determining policy regarding education and the profession's responsibility for carrying that policy into effect.

Public-Profession Communication

The profession should strengthen its program of communication with the public specifically to the end that its Professional Standards Movement is effectively and appropriately interpreted. One of the responsibilities of every profession is to keep the public informed of its policies and procedures with respect to the development and enforcement of standards of professional practice. That the education profession depends upon public sanction for its support makes such communication especially important.

In order properly to interpret essential professional processes, it is necessary to develop public awareness of the general and technical skills which make up teacher competence. With such awareness the standards program of the profession becomes more meaningful to the public. To the degree that the profession is successful in defining competence and assuring the public of its attainment and enforcement, it merits the privilege of professional autonomy with its attendant responsibilities. Public relations efforts of professional organizations should be evaluated against their effectiveness in achieving this end.

The profession's obligation is clear: to keep the public informed of its professional standards goals and to render public accounting of the adequacy of its professional machinery. Accounting to the public is a function of all members of the profession. Indeed, the teaching profession should cherish and foster its close relationship to the public, for mutual understanding between educators and their constituents is basic to our democratic way of life.

Conditions That Promote
Professional Accountability

The following conditions must be met before the profession can become accountable for its members:

Public policy, which makes provision for establishing and maintaining a fully prepared person in every professional position, including agreed-upon formal commitments and explicit rules and regulations governing relationships between the public, the profession, and individuals of either body, and guaranteeing justice to all concerned.

Public and professional insistence upon the conditions necessary for professional performance, including the professional obligation to decline responsibilities where conditions, misassignments, or maltreatment seriously impair the likelihood of professional performance.

Allocation by the public and acceptance by the profession of responsibility for adequately preparing professional personnel and being accountable for their continued competent performance and ethical behavior.

Establishment of appropriate professional and legal sanctions, as well as administrative procedures and machinery, for carrying out the responsibilities of being accountable for competent performance and ethical behavior.

Creation by the profession of an agreed-upon single code of ethics which can be used as a point of departure in administering the enforcement of ethical conduct.

Creation by the profession of agreed-upon definitions of competence which can be used as a point of departure in administering the enforcement of competent performance.

Development and implementation of a systematic program of educational research.

All these conditions are essential if competent educational services are to be guaranteed. These are minimums in a total program and their universal establishment requires joint endeavor by the public and educators everywhere.

Evolution of a Professional Entity

If the profession is to fulfill its role in bringing about these conditions, it must operate as an entity, for autonomy cannot be bestowed without an entity to receive. In addition, there must be a specific vehicle occupied with creating and maintaining such an entity. The teaching profession as it has been operating is not an entity but a loosely federated group of major segments, each with a variety of further subdivisions or components, each performing certain tasks often with little or no co-ordination or relationships with others in "the profession." Some envision the profession as an organization. Rather, it should be thought of as an abstraction, an entity having a series of major segments, each with a number of component groups and each with responsibilities and concomitant authority. This entity must have the proper checks and balances within it, as well as a structure of relationships among the segments and components, so that they comprise a cohesive whole.

Any professional body can be divided into major segments. In the case of the teaching profession, there are at least five major segments:

1. Those who teach or carry out other professional activities in preschool programs and in elementary and secondary schools.
2. Those who teach or carry out other professional activities in colleges and universities.
3. Professional personnel in state departments of education and other governmental agencies such as the United States Office of Education.
4. Professional personnel in organizations directly related to teaching at any level.

5. Professional personnel in voluntary accrediting agencies involved with accreditation of educational institutions.

Each of these segments could be divided into further components in terms of functions performed by their respective specialists. For example, consider the first major segment which includes practitioners in elementary and secondary schools. In addition to those who teach in special areas or at specific grade levels, there are also administrators, supervisors, counselors, librarians, and research personnel. In like manner, the other major segments could be divided. Regardless of the segment or component any practitioner fits into, he should have a precise understanding of his relationship to and responsibility for the profession as a whole.

If teaching is to become an autonomous entity, it is imperative that certain procedures and machinery must evolve which will fix appropriate professional responsibilities and concomitant authority with each of the respective segments of the profession. For example, at the moment the responsibility for determining who may become a member of the teaching profession is certainly far from fixed. Many begin teaching without ever having to acquire any recommendation from a professional school or college or its equivalent. Responsibility for preparation of teachers for all levels should be fixed with a professional college or its equivalent and there should be no way to enter the profession other than through an approved program. This means fixing responsibility with and granting accompanying authority to certain institutions for such preparation. These institutions should be subject to checks and balances; they should not operate without reference to the public welfare and the interests of the profession as an entity. To this end the profession has placed major emphasis on developing appropriate accrediting procedures.

Among the segments of the profession, a system of checks and balances must be created to ensure the co-ordination necessary to the interests of both the profession and the public welfare, which interests are inextricably related. These checks and balances must be designed to reduce the chances that any segment of the profession could hold veto power over any other segment or individual in the profession. They must also encourage optimum levels for discharging fixed responsibility.

A profession is more than an organization. Developing a profession calls for creation of formal machinery and establishment of an effective communication system among the various segments. Some agency must assume responsibility for bringing about its evolution.

There must be a reasonably well-defined organization or group of organizations responsible for the pattern which is to develop, for what is everybody's business is likely to become nobody's business.

This is apparently a delicate point among various segments of the teaching profession, particularly if one defines the profession as including all those engaged in any professional activity in any of the segments mentioned. Patently, any agency, organization, or group of organizations which would endeavor to establish a pattern for developing an entity must be a balanced composition of various divisions of the profession and also be subject to checks and balances. To assume that a profession should attempt to guarantee competent performance and ethical behavior of practitioners, unless there is some co-ordinating agency, seems clearly illogical.

It is one thing to carry out the specific responsibility that a given assignment within the profession requires and quite another thing to accept the broad responsibility of practicing within a professional framework. No professional person is independent of the functioning of the other components if he is to have optimum conditions in which to practice his own professional activities. And this means an organizational pattern which crosses state boundaries. Therefore, it seems logical that the appropriate vehicle for pressing toward a professional entity is the National Education Association, working in conjunction with the various state education associations.

At this point, the advancement of standards to create an autonomous profession may appear to have elements of the chicken-egg argument. Which comes first, autonomy or the professional entity? In reality, the two must evolve simultaneously. In the past, the teaching profession has gained its rights and privileges piecemeal. This has led to a well-established but not always fruitful approach to problem-solving by first setting up a priority system. Unfortunately, when priorities are established often the top few items receive attention and the others are forgotten. If teaching is ever to become a profession, a minimum plan, including procedures and machinery for accomplishing this end, should be developed. This means that all parts of such a minimum plan should be attacked simultaneously, with no "priorities" in the usual sense. By facing various problems and situations *in toto*, the proper context for the task of creating a professional entity may be established. To repeat, if teaching is to become a mature, autonomous profession, the total condition should be attacked with a total plan of action toward a comprehensive concept of solution.

Seven conditions necessary before the profession can be fully accountable for the performance and ethical behavior of its members have been suggested (see pages 207-8). Some, it is understood, cannot be accomplished by the profession itself; public education, after all, is a state function. It has also been emphasized that certain intraprofessional requirements for the development of an autonomous professional entity must be met. We wish now to suggest a structure which can evolve from what already exists and which we believe would serve very well as the machinery by which the conditions necessary to achieve a mature profession can be reached.

The Role of the State: Its Relationships With the Profession

Every state has certain powers to establish conditions of entrance into the teaching profession. The conditions which the states have established have usually been in line with the interests of the teaching profession. The United States Constitution requires that any conditions a state imposes be administered equally and fairly.

Responsibility for formulating and administering major policies in public education is generally delegated to the representative state departments of education. As specialized educational agencies, state departments of education are created by constitutional or statutory law to ensure expertness in those areas requiring professional judgment and competence. In general, state departments of education are composed of a state board of education comprised of laymen, a professional chief state school officer, and a professional staff. The boundaries of power and responsibility vested in these departments are established by state legislatures. Thus, the wishes of the people with regard to education may always be made known through representative government. That this continue to be true is fundamental.

Although state departments of education have many functions, those most directly related to the teaching profession include:

Determining who shall be granted a license to teach, what provisions shall pertain in granting the license, and on what grounds it may be revoked.

Determining how and which institutions shall be accredited to prepare candidates for the profession.

Delineating rights unique to the teaching profession, for example, those related to tenure, minimum salaries, student-teacher ratio. These vary in each state.

With few exceptions, authority for certification of teachers and accreditation of teacher education programs is vested by state statute in state departments of teacher education. In most cases, such departments are governed by lay policy-making boards. Procedures in exercising this authority and requirements for certification and accreditation vary to the point of creating national confusion.

A state department of education is in reality an educational institution, and its staff members constitute an important segment of the teaching profession. Since it has a professional chief officer and a professional staff, the point can be made that the certification of teachers and the accreditation of teacher education is now largely in the hands of selected professionals. But true professional autonomy cannot evolve when one segment of the profession is saddled with responsibility for developing and enforcing standards that affect the entire profession. Autonomy cannot evolve unless each segment is subject to the checks and balances that apply to all other segments. To put it another way, an entity does not exist until all segments are subject to the checks and balances of the total profession.

In most states, state departments of education have created advisory councils on teacher education and certification. These councils have come into being primarily because of the need to co-ordinate the activities and interests of the various segments of the teaching profession in a variety of professional affairs. Each of these councils has its own unique origin and history. A few have quasi-legal status and, therefore, are mandatory. However, such a council usually has been created by the state board of education to secure expert advice on policy regarding teacher education and certification from a group of professional people broadly representative of the teaching profession. These councils make many recommendations regarding teacher education, accreditation, and certification, and they have varying degrees of influence depending upon the particular state considered. Some are too large to be effective; others have but little responsibility; some are highly effective. The whole trend is extremely important and is moving in a constructive direction.

It can thus be said that the profession is already widely represented in matters of teacher education and certification in many states. Furthermore, it might be argued that a structure prevails in many states whereby the profession either is or could be adequately involved. Is this now what is desired?

To have a structure does not necesssarily ensure desired function. The evidence is clear that the teaching profession as a whole has not been in a position to assume responsibility for the accreditation of teacher education and the certification of teachers. Indeed, the role assumed by the profession has often been that of critic rather than creator of the conditions necessary for the acceptance of greater responsibility, both individually and collectively, for improvement in teacher education, accreditation, and certification. Many factors have contributed to this negative role, e.g., absence of adequate arrangements for reciprocity among states, over-dependence upon technicalities rather than upon broad general requirements, and ignorance of the historical facts about certification and accreditation. Another factor has been the still-prevailing but slowly dying idea that anyone with a clear understanding of a subject can teach it; therefore, professional requirements are unnecessary. Inertia and vested interests have sometimes inhibited improvement of accreditation and certification procedures. The profession itself, if it is to be accountable for its own, must be responsible for accreditation of preparatory programs and certification of professional personnel.

It is recommended that every state legislature in the United States establish a professional standards board of seven to eleven members as an adjunct to the office of the chief state school officer, but charged with responsibility for accreditation and co-ordination of teacher education programs and certification of professional personnel.

Members of such a board should be broadly representative of all levels and areas of the teaching profession and could be appointed through a variety of methods, depending upon established precedents in any given state. However, all appointees to such professional standards boards should meet certain criteria, including minimum qualifications as established by the respective state education associations working in co-ordination with the chief state school officer. All appointments should be those which have the sanction of the organized profession in the state. Such appointments should be staggered so as to insure continuity of the board.

Care should be exercised to create that mechanism which promises to work best in each state. That states do vary is illustrated by the ways in which the chief state school officer is named: in twenty-two states the chief state school officer is appointed by the state board of education; twenty-three states elect theirs by popular ballot; in five states the chief state school officer is appointed by the governor. However, the trend is toward the state board of education having power to appoint. In the past few years the number selected this way moved from eight to twenty-two. This trend is in keeping with removing this office as far as possible from the influence of partisan politics. Even so, the profession itself should be more closely involved in the discharging of certain legal responsibilities. As proposed here, establishment of professional standards boards appears to be one way to guarantee that professional involvement will be expected and that the public welfare will be protected by having decisions made by those best qualified to make them.

The professional standards board should have broad duties related to the accreditation of teacher education, procedures for licensure, and revocation of teachers' licenses. This board should also have responsibility for investigating and making recommendations concerning the misassignment of teachers. It would also be required to maintain liaison with a commission on professional practices and with the state commission on teacher education and professional standards, both of which are discussed later in this chapter. The two commissions would be strictly professional commissions created by state education associations, whereas the professional standards board would be legal since it would be an adjunct to the office of the chief state school officer. It should be noted, however, that a board is not professional merely because it has been legally established. There is considerable precedent for such legally constituted boards composed entirely of professional personnel.

The administrative responsibility of the chief state school officer for the professional standards board would, in most cases, be delegated to a director of teacher education and certification and his staff. The functions of the professional standards board would be specifically defined whereby only major decisions would have to receive the direct approval of the state board of education. However, the lay state board would have veto power over any policy decision made by the professional standards board. The relationship of education to the public welfare is so important in a democratic society that final authority must be clearly vested with the people and their representatives. Although the professional standards board being recommended here would be composed of professional personnel, members must at all times be keenly aware that they are a legally constituted body, created for the purpose of providing the state with a high degree of expertness in matters vital to the public welfare.

The professional standards board should be empowered to establish standing committees or commissions, or both, as appropriate in each state. Procedures with respect to assignments to commissions and committees would necessarily vary. For example, a commission might be established to study and make recommendations regarding the preparation of elementary- and secondary-school teachers. This commission might utilize individual study teams in each of the various subject-matter areas or in cutting across all areas. Such a procedure would facilitate official involvement of liberal arts personnel in the preparation of teachers. While such teams would be called upon regularly to report studies and make recommendations, they would be free to present recommendations at any time.

Procedures for revoking a certificate should also be a function of this professional standards board. Accreditation of institutions of teacher education should be another of its functions. Of course, as the National Council for Accreditation of Teacher Education enlarges its scope, accreditation of teacher education will become less a problem for certification bodies and complete reciprocity among states will become a reality. Even so, legal responsibility for accreditation will and should remain with the states.

If every state were to have some such professional standards board, including the proposed committees or commissions with study teams as suggested, the establishment of consistent national standards would be facilitated. With such a board, for example, national organizations representing special instructional areas could communicate with an official state body, which would have a study team through which its own members could contribute to the solving of problems and the resolving of issues in teacher education and certification.

There are many ramifications of the above suggestions. If professional standards boards were developed, it is believed that the profession itself, in accepting responsibility for its own affairs in teacher education and certification, would assume greater leadership. We know that regulatory authority alone does not bring fruitful results. There must be professional responsibility which in turn demands leadership. This means that a director of certification should have opportunities to do research and to be out in the field; he should not be tied to a desk counting noses and college credits.

Professional Sanctions

Educators, individually and in the corporate professional body, are obligated to devise and administer a program to assure enforcement of standards of performance. Ultimate professional autonomy rests on public sanction and faith in the machinery for enforcement. No profession has acquired nor can it maintain autonomy without public approval. On the other hand, adequate development of standards of performance and their enforcement can be fostered best by an autonomous professional group.

It is recommended that the National Education Association and the affiliated state and local associations establish commissions on professional practices to provide the profession's internal machinery for enforcement of standards.

The public has a right to expect the professional organization of teachers to lead the way in the development and enforcement of standards of practice. A competent educator expects and encourages public co-operation in defining outcomes to be achieved from the educational institutions established and supported by the public. But the professional educator must be responsible for prescribing procedures to attain them. Thus, enforcement of standards of competence will advance the profession and, at the same time, serve the professional needs of its members and of the public—a fundamental purpose of any professional organization.

Society accords special status to those professional groups which can demonstrate successful enforcement of standards. Prestige, freedom to conduct their own professional affairs (autonomy), and recognition of the social and economic value of their services accrue in public opinion as standards of practice are agreed upon and enforced.

The principle of professional autonomy requires that important tasks be assigned to those with special qualifications and immediate concern for results. Those accepting responsibility are entitled to freedom from outside interference while satisfactory results are obtained.

Standards of Competent Practice

The profession has three essential tasks in developing and maintaining standards for competent practice.

First, an acceptable definition must clarify, for the profession and for the public, what competences the professional educator is expected to maintain. Rather than limit this definition to the classroom technician stereotype, it is imperative that the larger concept of the educator's total professional role in society be described. This task is outlined in a later proposal.

This definition must be synthesized from the mass of experience represented by selected individuals in our profession. An unrealistic vision of what it is hoped these competences might become will not suffice, because the profession must be prepared to rise or fall in terms of progress made in requiring every member to attain them. Agreed-upon criteria of competence thus become an expression of serious commitment.

Second, with a definition of professional competence as a basis, agencies of the profession should proceed to develop and enforce standards of practice. The profession, however, must see to it that the standards are known and supported, both within the profession and by the public. It must be made very clear that the maintenance of adequate standards does not mean standardization. Particular attention, therefore, must be given to enforcement of minimum standards so that, within the profession, decisions can be rendered on the adequacy of professional performance.

Third, machinery for enforcement should be supplemented by a broad, positive program designed to encourage higher standards of practice. Specific contributions of many agencies and institutions must be brought to bear on the individual practitioner. The accumulation of case studies involving questionable competence to practice is a necessary procedure of a commission on professional practices.

Standards of Ethical Practice

Regulation of ethical practice is an essential part of a program to ensure competency of personnel. The profession has two major responsibilities in this standards field.

First, ethical behavior must be defined in such a manner as to provide a foundation for practical interpretation by members and agencies of the profession. Earlier attempts to define ethical behavior have resulted in the several current codes of ethics among state and national professional associations. Using these efforts as a basis, there is now a clear need to agree upon a single code that can be a guide for all members of the profession. A code of professional ethics is not easy to formulate. Any such code must be developed within the profession by its most experienced and capable leaders. Formulation of such a code requires clarification of what is competent and socially responsible behavior. The code also must be in harmony with the framework of social attitudes, desires, and controls. Accordingly, it will be as difficult as it is now important to develop a code which will receive wide support.

Second, the profession must provide a mechanism for interpretation and enforcement of ethical standards. One distinction of a worthy professional organization is the education of its own members with respect to professional ethics. While the development and clarification of a code of ethical practice may rest finally with the larger national unit, every state, local, and specialized organization must stimulate and counsel its members to study and implement proper ethical procedures in given circumstances.

Enforcement of ethical standards involves both defense and disciplinary action.   The profession must provide at local, state, and national levels the necessary agencies and prepared personnel to carry out these activities.   Defense of members unjustly accused of unethical conduct should be based upon the existence of a specific code of acceptable behavior which is generally understood and agreed to.   If final judgment in a case is based upon accepted principles, it will be recognized both within the profession and among the public generally.

Unprofessional behavior on the part of a member can cause widespread professional damage that may considerably weaken public confidence, which is the basis for the profession's freedom to conduct its own affairs.   It is imperative, therefore, that the profession have some means by which it can correct unprofessional behavior.   Disciplinary action is the necessary counterpart of defense action, and the means by which it can be taken is an area to which significant organizational effort ought to be directed.   As a final disciplinary action the profession should retain and exercise the right to suspend or expel members on the basis of appropriate findings indicating gross abuse of professional privilege.

Professional integrity requires that there be standards by which professional behavior can be judged and that these standards be widely known and rigorously applied.   Hence, the profession and professional organizations can be judged in terms of their support and use of a code of competent practice, including ethical behavior.

Development of Machinery to Enforce Standards

In the development of machinery for enforcing standards, the leadership responsibility of professional organizations is clear and inescapable.   All levels (national, state, and local) and the major specialized professional organizations have roles to assume.   These roles are not expected to be mutually exclusive, but some distribution of function and responsibility must be made for effective implementation of the program of standards.

The outline below suggests how responsibility for internal development and enforcement of standards may be allocated.

National Education Association.   The NEA should designate a single agency within its structure to provide nationwide leadership and responsibility in development of standards of professional practice and ethical conduct.   Such an agency should have the stature of a commission and could be titled the NEA Commission on Professional Practices.

Such a commission should become effective in supplying an essential unity among the variety of state, local, and specialized organizations. In the delineation of some of the specific roles of this commission below, there is one precaution: There must be a balance between central co-ordination on the one hand, and safeguarding of the initiative and motivation of state, local, and specialized organizations on the other. As long as substantial powers remain with these groups, their interest and action will be virtually assured. The commission on professional practices should seek the counsel and co-operation of state, local, and specialized groups in carrying out its roles.

Specifically, because of the way education is organized in the United States, the national commission must be primarily concerned with the creation of adequate procedure as well as with providing assistance in individual cases. Although the national commission should be vitally concerned with competences and ethics (especially as they relate to having standards which provide intelligent frames of reference), any case which has legal implications must necessarily be dealt with directly at the state and local levels. This does not preclude consulting assistance from the national level; it implies quite the opposite. Consultation should become a major function of the national commission. The national commission on professional practices should:

Develop a program national in scope for the adoption and enforcement of standards of practice.

Develop a single national code of ethical practice.

Provide national leadership in research on standards, including accumulation of case material and the application of research findings.

Encourage development of state commissions.

Set up the machinery for the establishment at the national level of a final appeal body on decisions involving internal enforcement of professional standards.

State Association. Each state professional association should maintain a commission on professional practices. Since educational authority in this country is the responsibility of the various states, the state associations and their local units become highly important in rendering this vital service to the profession and to the public in the enforcement of high standards of professional practice and ethical conduct.

As at the national level, this state commission must provide for proper recognition of and participation by the various state specialist organizations and established local organizations within the state. The state commission on professional practices should:

Develop a state-wide program for adoption and enforcement of standards of practice.

Develop a state-wide program for enforcement of a national code of ethics.

Encourage and support local professional associations in developing local or regional commissions on professional practices.

Provide machinery by which local or regional commissions refer special studies or cases on an appeal basis to the state commission.

Provide facilities for necessary state research and communication in professional practices enforcement, including the publication of case studies for review and study.

Provide direct liaison with the state's board of professional standards.

Local Associations. The local or regional professional organizations will bear heavy responsibility in the professional practices and ethics enforcement program. Because state and national commissions cannot conceivably carry out necessary processes in a profession so widespread, the ultimate success of the program is dependent upon the effectiveness with which practitioners are organized at the local level. Local or regional associations must be so organized that they can maintain a standing committee or commission on professional practices. This commission may be structured on the basis of community, county, or regional jurisdiction depending upon geographic and other considerations of size and resources.

The status and operations of the local commission must be established with due consideration for relationships with school governing boards and professional organizations within its geographic area. In carrying out the roles suggested below, the local commission also may call upon the resources of regional and state groups. Local commissions should:

Undertake local studies involving enforcement of standards of practice. (Studies may be requested by the local school board, the professional organization, or the individual member.)

Refer appeal cases to special regional or state commissions.

Provide for local interpretation and communication, both to the profession and, as necessary, to the public in matters involving standards of practice and their enforcement.

Associations in Specialized Areas. The specialized educational associations at the national, state, and local levels have a co-operative role to play in development and enforcement of standards. These organizations usually are either subject-centered (music, mathematics, physical education) or function-centered (principals, superintendents, librarians, supervisors). These organizations at the national, state, and local levels should:

Be called upon to assist in the development of some specifics in the national code of ethics. (Special situations arise, for example, with respect to administrators or music teachers or coaches, and others, which may need specialized attention.)

Be urged to develop standards of professional practice at the national and state levels for the comprehensive professional association.

Develop supplementary machinery for raising and enforcing standards of professional and ethical practice in liaison with the state or national organizations.

At all levels be called upon to represent their specialized group on expert panels or commissions where an investigation is being made involving a member of their specialization.

Procedures for Professional Practices Commissions

Investigating, recommending, and reporting on specific cases involving disputed professional practices, alleged incompetence, or unethical practice are the main procedures through which the commission can effectively interpret and enforce standards. It will be necessary that commission procedures be clearly defined, published, and available to all members of the profession. All procedures should avoid misuse of publicity. Although there may be occasional studies that merit public attention, every effort should be made to restrict case studies to the professional family. When reporting seems necessary, it should be confined to professional journals or special commission publications.

Initiation of the Case Study. How studies are to be initiated should be clearly spelled out. The commission should receive referrals from specified sources such as a governing board of a school district, an individual practitioner whose practice is under question, a professional group, or any individual or community agency with bona fide interest in school affairs.

Professional organizations should have available specially prepared staff personnel to assist in careful identification of a proposed case study. Although local commissions may not maintain staff for this purpose, it is expected that regional, state, or national associations could assist the local effort at this point. Staff assistance should be available to facilitate gathering of information, arranging for commission hearings, and if desired, implementing commission decisions and recommendations.

Hearings. The commission should determine the nature and extent of investigation following a preliminary inquiry. Hearing procedures should be planned so that all testimony can be recorded. Interviews should be scheduled with clear rules of procedure regarding use of evidence. Hearings should be private and confidential with only commission members, special committees, essential staff interviewers, and interviewees present.

Reports. Commission members should determine their findings and prepare a report describing the case study, the issues, and the commission's recommendations. The commission should determine the distribution of its report and should avoid undue publicity.

Defense and Discipline. Whether the commission recommends defense or discipline following a study, how the recommendations of the commission are to be implemented should be clearly stated. Final authority to carry out the recommendations of the commission should rest with the executive board of the professional association maintaining the commission. It is at this point that liaison with the state's professional standards board will be useful and effective.

Panel of Experts. Commissions at the state and national levels should maintain panels of prepared experts—practicing members of the profession—to assist in case studies. Depending upon the nature of the inquiry into ethics or standards of practice, suitable personnel should be drawn from the panel in formulating special committees to render specialized aid. Members of specialized professional groups may be of particular service on a panel. It is proposed that the local commission should make preliminary studies and seek advice of state commissions in most cases. A major function of the local commission should be to determine whether a case merits calling upon the state commission for a special committee composed of members from the panel of experts. Discretion should be used, especially in delicate local cases, to ensure objectivity. This probably means acquiring the judgment of a special committee selected from outside the immediate administrative jurisdiction of any given case. Even in cases which a local commission might feel competent to handle, counsel should be acquired from the state education association.

Appeals. Provision should be made so that in certain instances decisions can be appealed to state or national commissions, or both. Appeal procedures should be clearly understood and controlled. Every effort should be made to establish and increase the effectiveness of local commissions.

Precedent. It is essential that commissions on professional practices provide for accurate recording and communication of the development, conduct, and results of case studies so that a body of precedent is established.

The Role of the Courts

In matters of professional discipline or defense where action on contractual relations with an employing authority is necessary or desirable, it is imperative that the profession have established procedures by which expert testimony can be rendered. In each state the profession must obtain necessary legislation to permit such testimony in courts of law. The profession, through its commission on professional practices, must maintain highly refined techniques for qualifying educational experts for this service. Although the right to give expert testimony is a very fundamental right, it is wise to keep certain decisions affecting the profession within the confines of professional machinery where persuasion is used as long as possible. When a case goes to court it should be clearly recognized that the decision made is no longer one located within the confines of the profession. Of course, this is sometimes necessary and even desirable. But careful consideration should be given to the problem of the appropriate use of the courts. This assumes wise legal counsel.

Relations with State Professional Standards Boards

Action taken by commissions on professional practices, when it involves disciplinary procedure and when it affects the granting, suspension, or revocation of the license, must be based on established clear relationships between the commission on professional practices and the state's professional standards board. The board in turn should be authorized to take action within a legal framework with safeguards both to the individual and to the public.

Only in the event that disciplinary procedures involve revocation of the license to practice is the state legal agency involved. Recommendations affecting the practitioner's license may originate within or without the profession. In either event, internal agencies of the profession must make the profession's recommendations to the legal agency. It is fundamental that the profession, through commissions on professional practices, have close and well-defined relations with the state professional standards boards.

Importance of Continuous Identification and Study of Problems

As conditions surrounding the profession change and new procedures evolve, it will become increasingly important for the organized profession to accelerate its efforts toward defining problems and suggesting policies and action programs in the areas of identification, selective admission and retention in teacher education, of accreditation of teacher education programs, of certification, and of professional performance and ethical behavior of practitioners. Therefore, state education associations should continue to encourage their commissions on teacher education and professional standards. State commissions should, in turn, encourage in a similar way the work of such local groups.

In particular, there should be a continued effort to bring about involvement and co-ordination of the efforts of all those who have contributions to make toward the improvement of the teaching profession and the service it renders. This should be done on the national, state, local, and institutional levels. Only a beginning has been made in this respect.

State TEPS commissions should epitomize co-ordination in that their constituencies should be broadly representative. Moreover, these commissions should be so created and established that continuity of their work is assured. A critical factor to the success of any commission is adequate professional staff to carry out the work of the commission.

Because it is imperative that the standards recommended in this report be based on policy devised by the corporate profession through appropriate democratic machinery, the evaluation of education association programs should be based on a realistic assessment of the degree to which standards are being realized.

It is recommended that the National Commission on Teacher Education and Professional Standards encourage and assist professional associations at all levels in giving immediate and regular attention to the assessment of their internal policy-making machinery.

Standards of professional service cannot be secured by silence or by apathy. The path to securing standards is a democratic process of decision-making. The only truly representative bodies through which the total profession can speak are in the professional education associations. If any professional policy is to be developed, it must be developed through these organizations.

Standards in any area of professional service, however, will not be improved simply because policies are developed and means for their implementation pointed out. The profession would be deluding itself if it set forth the thought that the improvement of professional standards will be any less arduous and difficult than progress on other fronts. Proposed policies and changes can be expected to run headlong into vested interests and stout opposition, both within and outside of the profession. In the years ahead professional gains considered imperative will be made only with insistent pressure and strengthened influence by the professional organizations.

Such influence depends upon comprehensive policy development and the machinery which precedes it. It is appropriate and imperative, therefore, that the National Education Association assume leadership of the complex national, state, and local comprehensive and specialist organizations in proposing procedures for the development of policy. These procedures must evolve from a consideration of:

The complexity of the pattern of educational organizations at the national, state, and local levels.

The range of activities, the geographic scope, and the educational function of this wide variety of professional agencies.

The need to preserve independence and autonomy of groups, while at the same time providing for their effective participation in overall policy development.

The principle that each of the varied organizations should develop policies on issues and problems primarily related to its own particular area of geographic or professional influence, rather than on broad questions of concern to the whole profession. The NEA's major policy decisions, on the other hand, should be related primarily to the many common interests shared by all members of the profession.

An Evaluative Mechanism

Just as educational institutions are accredited, it now seems apparent that professional organizations should devise among themselves a similar evaluative mechanism. Procedures, including adequate instruments, could be developed for self evaluation of various professional associations at all levels. There are, among all these groups, identifiable and sufficiently common characteristics which are essential to their professional status. These characteristics can be the basis of evaluative instruments. Details of procedure and content of the instruments could be varied, depending upon the organization and its sphere of responsibility. On a voluntary basis, any one of the varied organizations could use these procedures and instruments in a self-appraisal program, which would attempt to measure the degree to which its program, services, and policy-making machinery exemplify the characteristics of a profession.

A Frame of Reference for Teacher Competence

The need for an authentic definition of the teacher's professional role has long been recognized. Although several studies are under way, at the national level no significant progress has been made in refining and establishing such a definition. Yet, in order to validate key professional procedures such as teacher selection, preparation, and licensure there is pressing need for an operational definition of the totality of teacher competence. Important decisions leading to action on professional standards assume that the nature of the teacher's tasks is definable.

It is recommended that the National Commission on Teacher Education and Professional Standards, in co-operation with other agencies, establish a comprehensive definition of teacher competence acceptable to the profession.

Construction of an acceptable description of teacher competence should take into account the major areas of the teacher's professional activity. The following areas of competence suggest the minimum essentials of a framework for the proposed definition:

1. Competence as a director of learning, as a counselor, and as a repositor of the culture. In these areas teachers possess a variety

of professional skills and knowledge for which general and technical preparation is necessary. Often overlooked is the teacher's role as a repositor of the culture which has extensive implications for standards of preparation and inservice education.

2. Competence as an administrator of the educational program. Each teacher has responsibilities for management of the educational enterprise. School organization, curriculum building, program evaluation, and other program developments necessitate effective participation by all professional staff members.

3. Competence as an educational service agent in the community. Teachers not only perform as interpreters of the educational enterprise but, having skills and knowledges not possessed by other citizens, they provide a specialized competence in solving educational problems of the community.

4. Competence as a member of the profession. In addition to the areas of technical competence suggested above, the teacher has important responsibilities in achievement of professional goals apart from the immediate educational or scholastic enterprise. These obligations require attention to such over-all concerns as standards for entrance and continuing membership in the profession, provision for educational and related research, and maintenance of the program of the corporate body of the profession.

However, it is apparent that a backlog of precedent needs to be established as to what constitutes competency in a variety of situations. This can be done when competences which constitute a frame of reference are agreed upon and some structures such as the professional practices commissions are established.

It is recommended that the National Commission on Teacher Education and Professional Standards begin immediately a program designed to establish such professional practices commissions at the national, state, and local levels, as described herein.

The Development and Implementation of a Systematic Program of Educational Research

In order to expand the knowledge which is fundamental to teacher competence and to the operation of the total educational process, many organizations, agencies, and institutions have conducted scientific inquiry into the various aspects of education. However, much of this research activity has been sporadic, under-financed, haphazard, and often not communicated to the practitioner. That efforts in the application of educational research findings to educational practice lag far behind is well documented.   This lag is due essentially to the failure of the profession to place sufficient emphasis on prosecuting research, on securing support for research in sciences basic to education, and on orienting research toward practitioner use.

It is recommended that the National Education Association give greater support to agencies interested in research and experimentation, and make every effort to assure the application of research findings in all phases of the educational enterprise.

Research Support

National, state, and local support for research may come from a variety of sources.   A portion of the general funds of the national association should be allocated to such endeavor.   Foundations, business, and industry are areas of support which need to be more carefully and persistently explored.   Well-conceived projects, carefully designed and written up with budget allocations, should be prepared for presentation to these agencies.   In addition, portions of available funds for research should be used for special grants on a direct or matching basis to research centers and universities.

Federal funds for educational research in the form of grants to institutions and government agencies should be increased.   A pattern similar to the National Institutes of Health might be feasible.   Certainly three things need to be done:

1. What is already known and what is underway in the field of educational research should be gathered in some center, probably through some technique of automatic storage. This should be continuous.

2. What is known should be studied (automatic storage would make this more possible) with an eye to discovering areas where new researches should be made.   Institutions with appropriate talent should be located and subsidized so as to make such research become a reality.

3. What research says should be disseminated to the practitioners in the field in ways whereby new knowledge and discoveries are effectively articulated with the main stream of American education.

Programs of research must be decentralized and at the same time co-ordinated so that talent may be used wherever it is located.   Colleges and universities should be the primary loci of research.   However, the three-pronged task suggested above is so gigantic that only through the strengthening and expansion of activities such as those now being carried on by the United States Office of Education can it be carried out. The organized profession should be in a strong position to give guidance and co-operation in the execution of this task.

Promotion and Conduct of Research

The profession, through its appropriate agencies, should give leadership in the promotion and conduct of educational research:

By issuing authoritative statements on educational research indicating problems needing attention and identifying agencies that might appropriately conduct the research. Statements should clearly identify the social need for solution of the specific research problem. The "why" must be made clear.

By giving particular attention to the validation of professional criteria for teacher competence. In order to merit continuing public support the profession must develop and accumulate tested procedures. Research efforts to this end cannot be left to piecemeal arrangements among unco-ordinated agencies.

By encouraging the formation of parallel efforts in state professional associations.

By encouraging research activity among the members of the profession.

By co-ordinating and co-operating with research efforts of other disciplines, particularly those representing areas basic to the study of education.

Application of Research

There exists a critical need to reduce "educational lag," that large gap between professional knowledge and educational practice. Concentrated attention should be given to this area. A nationally co-ordinated program for dissemination, application, and implementation of research findings should be established. The larger national specialized associations, most state associations, and those local groups engaged in this same enterprise should have liaison with the national educational research groups.

If the lag is to be reduced, it is imperative that the profession make more insistent efforts than ever before in creating and using new ways to stimulate the application of research findings. To this end there is need for field service personnel whose sole task would be to promote and expedite the application of research findings in the schools and in the profession.

One of the major commitments of a professional education organization, therefore, is to preserve, expand, and utilize the body of special knowledge and insight of which the profession is custodian. It also should cultivate in teachers a more sensitive respect for and allegiance to this foundation of their work. An educational organization, therefore, may be appraised in terms of the effectiveness with which it cultivates professional knowledge among its members, assists and contributes to increase in knowledge, and contributes to dissemination and application in practice of available knowledge.

Summary

The Committee on the Advancement of Professional Standards has attempted to establish the need for the evolution of a professional entity for the teaching profession. Obviously, the major vehicles for accomplishing this will be the National Education Association and the various state and local education associations.

Such an entity will evolve only by better fixing certain responsibilities with the appropriate major segments of the profession and establishing appropriate formal and informal relationships among these segments. Creating such an entity will include a variety of checks and balances which will assure greater individual freedom and exercise of individual competence of all professional personnel. In particular it is the teacher-student relationship and the right to prescribe individual methods which are the vital center. These must be guaranteed the competent practitioner. Thus, the machinery and rationale for such relationships suggested in this chapter are directed to this end.

The teaching profession's relationship to the public is particularly unique, and safeguards for strengthening this relationship have been advocated. Recommendations herein make provision for more effectively guaranteeing that decisions in the public interest be made by those most qualified to make such decisions. Moreover, it is suggested that the teaching profession establish a nationwide approach whereby it can become accountable to the public for competent performance and ethical behavior of its members.

Most of the suggestions made here will require diligence, hard work, and support of educators at all levels. Quite probably, and logically, the major responsibility for their innovation will fall upon the National Commission on Teacher Education and Professional Standards and the parallel state commissions.

CHAPTER 9

The Teaching Profession in the Decades Ahead

THE NEW HORIZONS PROJECT has been concerned with goals for the teaching profession. Goals have been conceived not as ends in themselves but as directional guides for action. As progress toward accomplishment of presently envisaged goals is made, it is likely that future prevailing conditions will cause new goals to emerge. Actually one of the important guiding directives for the teaching profession, as for all educational planning, is ability to respond to modified conditions brought about by new knowledge, new purposes, or new demands growing out of changes in a community or in a world society. It is, therefore, to be expected that present goals, while providing adequate guidance for the years immediately ahead, will change as conditions surrounding the teaching profession take on new dimensions.

Throughout the preceding chapters some goals have been stated explicitly, others have been implied. Not all the recommended goals are new, for the profession has long been moving toward valid and desirable goals which will continue to provide direction for the future. What is needed with reference to such persisting goals is more widespread commitment to them and acceleration of efforts in working toward their achievement. There are, however, in the preceding pages of this report recommendations that suggest new goals. These need careful study by the profession. When new goals are found to be worthy, plans of action should be evolved so that their full meaning is understood, so that positive steps toward their accomplishment may be taken.

In the committee reports (Chapters 4-8) specific recommendations have been discussed in each of the areas encompassed by the project (selection, teacher education, accreditation, certification, and advancement of professional standards). Minimum attention has been given to the interrelationships among suggestions in the various parts and to the "image of the whole" of the Professional Standards Movement. For both the profession and the public it is important to perceive the whole image of the profession's efforts to advance toward self-discipline. If any part of the whole is weak or fails to function properly, action on the parts may even be dangerous. For example, to base licensure for teachers on recommendation from NCATE-accredited colleges and universities has inherent dangers unless standards and procedures are such as to guarantee accreditation only to those institutions which conduct teacher education programs of high quality. It is perfectly clear that, until all parts of the Professional Standards Movement are functioning and in appropriate relationship, the profession dare not hope to move rapidly toward legitimate autonomy. Nor can the public be expected to place complete confidence in the profession's ability to assume fully its responsibility for the quality of education in these United States.

The purpose of this concluding chapter is to present an "image of the whole" as created by the recommendations of the project. This image is presented in outline form. The reader is encouraged to return to earlier chapters for detailed analysis of any points appearing in the summary outline.

An Image of the Teaching Profession as Revealed Through Its Development and Enforcement of Professional Standards

I. *The center of this profession is the teacher; other educational specialists complement the teacher and his work. Teachers and other specialists are professionals:*

A. Who have been carefully selected and are fully qualified to perform their respective roles.

B. Who are committed to professional service.

C. Who behave as scholars, perform with excellence.

D. Who individually and with others share their profession's responsibility for the quality of service rendered.

II. *The core of the Professional Standards Movement is the profession's commitment to the central purpose of providing the best possible educational opportunity for all:*

A. By assuming its full share of responsibility for the achievement of this central purpose through rigorous self-discipline.

B. By encouraging continuous study, experimentation, and research with regard to both its internal affairs and the many facets of its social service.

C. By protecting appropriate freedom for individuals and groups.

D. By holding high standards of admission to and continuing membership in the profession.

E. By maintaining high expectancies of individual members in the discharge of their obligations to the profession and to the particular service rendered.

III. *The center of the professional standards program is the continuous selection and preparation of all professional personnel.*

A. A total program of identification and selection begins in the elementary school and continues throughout the careers of educators.

1. The selection program will be effective in the elementary school:

   a. when teachers demonstrate exemplary personal and professional behavior.

   b. when children showing special interest in and capacity for teaching are identified and encouraged.

   c. when children's questions about teaching are responded to with sincerity and adequate, appropriate information.

   d. when opportunities to explore teaching are made available to those expressing a desire to explore education as a career.

2. In the secondary school, the program of selection will be effective:

   a. when teachers and other educators demonstrate exemplary personal and professional behavior.

   b. when provision is made for students especially interested in and able to pursue careers in education (the Future Teachers of America can be an excellent vehicle for this):

> (1) to secure appropriate and accurate information about teaching and other educational careers.
>
> (2) to explore teaching through direct experience in teacher roles and in association with effective teachers.
>
> (3) to secure appropriate information about institutions and programs of teacher education.
>
> (4) to take the initial steps in co-operation with institutions of higher education for admission to college.

c. when study of education and the school as a social institution is made a part of the work in social science for all students.

3. The program of selection will be effective in colleges and universities, graduate and undergraduate:

a. when teachers and other educators demonstrate exemplary personal and professional behavior.

b. when interested students are provided opportunity early in their programs to explore education as a career through direct experience with the role(s) they may eventually perform. (The Student National Education Association can be an effective vehicle in this regard.)

c. when study of education and the school as a social institution is made a part of the work in general education for all students.

d. when standards for admission to professional preparation are rigorously applied.

e. when careful selection is made a continuous and integral part of the professional program:

> (1) by full utilization of validated instruments and procedures in securing data relevant to wise decisions by both students and their advisers.
>
> (2) by careful recording and analysis of behavior by both students and advisers as additional data to be employed in making decisions.

(3) by appropriate utilization of counseling services, both the general guidance of college teachers and the specialized services of psychologists, psychiatrists, doctors of medicine, and other experts.

f. when central responsibility for the selection process is lodged in the department or school of education:

(1) with policies and procedures determined by total faculty action.

(2) with final decisions affecting selection made by a faculty committee representative of all phases of the student's program.

g. when the final stages of the selective process include administration of a comprehensive examination in background knowledge and a requirement of demonstrated competence appropriate to a beginning practitioner in the role for which the student has been preparing.

h. when institutional recommendation of candidates is based on adequate data.

i. when institutions are held accountable for the quality of performance of their graduates.

4. Continuous selection during service will be effective:

a. when those interested in and competent to pursue preparation for roles other than those being performed at the time are identified and encouraged.

b. when the profession enforces standards of ethical conduct and standards of practice through systematized procedures:

(1) for protecting its members from unwarranted abuse, from working conditions that preclude effective performance, and from unnecessary and undesirable restrictions on freedom as professionals.

(2) for protecting the profession and the public it serves from unscrupulous or incompetent practitioners.

B. A total program of preparation begins in the elementary school and continues throughout the careers of educators.

1. Preparation for careers in education is effective in the elementary school:

a. when teachers demonstrate exemplary personal and professional behavior.

b. when educational opportunities provided children are of the highest quality.

2. In the secondary-school preparation for those who will choose careers in education is effective:

a. when teachers and other educators exemplify desirable personal and professional behavior.

b. when educational opportunities provided secondary-school youth are of the highest quality.

c. when colleges and secondary schools co-operate in offering special assistance to students who are interested in and have the necessary qualifications to pursue careers in education:

(1) by providing opportunity to take tests, to fill out inventories, and to engage in other activities related to diagnosis and prognosis.

(2) by providing consultative services both in high schools and on college campuses.

3. Preservice collegiate preparation of teachers is effective when every institution purporting to prepare teachers:

a. is committed to total institutional responsibility for the teacher education program.

b. is staffed only by fully prepared educators who perform with excellence.

c. carries on continuous experimentation and research on its own program and in the many facets of educational service for which it prepares practitioners.

d. meets standards for professional accreditation and surpasses those standards where possible.

e. relates to other segments of the teaching profession in appropriate ways, contributing to and accepting contributions from educators working at all levels and in all functions of education.

f. has a teacher education program that is a distinctive organization of learning experiences, in large part individually designed for each prospective teacher, and characterized:

(1) by a broad liberal education.

(2) by content that is selected on the basis of its relevance to decisions the teacher must make and implement as a person and as a professional.

(3) by specialization that includes study of the teaching field both as a discipline and as an area to be taught to others.

(4) by an internship, in addition to student teaching and other laboratory experiences, as an integral part of the program.

(5) by appropriate use of both qualitative and quantitative evaluation of student progress.

(6) by direct attention to responsibilities incumbent upon members of the teaching profession.

(7) by students' assuming major responsibility, under guidance, for their own learning.

g. admits students to and retains them in the program on the basis of specifically stated criteria and procedures of selection.

4. Graduate preparation of professional personnel is effective when characterized by the same principles as preservice preparation, with special emphasis:

a. on individually designed programs.

b. on continuing liberal education.

c. on direct experiences, including an internship, in roles which the educator is preparing to perform.

      d. on continuing work in the teaching field or other area of specialization.

  5. Continuing inservice education of professional personnel is effective:

      a. when schools and colleges co-operate in carrying on inservice education.

      b. when programs are individually designed.

      c. when opportunities for liberal education are available throughout the career of the educator.

      d. when personnel responsible for continuing education are fully qualified and competent in the performance of their roles.

      e. when the motivation for continuing education is excellence of performance as a professional.

IV. The three essential processes of enforcement of professional standards are accreditation of preparatory programs, licensure of professional personnel, and rigorous application of standards of practice.

  A. Professional accreditation of preparatory programs shall have reached its full significance:

    1. When the profession's agency for accreditation, the National Council for Accreditation of Teacher Education:

      a. is adequately supported by the profession.

      b. has a constituent membership that is fully representative and provides for free flow of information to and from all segments of the profession.

      c. engages in continuous study of its standards and procedures.

      d. assumes responsibility for dissemination of information concerning its policies, standards, and processes, both to the profession and to the public.

      e. provides for specific preparation of evaluators and employs only those who are so prepared.

      f. provides maximum service to institutions in minimum time.

g. requires regular interim reports from accredited institutions.

h. applies standards rigorously, approving only those institutions of high quality.

2. When standards for accreditation:

a. are based on continuing study, research, and experimentation.

b. are stated in terms that facilitate understanding of them and appraisal of programs in relation to them.

c. may be viewed as stimulating improvement as well as regulating practice in institutions.

d. not only provide for, but actually require institutional experimentation with varied approaches to the preparation of professional personnel.

3. When every professional educator:

a. is committed to abiding by the standards of accreditation.

b. assumes responsibility, individually and with others in the profession:

(1) for building understanding of accreditation standards and procedures within the profession and among the public.

(2) for contributing in various ways to the development of better standards.

(3) for preparation of and participation by representatives as team members in evaluation of institutional programs.

4. When the only preparatory programs available to prospective candidates at any level are those accredited by the NCATE.

5. When licensure, employment as an educator, and membership in the profession can, with confidence, be based on the candidate's recommendation from a professionally accredited institution anywhere in the nation.

B. Licensure of professional personnel will be effective:

1. When the state maintains its authority to administer the issuance of licenses to teachers, but delegates to the profession responsibility for determining standards to be employed in licensure.

2. When the only purpose of legal licensure is to provide visible evidence that the candidate is competent as a beginning teacher.

3. When other purposes, now too frequently applied to licensure, are achieved:

   a. by accreditation of institutions and programs ensuring that candidates have been carefully selected and well prepared and are competent as beginning teachers.

   b. by institutional accountability for their recommendations of candidates for licensure.

   c. by wisdom of school and college officials in assignment of functions to personnel.

   d. by professional conduct by individuals in assuming only those assignments for which they are prepared and competent.

4. When the state issues only one license, the initial entrance license for teachers, based:

   a. upon completion of an NCATE-accredited program of preparation.

   b. upon recommendation by the preparing institution on the basis of demonstrated competency as a beginning teacher.

   c. upon recommendation of teaching competence by the appropriate organization of teachers.

5. When specialized licenses beyond the basic one are developed and administered by the profession itself through its various associations of specialists.

C. Enforcement of standards of ethical conduct and professional practice will be effective:

1. When members of the profession view their responsibilities for their own conduct and for that of their professional associates seriously and realistically enough to take action in evaluation of themselves and their peers.

2. When acceptable definitions of competency are developed and used as points of departure in examination of practice.

3. When a single national code of ethics is formulated and used as a point of departure in examination of ethical behavior.

4. When appropriate machinery for dealing with both defense and disciplinary cases is evolved and in operation at local, state, and national levels.

V. *The chief requisite to success in the Professional Standards Movement is leadership by the National Education Association.*

  A. Certain imperatives emerge from this summary of recommendations.

    1. Nothing less than a total approach to professional self-discipline will suffice.

    2. Co-ordination of the many segments of the teaching profession and of the many functions to be performed by professional educators dare not longer be delayed.

  B. The National Education Association is the logical and the only adequately representative group to assume leadership in the development of an autonomous, total teaching profession.

  C. The NEA will effectively discharge its leadership obligation:

    1. When the organization is an influential model of professional association:

      a. in greatness of purpose.

      b. in democratic structure and operation.

      c. in co-ordination of people, ideas, and functions.

      d. in machinery for policy formation and implementation.

      e. in communication and relationships with the public.

2. When its structure is modified so that every segment of the teaching profession:

   a. is adequately represented.

   b. has co-operatively developed and fixed responsibilities and authority.

   c. has open channels for contributing to and profiting from the total profession.

D. Recommendations of the New Horizons Project suggest specifically that the NEA, through appropriate departments, commissions, and committees, and through affiliated state and local associations, should:

1. Assist in the development of state professional standards boards so that proper professional involvement in development and enforcement of standards in teacher education and certification may be assured.

2. Assume leadership in the development of professional practices commissions on the state and local levels so that the profession may better exercise its responsibility for the conduct of its members.

3. Facilitate the development of a single national code of ethics and standards of practice.

4. Take leadership in the development of machinery at the national level for fundamental research and experimentation, the dissemination of findings from the same, and the stimulation toward application of findings in practice.

5. Develop a systematic plan for appraisal of its own internal operations and assist state and local associations in similar appraisal of their internal operations.

VI. *Within this total image of a profession moving vigorously toward self-discipline and the attendant autonomy, the National Commission on Teacher Education and Professional Standards and its affiliated state TEPS commissions continue to have fundamental leadership responsibility. This responsibility will be discharged effectively:*

A. When the NCTEPS and its affiliated state and local commissions exercise, even more forcefully than in the past, leadership in identifying problems, in analyzing issues, and in suggesting policies and action programs in the areas of identification, of selective admission and retention in teacher education, of teacher education programs, of accreditation, of certification, and of professional performance and ethical behavior.

B. When recent commendable efforts to involve all segments of the profession in consideration of pertinent policies and practices are increased and made the expected *modus operandi* rather than the exceptional practice:

1. By structuring the national, state, and local commissions so that they are truly representative of all segments of the profession.

2. By performing as models of appropriate co-ordination of effort.

3. By involving all segments of the profession in deliberations such as are characteristic of state, regional, and national conferences.

C. When the NCTEPS and its affiliated groups become influential "relators" of the suggested professional standards boards and professional practices commissions, the state boards of education, the public, and the profession, one to the other.

D. When greater responsibility is assumed by the NCTEPS and its affiliated state and local commissions for interpreting the Professional Standards Movement, both to the profession at large and to the public.